CALLING IN TODAY'S WORLD

Calling in Today's World

Voices from Eight Faith Perspectives

Edited by

Kathleen A. Cahalan *&* Douglas J. Schuurman

WILLIAM B. EERDMANS PUBLISHING COMPANY

GRAND RAPIDS, MICHIGAN

Wm. B. Eerdmans Publishing Co.
2140 Oak Industrial Drive N.E., Grand Rapids, Michigan 49505
www.eerdmans.com

22 21 20 19 18 17 16   1 2 3 4 5 6 7

Library of Congress Cataloging-in-Publication Data

Names: Cahalan, Kathleen A., editor.
Title: Calling in today's world: voices from eight faith perspectives /
edited by Kathleen A. Cahalan & Douglas J. Schuurman.
Description: Grand Rapids : Eerdmans Publishing Company, 2016. | Includes index.
Identifiers: LCCN 2016013063 | ISBN 9780802873675 (pbk.: alk. paper)
Subjects: LCSH: Vocation.
Classification: LCC BL629 .C35 2016 | DDC 204/.4—dc23
LC record available at https://lccn.loc.gov/2016013063

To my husband, Donald, whose stewardship
of creation is a gracious calling

Kathleen A. Cahalan

To my wife, Kathy, whose faithful fulfilling
of her callings is exemplary

Douglas J. Schuurman

Contents

Preface

KATHLEEN A. CAHALAN AND DOUGLAS J. SCHUURMAN

"What does a Buddhist think about calling?" "Does a Jew have a similar sense of calling to a Christian?" "Do you know of any books on vocation from the perspective of other religions?" In the past several years, both our students and colleagues who teach at other colleges and universities have asked each of us these kinds of questions.

As two Christian theologians, one Catholic and one Protestant, we had to answer our students, "I don't know. Good question." And to our colleagues looking for a comparative theology of religion text, we had to say, "No, I don't think so." Both of us have been working on a theology of vocation, within the Christian tradition, for several years, but we did not know how adherents in other traditions would respond to the question, "Do you have a sense of calling in your life?"

Do other religions have anything like the concept of Christian vocation? It is important to note at the outset that other religious traditions do not have terms such as "calling" or "vocation."[1] Rather than finding an equivalent, we asked scholars and practitioners of other traditions the following question: "Does your tradition have anything *like* the concept of vocation in the Christian tradition? And if so, how do people live out a sense of calling as a Muslim or a Hindu?" We had to ask people to search their tradition's sacred texts, key figures, practices, and concepts to see if there was anything analogous to vocation in the Christian tradition. Together our efforts form the basis of this book.

---

1. *The Compact Oxford English Dictionary,* 2nd ed. (Oxford: Oxford University Press, 1991), defines "calling" and "vocation" with nearly identical entries (pp. 202 and 2246). Following the OED, we use "vocation" and "calling" interchangeably.

We believe there is a significant need for a book that treats the concept of calling, or vocation, from multiple faith perspectives. Partly owing to programs focusing on the theological exploration of vocation, supported by the Religion Division of Lilly Endowment, Inc., the theme of vocation in Christian thought and practice has been given extensive consideration in US colleges, universities, and churches.[2] It is time we expand that discussion to include other major world religions. We hope this book will lead to greater understanding of one's own religious tradition and of the faith traditions represented in this volume. And we hope that better understanding will increase and improve efforts to build a better, more humane world.

The primary intended audience for this book, then, is college and university students, persons preparing for leadership positions in their communities in divinity schools, and those who currently are in leadership positions in their religious communities. We hope this volume will be used as a textbook for courses in comparative religion, religious ethics, or professional identity and ethics. Our secondary audience is anyone who is curious about vocation or calling in one or more of the traditions treated in the volume.

As the United States increasingly becomes more religiously diverse, members of various faith communities meet each other in college classes, workplaces, neighborhoods, volunteer organizations, and elsewhere. They join hands in working for justice and peace and in promoting the ecological health of the planet. For example, the leader of the Roman Catholic Church, Pope Francis, in June 2015 delivered a teaching on how Catholic Christians should treat the environment, but he also appealed to "the whole human family" for a "new dialogue."[3] The interfaith response to his encyclical has been overwhelming from groups such as the Coalition on the Environment and Jewish Life, Green Muslims, the Buddhist Peace

2. The "Network for Vocation in Undergraduate Education" (NetVue) promotes the theme of vocation among its 178 institutional members, helping to create a ripe audience for materials on vocation. See its website, accessed July 10, 2015, http://www.cic.edu/Programs-and-Services/Programs/NetVUE/Pages/View-the-NetVUE-Members.aspx. NetVue is beginning to emphasize interfaith discussions of vocation as seen in the titles of recent NetVUE-supported conferences, "Vocational Explorations in a Multi-Faith World: Cultivating Informed Engagement Across Faith Traditions in Undergraduate Education," hosted by Calvin College, Sept. 20–21, 2013, and "Interreligious Reflection on the Vocation of Sustainability," hosted by Luther College, March 7–8, 2014.

3. See Pope Francis, *Laudato Si' of the Holy Father Francis on Care for Our Common Home*, nos. 13, 14, accessed July 9, 2015, http://w2.vatican.va/content/francesco/en/encyclicals/documents/papa-francesco_20150524_enciclica-laudato-si.html.

Fellowship, and a group of young adults, the Emerging Leaders Multi-Faith Climate Convergence, who attended the *Una Terra, Una Familia* (One Earth, One Family) March on June 28, 2015, in St. Peter's Square together.[4] Each tradition has been calling upon its members to work with others from diverse faith traditions to advance humanitarian causes and reforms at home and worldwide. If we want to work together on important social issues, we need ways to get to know and understand the beliefs and practices of diverse religious communities.

"Calling" and "Vocation" as Christian Concepts

"Vocation" and "calling" are Christian concepts. They do not appear in other religions. Before we articulate concepts of calling, or their analogues, from the religions represented in this book, it is necessary to note what we do and do not mean by calling. Since popular conceptions of calling no longer reflect central aspects of the Christian tradition from which they emerged, it will be helpful to compare and contrast the popular from originating ideas of calling. We focus here on the Christian tradition because of its influence on modern Western culture, and we focus on modern Western culture because it shapes the worldview of our intended readers.

In the Christian tradition the idea of calling has been central for shaping how believers understand their relation to God and how that relation shapes how they live in this world. For Christians in the early church and Protestant reformers in the sixteenth century, calling was an expansive, all-encompassing idea. It united faith and worship to every significant social sphere of a person's life. Christians had a sense that God was calling them in every part of their daily lives—at home, at work, in the neighborhood, and at church, according to Martin Luther. Their many callings were to follow in the way of Christ, blessed with gifts from the Holy Spirit, attentive to the needs of others and the responsibilities of their roles.

For a variety of social and cultural reasons, the meaning of "calling," and especially "vocation," in the modern world came to refer primarily to paid work, and often it came to refer more narrowly to the service pro-

4. For a list of religious organizations working on the environment, see Interfaith Power and Light, accessed July 14, 2015, http://www.interfaithpowerandlight.org/resources/other-organizations/. See GreenFaith: Interfaith Partners for the Environment for information on the Multifaith Climate Convergence, accessed July 15, 2015, http://www.greenfaith.org/.

fessions or to prestigious occupations. Today's popular usage emphasizes the language of personal meaning, purpose, fulfillment, and direction, as evidenced by the numerous books about "calling."[5] Clearly the concept is not dead. However, it lacks the deep religious and moral connotations it has in a Christian context as being rooted in God's initiative, as demanding something from us, and as being oriented not to our self-enhancement but to our radical self-giving in love. Certainly Christians are not opposed to meaning, purpose, and fulfillment, but from a Christian theological point of view calling has always meant that we find our meaning, purpose, and fulfillment in God. However, calling has now become largely secularized, stripped of its religious and spiritual meaning.

Several reasons account for the loss of Christian understandings of vocation. First, many Christians associate the terms with church-related or monastic roles, such as a call to become a pastor, missionary, priest, or nun. Second, many think that church leaders have heard an audible voice from God or have had a miraculous encounter with God calling them to become a pastor or priest, and thus many Christians conclude that God has not called them. Third is the common notion that God has a rigid, highly detailed "blueprint" for each person's life. Within this blueprint, God calls individuals to a single specific place of work, and to no other, or has a particular person in the blueprint for one's spouse, for those called to marriage. Christians who hold this view are highly anxious that they might miss their one and only chance to heed God's call.

But these common conceptions of Christian vocation, which do have roots in the tradition—callings are for religious leaders, come about through divine direct communication, and are fully formed—miss the mark. They lose the biblical insight that every significant social relation constitutes a calling, including paid work, but also being a friend, aunt, uncle, child, parent, student, and more. As Christian theologians, we want to emphasize that God's callings are much more mundane, are mediated by the world's needs, and require individual and communal discernment.

If you are a Christian reading this book, you will find that the Christian tradition has a long and varied history of thought and practice to draw upon in figuring out what it means to say that God calls us.

---

5. See for example Gregg Levoy, *Callings: Finding and Following an Authentic Life* (New York: Three Rivers Press, 1997); Diane Dreher, *Your Personal Renaissance: 12 Steps to Finding Your Life's True Calling* (Cambridge, MA: Da Capo Press, 2008); or William Damon, *The Path to Purpose: How Young People Find Their Calling in Life* (New York: Free Press, 2008).

But what if you are not a Christian and this tradition is not your context for understanding calling? You may find the secular sources noted above to be helpful, but what if you want to know if calling makes any sense in the Confucian tradition, or for contemporary Buddhists and Muslims? The chapters in this book invite you to consider what your tradition (if it is included here, since this is not an exhaustive list of religious traditions) says about calling. We also invite you to appreciate what other traditions have to offer and to support each other's sense of calling.

Chapter and Author Overview

The goal of this book is to bring other faiths into conversations about callings. These faiths include the "Abrahamic religions," Judaism, Christianity, and Islam. We also include the major Asian religions, Hinduism, Buddhism, Confucianism, and Daoism. We have also included a chapter exploring how a secular humanist might understand calling, since this is a major voice today in Western secular societies. With approval of all the volume's contributors, we decided to have two chapters treating the Christian tradition, one on the Catholic tradition and one on the Protestant tradition. Because of how formative the Christian traditions have been for the culture of our primary intended readers, treating two major streams of Christianity was deemed important.

Calling is a strange notion for Jews. Certain notions of calling, such as God's direct communication or the calling of religious leaders, is foreign to the post-biblical Jewish tradition, as Rabbi Amy Eilberg explains in her chapter, "*Hineini* (Here I Am): Jewish Reflections on Calling." Furthermore, Judaism holds the identity and formation of the community as its central task and to speak of calling is not, then, about individuals but about the whole people of Israel. Nevertheless, Rabbi Eilberg searches Rabbinic and Hasidic texts to discover ways in which Jewish thinkers have considered dimensions of an individual seeking guidance from the divine.

In "Called to Follow: Vocation in the Catholic Tradition," Kathleen Cahalan explores key aspects of calling stories that include discernment, identifying gifts, searching, receiving a message, taking up service to one's neighbor, and a taking on a new name. Historically, Catholicism embraced an understanding of vocation that distinguished those called to religious life in a vowed community or to religious leadership (e.g., priests) from lay individuals, but today Catholic theologians focus on calling that embraces all work and life commitments.

Douglas J. Schuurman in "To Follow Christ, to Live in the World: Calling in a Protestant Key" explores Luther's revolutionary notion that Christians share a common or general calling, that is, to be the Body of Christ, and they have particular callings, ways in which they live out the love of neighbor and God in their particular roles as teachers, grandparents, accountants, and friends. Schuurman uses the German Lutheran pastor and theologian Dietrich Bonhoeffer to exemplify key aspects of Protestant calling.

Muslims, like Jews and Christians, have a strong sense of calling as a people. John Kelsay, a scholar of Islam but not himself a Muslim, describes the foundational sense of calling in Islam, which means "the submission" to God, which is a person's first response to God's callings. In "Divine Summons, Human Submission: The Idea of Calling in Islam," Kelsay explores the Islamic sense of calling through three significant figures: the prophet Muhammad (569–632 CE), the philosopher and theologian Al-Ghazali (1058–1111 CE), and US civil rights leader Malcolm X (1925–1965).

In "Worship, the Public Good, and Self-Fulfillment: Hindu Perspectives on Calling," Anantanand Rambachan explores two concepts from the Bhagavadgītā that can be related to calling. *Svabhava* refers to one's own nature and the work that flows from the intrinsic nature of each human being. For the Hindu, this work is a form of worshiping God. The living out of *svabhava* is referred to as *svadharma,* which means that all individual lives and work have a social and cosmic significance because each contributes to the harmony and well-being of all.

A Buddhist is not called to be a Buddhist per se, according to Mark Unno in his chapter, "The Calling of No-Calling: Vocation in Nikaya and Mahayana Buddhism." If one were to identify an analogy to calling in early Nikaya Buddhism, the calling is to attain liberation, or *mokṣa,* from the bonds of suffering and awaken to *nirvana.* In Mahayana Buddhism, the calling is to manifest compassion for all beings in order to bring them to awakening first, and only then to attain awakening for oneself.

Mark Berkson explores two Chinese traditions in "The Cultivation, Calling, and Loss of the Self: Confucian and Daoist Perspectives on Vocation." For both, a sense of calling would begin with the core concept of Dao (the Way), but with distinct emphases: Confucians emphasize the social aspects of the Dao, perfecting moral character in order to create a harmonious society, and the Daoists (with a focus here on Zhuangzi) highlight the movement and activities of the natural world, suggesting practices that will enable one to live effortlessly in harmony with nature.

In "Vocation without the Supernatural: Calling in Secular Traditions," Edward Langerak explores how secular humanists today might explain the reasons for living a moral life, for finding meaning and purpose in life, and for living out a sense of calling through the experiences of gift, gratitude, and fulfillment.

Our Common Inquiry

As we noted above and the chapter descriptions portray, you will not find an exact equivalent of the Christian notion of calling or its secular usage today in other religions. In order for authors to explore this concept and for readers to be able to compare and contrast key ideas and figures, we have organized our chapters around the following list of questions:

1. Briefly describe the tradition and focus for this chapter. What are some of the key texts and persons who have developed this religion's views of "calling"? What is a story that captures the tradition's notion of calling?
2. What concepts and key terms in the tradition relate the Divine/Transcendent/Ultimate to a sense of calling? How does or should a sense of calling affect how adherents of this faith understand their life in this world and how they live and act in daily life? Actions include work performed for pay, but should not be limited to such work.
3. How do human beings come to know what the Divine/Transcendent is calling them to be and to do in this world? What audio, visual, or other sensory imagery conveys and expresses experiences of being "called" by God? How do human beings relate work and commitments in the world to what they value as having ultimate meaning? Are there persons in this tradition who guide others in these matters (rabbis, pastors, teachers, gurus, etc.)?
4. What practices and modes of thought help sustain a vital sense of calling in this tradition?
5. What aspects of modern life and culture make it difficult for members of this faith community to relate a sense of calling to life amid varied social spheres (paid work, home life, stage in life, civic and social communities, etc.)? What aspects of modern life provide opportunities to

deepen and extend callings that connect "the divine," or "the ultimate," and worldly life?

6. What concepts and practices related to calling need to be retrieved to help this religion's adherents live faithfully in the modern world? What features need to be revised and reformed in light of modern challenges and possibilities?

Each author decided how best to address the six topics listed above. Some authors, you will find, follow the ordering rather closely; others do not, though in some way each topic is addressed. Some dwell much longer on one or two topics identified in the template than on the others, but still include some insights about the others. Each author uses stories, both ancient and contemporary, to illuminate how people live out a sense of calling. We hope the template will make it easier for readers to compare the traditions represented in this book.

We hope that this book will enable better understanding of major world religions on this important topic, as well as a better grasp of one's own religious tradition. The goal is not to find a common denominator, or one understanding of calling, to which all religious diversity can be reduced. Instead, it is to set forth a nuanced view of the religious and moral issues surrounding the concept of calling, or its analogues, in a way that respects the particularity and integrity of that tradition. We expect to find some similarities and differences that will further illuminate the realities underlying the ideas we treat.

Our thanks go to each of the authors for entering into this venture with us. We also thank the Collegeville Institute Seminars, hosted by the Collegeville Institute and funded by Lilly Endowment, Inc., who supported two gatherings of the authors to discuss our essays and further our thinking about calling.[6] And we thank our students and colleagues who kept pressing us to consider vocation from an interfaith perspective. It has proven to be a fruitful dialogue for us and we hope for our readers.

---

6. For information about the Collegeville Institute Seminars and its resources on vocation, see its website, accessed July 14, 2015, http://collegevilleinstitute.org/the-seminars/.

Contributors

Mark Berkson is professor and chair in the Department of Religion at Hamline University. His work on Confucian and Daoist thought has appeared in numerous books and journals. His lecture series for the Great Courses, *Cultivating Literacy for Religion,* was released in 2012. His current project is *Death, Immortality, and the Afterlife: A Comparative Perspective.*

Kathleen A. Cahalan is professor of theology at Saint John's University School of Theology and Seminary and director of the Collegeville Institute Seminars. She is editor, with Gordon Mikoski, of *Opening the Field of Practical Theology* (Rowman & Littlefield, 2014), author of a book tentatively titled *Call It What It Is* (Eerdmans, forthcoming 2017), and coauthor, with Bonnie J. Miller-McLemore, of a book tentatively titled *Calling All Years Good: Vocation across the Lifespan* (Eerdmans, forthcoming).

Amy Eilberg, the first female rabbi ordained in Conservative Judaism, teaches and practices interreligious and intra-Jewish dialogue. She is the author of *From Enemy to Friend: Jewish Wisdom and the Pursuit of Peace* (Orbis, 2014).

John Kelsay is Richard L. Rubenstein Professor of Religion and Bristol Distinguished Professor of Ethics at Florida State University. He is former president of the Society for the Study of Muslim Ethics. His most recent book is *Arguing the Just War in Islam* (Harvard University Press, 2007).

Edward Langerak is professor emeritus of philosophy at Saint Olaf College, with specializations in ethics and social and political philosophy. His most recent book is *Civil Disagreement: Personal Integrity in a Pluralistic Society* (Georgetown University Press, 2014).

Anantanand Rambachan is professor of religion at St. Olaf College, specializing in the Hindu tradition and interreligious dialogue. His most recent book is *A Hindu Theology of Liberation: Not-Two Is Not One,* SUNY Series in Religious Studies (State University of New York Press, 2015).

Douglas J. Schuurman is professor of religion at St. Olaf College, specializing in Christian ethics and theology. His most recent book is *Vocation: Discerning Our Callings in Life* (Eerdmans, 2004).

Mark Unno is associate professor in the Department of Philosophy at the University of Oregon. He is editor of *Buddhism and Psychotherapy across Cultures: Essays on Theories and Practices* (Wisdom Publications, 2006) and author of *Shingon Refractions: Myoe and the Mantra of Light* (Wisdom Publications, 1997).

Hineini (Here I Am)

Jewish Reflections on Calling

Amy Eilberg

Early in the twenty-second chapter of Genesis, during which God commands Abraham to sacrifice his son, God calls to Abraham, saying simply, "Abraham!" Abraham responds with a terse answer, rich with meaning: "Here I am" (in Hebrew, the single word *"Hineini"*). Rashi[1] comments that Abraham speaks in the language of humility and of readiness. Before hearing what God will ask of him, Abraham is ready to accept the call.

While visiting my stepson who was spending a year in Israel, my husband and I had the opportunity to visit a place I had long admired: the School for Peace at Neve Shalom/Wahat al-Salaam/Oasis of Peace, located between Tel Aviv and Jerusalem. Neve Shalom/Wahat al-Salaam would be a remarkable place anywhere, but especially in the midst of one of the most intractable conflict zones in the world. It is a village created as a living exercise in coexistence for Israeli Jews and Israeli Arabs.[2] The community is home to more than one hundred families who live together, raise their children together, and work together for peace and understanding between Jews and Palestinians around the region.

The town houses the world-renowned School for Peace, which serves as a laboratory, educational center, and think tank for peacebuilders from around the region and around the world. The school's signature program is a three-day residential encounter program for high school juniors from Jewish and Palestinian schools within Israel. As the school systems in Israel are almost completely separate, the group of approximately one hundred

---

1. Rabbi Shlomo Yitzhaki, preeminent biblical commentator, eleventh-century France.
2. Father Bruno Hussar, a Jewish-born Roman Catholic priest, created the village in 1970.

sixteen-year-olds who attend each workshop—half of them Jewish Israelis and half Israeli Palestinians—have virtually never before met "the other" in a positive context.

During their three days together, the young people begin by discovering the commonalities in their language and culture, a key to uncovering one another's common humanity. As the program unfolds, the participants actively engage the dynamics of the conflict that defines all of their lives. Highly trained facilitators employ a sophisticated educational methodology that attends to and redirects power dynamics within the group that mirror those outside the sheltered environment of the school.

My husband and I watched from behind a one-way mirror as the young people settled into their groups together, learned one another's names, and negotiated about the names they would give to their groups. In any other circumstance, this would have been a simple set of icebreakers at the beginning of a youth group conference. But there was nothing simple or ordinary about this encounter.

Far too soon, the person who had brought us said that it was time for us to go. For my part, I was riveted to the floor, gripped by a powerful instinct to roll up my sleeves. Every time I told the story of what had happened to me that day, I found myself reaching for my sleeves. Although the God I believe in does not communicate like a human being or literally send messages to individuals, I felt a visceral sense of having been called by God to roll up my sleeves and find some way to help with peace in the Middle East and around the world.

This experience initiated a so-far ten-year journey of orienting my life around the desire to serve the cause of peace.[3] How are we to understand such experiences? Did the Creator of the universe actually intervene to instruct me to change the direction of my professional life? Was my sense of divine call simply my own psycho-spiritual explanation for an emotionally powerful experience? Was this turn of events a Jewish story, comprehensible in the context of Jewish theology? Did it bear any relationship to the stories of biblical figures who responded *"Hineini"* ("Here I am") to a perceived summons from the divine?

I daresay that a survey of rabbis and Jewish scholars on the subject of "vocation" or "calling," understood to be direct divine communication or direction to human beings, in Jewish tradition would reveal a decisive

---

3. I describe this journey in my book, *From Enemy to Friend: Jewish Wisdom and the Pursuit of Peace* (Maryknoll, NY: Orbis, 2014).

majority responding that Judaism has no such concept. On the other hand, if we consider the concept of calling as described by Schuurman in terms of the Protestant reformers,[4] as the obligation to live in faithfulness and devotion to God and in accord with sacred values, the concept resonates deeply with central Jewish principles and practices. If calling refers to a sense of meaning, purpose, and identity deeply rooted in the sacred, then it is simply another name for the kind of religious life that Jewish tradition describes and prescribes.

Jewish religious life, as classically understood, is characterized by adherence to *halacha*/Jewish religious law as a way to serve God. This way of life includes sanctification of everyday experience through prayer, blessing, and observance of the *mitzvot* (commandments), regular study of sacred text, and a life of service, all grounded in sacred community. For traditional Judaism, a primary goal of life is to orient oneself to the holy, as much as possible, on a moment-by-moment basis.

For many contemporary Jews who no longer consider themselves bound by Jewish law, connection to fellow Jews around the world and to Jewish history serves as a primary source of personal meaning and identity. In recent decades, the ancient concept of *tikkun olam* (repair of the world) has been refashioned to describe a broad range of social justice work at home and abroad and has commanding power in many Jewish lives.

In the sections that follow, I will first explain why the concept of calling seems foreign to so many Jews and then offer descriptions of a life lived in relationship with God from within Jewish sources.

The Jewish Tradition

Contrary to popular belief, Judaism is by no means synonymous with the Hebrew Bible. Rather, the Hebrew Bible is the foundation on which Jews in different times and places over twenty-five hundred years since the biblical period have constructed the diverse set of texts, beliefs, practices, and communal phenomena we know as "Judaism." As one scholar puts it,

> Judaism is the religious expression of the Jewish people from antiquity to the present day as it has tried to form and live a life of holiness before

---

4. Douglas J. Schuurman, *Vocation: Discerning Our Callings in Life* (Grand Rapids: Eerdmans, 2004).

God. . . . Never static, Judaism has changed and challenged its adherents for over two millennia, even as it has been changed and challenged by them in different circumstances and times. . . . Judaism [is] a religion rooted in the Bible—in terms of its beliefs and behaviors, history and hopes—yet radically transformed by the ongoing teachings of the sages.[5]

As such, anything we say about Judaism must begin with the Hebrew Bible, but must also carefully examine sources and perspectives from the Rabbinic period,[6] when Judaism as a post-biblical religion was created; the medieval period, from approximately 700 CE to 1750 CE, during which codes of Jewish law, works of philosophy, and Jewish mysticism emerged; and the modern and contemporary periods.

As we consider the enormous chronological and geographical scope of Jewish sources, it becomes clear that any simple statement of what "Judaism" says about a particular issue is facile, if not downright false. Some scholars go so far as to describe a series of "Judaisms,"[7] or a "family of traditions," which share significant similarities but also have enormous differences based on geography, history, and orientation,[8] much as many "Christian" principles are articulated and understood somewhat differently in Catholic Christianity, Orthodox Christianity, and the various denominations of Protestantism. I will draw most heavily on biblical and Rabbinic sources, which are most central to the formation of Judaism as a religion, but I will consider medieval, modern, and contemporary perspectives as well.

I will describe principles and practices that are widely recognized as central to Judaism as we know it, but I will also write from my particular vantage point as a twenty-first-century spiritual teacher. I am one of a growing number of rabbis who, since the 1980s, have worked to reinvigorate the spiritual core of Judaism that had been eroded by the Enlightenment's philosophy of rationalism and twentieth-century Holocaust trauma. Throughout my career, I have worked to encourage Jews, even those long

5. Michael Fishbane, *Judaism* (San Francisco: Harper & Row, 1987), 12.

6. I capitalize the words "Rabbis" and "Rabbinic" when describing the rabbis of the formative period of Rabbinic Judaism, from the first century BCE through the seventh century CE, but not when referring to contemporary rabbis.

7. Jacob Neusner, *The Way of Torah: An Introduction to Judaism*, 6th ed. (Belmont, CA: Wadsworth, 1997), 15.

8. Michael L. Satlow, *Creating Judaism: History, Tradition, Practice* (New York: Columbia University Press, 2006), 6.

alienated from Jewish tradition, to reclaim religious practice—for the sake of personal spirituality, well-being, and connection. My work has been to help Jews turn to the tradition for personal support and comfort and also to listen for the voice of the Holy in shaping their daily lives. As indicated in my story above, I have fashioned my own life and work in response to my best understanding of what God was calling me to do at a particular time. My reading of Jewish sources and my understandings of Jewish spiritual life flow from this body of work and life perspective.

Calling in the Jewish Tradition

Calling as Foreign to Judaism

As indicated, a great number of Jewish scholars and rabbis would likely say that Judaism has no concept of vocation or calling. There are four primary reasons why this is the case.

First, the Rabbinic tradition asserts that direct communication between God and human beings ended with the last of the literary prophets, as in the statement, "After the death of the last prophets, Haggai, Zechariah and Malachi, the 'holy spirit' (i.e., prophecy) ceased among the people of Israel."[9] One may well say that this statement, authored by early Rabbis of the post-biblical period, was self-serving. These Rabbis were in the midst of the monumental task of creating a Judaism that could survive and thrive after the destruction of the Temple in Jerusalem in the year 70 CE. One of their central tasks was to establish their own authority in the absence of the Temple priesthood and as the biblical period grew more distant.

Nonetheless, this view became authoritative. The predominant position of classical Jewish sources is that after the deaths of the literary prophets of the Bible, God never again spoke directly with individuals. Thus, the notion of God communicating God's specific desire for a particular person's life choices is foreign, if not vaguely offensive. A suggestion that God had communicated direction for an individual's life in a supernatural act of divine "speech" would seem arrogant or foolish in a Jewish context.

Second, Jewish religious life is highly communitarian. While individ-

9. Tosefta Sotah 13:4. Strikingly, however, the text there continues to describe the possibility of the "holy spirit" coming to certain particularly gifted scholars of the Rabbinic period.

uals of course carry on their own life of prayer, sacred study, and practice, Jewish teaching is predominantly expressed in the collective. The biblical system of *mitzvot* (commandments), generally speaking, applies to all Jews. Based on biblical law as elaborated by the Rabbis, Jews are required to pray three times a day, observe the laws of *kashrut* (rules for kosher eating), celebrate the Shabbat (Sabbath) and holy days, as well as adhere to a wide range of ritual, ethical, communal, and interpersonal practices. These requirements are equally binding on all Jews (with occasional exceptions for children, women, and those who are physically unable to observe them).

Jewish sources have a great deal to say about what God wants of us, as in the much-beloved teachings, "And now, O Israel, what does the Lord your God ask of you but to revere the Lord your God, to follow in all of God's ways, to love and serve the Lord your God with all your heart and soul, keeping God's commandments and laws, which I enjoin upon you today, for your good" (Deut. 10:12), and "God has told you, O human being, what is good, and what God requires of you: only to do justice, to love kindness, and to walk humbly with your God" (Micah 6:8). But these life-defining commands are addressed to all Jews (the presumed audience for Jewish sources), not to any individual in particular.

Third, one commonly held view of religious vocation—a call to religious leadership—is completely absent in Jewish life. A rabbi is a person (formerly, a man) who has attained a high level of knowledge of Judaism and is therefore charged to teach the riches of the tradition to others. There is no sense of a "calling" to this "ministry," nor any sense that rabbis are different in any way than any other Jews.

Finally, the words "vocation" and "calling" have a discordant sound to many Jews because enormous numbers of contemporary American Jews do not believe in God, at least in the kind of personal God who could communicate desire or commands to human beings. I will have more to say on this point below. For now, suffice it to say that these four potent factors lead many—especially those holding a narrow view of vocation—to conclude that Judaism has nothing to say about it.

General Calling in Judaism

However, Jewish sources contain many expressions that are comparable to the broader notion of vocation expounded in the Protestant tradition. This is particularly so in the arena of "general," as distinct from "particular" vocation, that is—direction for life addressed to all Jewish human beings rather than uniquely to any individual Jew.

We might begin with the biblical commands that the Israelites are to be "a kingdom of priests and a holy nation" (Exod. 19:6) and the essential exhortation, "Be holy, for I the Lord your God am holy" (Lev. 19:2). These are fundamental instructions for fashioning a life of holiness in response to God's command. These directives apply to all members of the Israelite community, and to their heirs, the Jewish people. In the first command, as in the foundational notion of a covenant binding the people of Israel to its God, the relationship is between God and the Jewish community. In the second, each of us must fashion our own life of holiness in imitation of God, but the command is the same for all of us, regardless of our particular gifts, challenges, interests, or preferences.

The Hebrew Bible pronounces and the Rabbinic sages elaborate on the notion that the basic goal of life for Israelites (and later, Jews) is to observe the *mitzvot* (commandments), as a primary path of service to God. The system of 613 commandments enumerated throughout the Hebrew Bible (some of them moot after the destruction of the Temple in Jerusalem) is easily misunderstood, and sometimes parodied, as a burdensome, slavish, and faithless attention to "the law." From a Jewish perspective, to observe the *mitzvot* is to live in relationship with God and to demonstrate faithfulness not only in creed but in deed—in religious rituals throughout the day and the year, and in every aspect of life. Abraham Joshua Heschel, the renowned twentieth-century philosopher, writes,

> A Jew is asked to take a leap of action rather than a leap of thought. He is asked to surpass his needs, to do more than he understands in order to understand more than he does. In carrying out the word of the Torah he is ushered into the presence of spiritual meaning. Through the ecstasy of deeds he learns to be certain of the hereness of God.[10]

Or, as another contemporary scholar puts it, "*Mitzvot* . . . [are] the heart of one's relationship with God."[11]

The Rabbis created an elaborate system of religious living known as

10. Abraham Joshua Heschel, *God in Search of Man: A Philosophy of Judaism* (New York: Farrar, Straus & Giroux, 1955), 283.

11. Edward Breuer, "Vocation and Call as Individual and Communal Imperatives: Some Reflections on Judaism," in *Revisiting the Idea of Vocation: Theological Explorations*, ed. John C. Haughey, SJ (Washington, DC: Catholic University of America Press), 44.

the *halacha* (literally, "way" or "walk"), based on the commandments given in the Torah, governing most aspects of behavior from the time of awakening in the morning to the moment before falling asleep at night. To accept this system as a way of life is to lace awareness of the divine through virtually every moment of the day, invoking God's presence in all of these moments, and sanctifying the most ordinary of daily activities.

Halachic living is all-encompassing, with no distinction between ritual and "secular" life. One performs these commandments whether or not one feels like doing them at a particular time. With a few exceptions, this way of life is incumbent upon all Jews—no more or less for rabbis.

Deeply related to the observance of *mitzvot* is a set of liturgical *berachot* (blessings). Each *beracha* (blessing) begins with the words, "Blessed are You, Lord our God, Ruler of the Universe," and continues by naming the act to be performed or experienced. There are *berachot* for consuming a wide variety of foods, sights, and scents, for a range of ritual actions and special life experiences, and even for bodily functions. The great sage Rabbi Meir, of the second century CE, taught that one is obligated to utter one hundred blessings every day. Technically, this refers to the recitation of liturgical blessings at many points throughout the day. More broadly, the intent is to pause at as many moments as possible throughout every day, remembering the presence and blessings of God, orienting one's life around these gifts and the obligations they create. Max Kadushin, a twentieth-century rabbi and scholar, refers to this transformation of everyday moments into invocations of the divine as "normal mysticism."

> Normal mysticism enables a person to make normal, common-place, recurrent situations and events occasions for worship. The food he eats, the water he drinks, the dawn and the twilight are joined to *berakhot* [liturgical blessings] acknowledging God's love. These daily common-place situations are not only interpreted in the act of worship as manifestations of God's love, but they arouse in the individual, in the same act of worship, a poignant sense of the nearness of God.[12]

Another central element of Jewish theology and practice is the process of *teshuvah,* or repentance. Narrowly speaking, this refers to an elaborately

---

12. Max Kadushin, *Worship and Ethics: A Study in Rabbinic Judaism* (New York: Bloch, 1963), 168. Throughout this chapter, I have left generic male language in place in direct quotes.

structured process for acknowledgment of sin, confession of wrongdoing, amends for harm done, and transformative work to become a person who could never again commit such an act. More broadly, the word *teshuvah* also means "turning" and "response," and as such refers to the lifelong process of turning away from that which impedes connection to God and turning toward a sacred way of life, as given to the entire Jewish people.

We see here an elaborate system of religious living that provides all members of the community with detailed but general direction for how to construct their lives, moment by moment. The meta-instruction is beautifully encapsulated in a second-century CE wisdom teaching, in which Rabbi Yosi says, "Let all your actions be for the sake of heaven."[13] Individuals are thus to build their lives around sacred teachings of the Torah as interpreted by the Rabbis, addressed to all Jews, without expectation that it would be possible or even appropriate to discern personal directives from God.

Particular Callings in Judaism

As indicated, Jewish teachings lean heavily in the direction of general instructions for living a righteous and faithful life, addressed to the entire Jewish people. However, there are places in the tradition that inspire a sense that divine guidance is available to individuals in their own lives.

With some frequency, Rabbinic sources report the intervention of a *bat kol* (literally, "daughter of a voice"), a disembodied heavenly voice, offering guidance on a matter of law or interpretation. This is generally an intervention to resolve an ambiguous legal situation or a dispute among rabbis. This is not the kind of personal communication with the Ultimate that would respond to an individual's prayer about a life decision, but it does represent a kind of direct divine-human communication.

The following imaginative Hasidic[14] text builds on a more personal notion of the *bat kol* in Rabbinic Judaism.

A *bat kol* (heavenly voice) goes out from Mount Sinai and calls, "Return, you wayward children." What, indeed, is this voice/*bat kol?* Apparently,

---

13. Mishnah *Avot* 2:12.

14. Hasidism refers to an ultra-Orthodox revival movement beginning among Eastern European Jewry from the second half of the eighteenth century onward. The Hasidic rabbis, or "rebbes," left a body of literature, including homiletical, exegetical, and philosophical works.

even though people don't hear this sound that comes each day, still the awakening to repentance is due to that announcement, that indeed, it is that voice that is heard. What then brings about this awakening to repentance each day? It is that we have heard this voice already at Sinai, "I am God . . ." (Exodus 20:2) and "You shall have no other gods before Me" (Exodus 20:3), spoken from God's very lips. This has been inscribed on our hearts, and from this arises the awakening each day . . .[15]

Here the *bat kol* issues a daily rebroadcast of the words originally given to the whole Jewish people at the start of the Ten Commandments. The content of the heavenly voice is general; it is the voice of God in the Torah. Yet this text prescribes how the individual is to attend and respond to the divine voice as articulated through the tradition. Thus, the general call becomes particular, with distinct impact on each individual's life.

Some Rabbinic texts speak of *ru'ach hakodesh* (literally "holy spirit"), referring not to an entity but to divine inspiration offered to a gifted individual, suggesting a capacity to foresee the future, and/or to receive direct guidance. This special gift is available only to extraordinary individuals, but it does evoke the possibility of individual interaction with God about a decision or life direction.

In some wisdom texts there is a suggestion of how to personally discern God's desire, addressed to all Jews, as in: "Rabban Gamliel used to say: 'Do God's will as if it were your own; so that God may do your will as God's own.' "[16] Here individuals are explicitly directed to discern the divine will for their lives and to fashion their lives around it. This text and others like it challenge the commonly held notion that Jewish sources speak always and only in the collective voice. Secular Jews tend to find such references to "God's will" foreign, offensive, and "un-Jewish," and would be surprised to find the phrase in a Jewish text at all. But its presence in a popular Rabbinic text challenges the predominant narrative according to which Jews access God only through collective prayer, ritual, and study.

In Hasidic sources one finds many explicit reflections on the inner life, including a process for aligning one's life with the desires of the Holy. Take, for example, the creative Hasidic etymology that connects the word *mitzvah* (commandment) with the Aramaic word *b'tsavta* (together), expressed here

15. *Kedushat Levi*, Commentary by Rabbi Levi Yitzhak of Berditchev (1740–1809, Poland).

16. Mishnah *Avot* 2:4.

by Heschel, himself an heir to the Hasidic tradition: "A mitzvah is . . . an act of *communion* with God. The spirit of *mitzvah* is *togetherness*. We know, He is a partner to our act."[17] According to this interpretation, the observance of commandments is not only a matter of law incumbent upon all Jews, but also a practice for living in a state of intimacy with God. As such, living within the collective system of Jewish religious practice is itself a path to personal closeness to God on a moment-by-moment basis throughout one's life.

The Hasidic masters were also deeply interested in the process of *devekut* (literally, "cleaving") or attachment to the divine. At its highest level this is an experience of mystical union with God, usually available only to particularly gifted rabbis or "rebbes." But the teachings also encourage ordinary individuals to place God at the center of their lives, as a constant source of guidance, orientation, and concern. According to Hasidism scholar Arthur Green, "Each person should seek to live a life of constant *devekut*, never allowing the mind to depart from God even for a moment," leading each individual toward an ideal of going "about their affairs without ever removing their minds from constant concentration on God."[18]

This process of cleaving or attachment to God is not described as facilitating communication or particular content, as in answers to a question about which career path to pursue or which individual to marry. Rather, it describes an ideal of constant orientation of one's life toward and with the divine.

Consider also the following striking Hasidic text, which explores the inner process of turning the heart toward God in repentance.

> Everything is from the Blessed One, even the stirrings to *teshuvah* (repentance, return, or reorientation). When a person repents/turns, the impetus comes from Above, as it says in the Zohar,[19] "The Blessed Holy One calls every day, 'Return, you wayward children' (Jeremiah 3:14)" but who listens to the call? But it is known that an angel is created from the word of the Blessed One, and this angel enters the heart of the person and introduces the inclination to repentance into the heart.[20]

17. Heschel, *God in Search of Man,* 287.

18. Arthur Green, *These Are the Words: A Vocabulary of Jewish Spiritual Life* (Woodstock, VT: Jewish Lights, 1999), 123–24.

19. The Zohar (literally, "Radiance") is the preeminent work of Jewish mysticism, authored by Spanish kabbalist Moses ben Shem Tov de Leon, who died in 1305.

20. Rabbi Dov Baer of Mezeritch (1700–1772, Poland), *Maggid Devarav leYa'akov,* "He Tells His Words to Jacob."

Like the source we saw previously, this Hasidic author, drawing from an earlier Jewish mystical tradition, imagines God calling out every day to humanity, with the biblical words, "Return, you wayward children," urging the return of all souls to their rightful orientation to the sacred. But, he continues, if we look around at the state of the world, it surely looks as if no one is listening to this divine call! And so God creates an angel that infiltrates each human heart, there gradually introducing the impulse to spiritual growth and righteous living. The text, then, becomes a poetic exhortation to each individual to listen deeply and personally to the voice of God.

Once again, the content of the divine proclamation is a repetition of biblical words, already part of the collective record of divine revelation. But with the introduction of the angel into each soul, it is clear that the collective words are to be received and responded to in a deeply personal way.

Similarly, Rabbi Yehudah Leib of Ger[21] offers a lyrical explanation of the divine "point" that resides within the human heart, and how that point must be cleansed and renewed each year through the prayer and ritual of the High Holy Days.

> There is a holy point in each Jewish person's heart. This is the living soul. . . . But over the course of each year, as we become accustomed to sinning, the material self overpowers and hides that holy point. We then have to seek compassion from the blessed Holy One, asking that this imprint in our heart be renewed on Rosh Hashanah (Jewish New Year). This is what we mean when we say [in the High Holy Day liturgy], "Inscribe us for life."[22]

In his writings, this Hasidic teacher frequently describes the "point," the locus of divine presence in the human heart, letting us know who we are supposed to be. But he teaches that the human heart regularly becomes occluded, making it impossible for the person to be true to his or her divine essence. Words of (communal) prayer are the vehicle by which the person can reconnect with his or her divine essence, back into a state of sacred alignment with God.

21. Prominent Hasidic rabbi in Poland (1847–1905).

22. Arthur Green, *The Language of Truth: The Torah Commentary of Rabbi Yehudah Leib of Ger,* trans. and interpreted by Arthur Green (Philadelphia: Jewish Publication Society, 1998), 343.

Closer still to a notion of individual calling, one finds in Hasidic literature a concept of *shlichut* (personal mission, life task, or purpose), given to an individual by God, as in the following twentieth-century Hasidic text:

> Every individual is a small world unto himself. . . . No person has ever been identical to another person since the creation of the world, and therefore each and every person has a special *sh'lichut* (mission), a distinctive purpose for which he was sent. . . . The beginning of all service is discovering for what particular purpose one was sent to this world.[23]

This text departs markedly from the predominantly collective voice of classical Jewish sources. Here we have an evocative description of the uniqueness of each human soul, the suggestion that each person has a particular mission to fulfill, and an exhortation to each soul to discern what that purpose might be.

In twentieth-century Jewish philosophy, one finds bolder expressions of the individual's role in discerning divine commands. Wrestling with the place of *halacha* (Jewish law) in the lives of modern Jews, Franz Rosenzweig[24] and Martin Buber[25] elevated the importance of the inner life of the individual, and transformed the collective voice of "commandment" into a sense of direct personal connection to the divine.

Rosenzweig famously wrote, "God is not a lawgiver. But he commands."[26] This was an expression of Rosenzweig's novel distinction between *gesetz* (law) and *gebot* (commandment), the difference between mere legislation and true commandment animated by divine love.[27] That is to say, Rosenzweig stretched the tradition's conviction that all of the *mitzvot* were literally given by God, suggesting that God "speaks" personally to the Jewish individual through the medium of the commandments. Thus, each of the commandments communicates the divine voice to each individual.

Rosenzweig went so far as to assert that the only part of the Ten

---

23. Rabbi Sholom Noach Berezofsky, or "Slonimer Rebbe" (1911–2000, Tel Aviv and Jerusalem), *Netivot Shalom (Pathways of Peace)*, "Paths of Knowledge" 6:2 (Jerusalem: House of Slonim, 1933).

24. Jewish philosopher in Germany (1886–1929).

25. Jewish philosopher, born in Austria, died in Israel (1878–1965).

26. Arnold Eisen, *Rethinking Modern Judaism: Ritual, Commandment, Community* (Chicago: University of Chicago Press, 1998), 196.

27. Eisen, *Rethinking Modern Judaism,* 198.

Commandments that was actually spoken by God were the words, "I am the Lord your God," or perhaps only the single word "I," "that is, the announcement of God's presence."[28] For Rosenzweig, while the content of the commandments is significant as the collective path prescribed for the Jewish people, what is most meaningful about the commandments is the love of the One who commands.

Buber takes this idea a step further, rejecting all traditional notions of the obligatory nature of the *mitzvot* (commandments) given in the Torah to all Jews. In fact, for Buber, observance of the collective *mitzvot* actually impedes personal relationship with God, which can only arise in a unique moment of "I-Thou" encounter between God and an individual. For him, to categorically prioritize the *mitzvot* given to the collective would be to block access to the immediacy of real, individual divine-human encounter. Buber's thought was disregarded by many Jewish leaders, as his utter rejection of the *mitzvot* puts him at odds with the mainstream tradition.

This set of materials has offered a challenge to the narrative according to which Jewish texts speak always and only to the entire Jewish people. Certainly, many texts (most often in Hasidic works) stress that individuals are to make unique use of wisdom teachings in the tradition for their personal lives. Some texts and concepts have demonstrated that there is at least a substratum or minority view in Jewish sources, suggesting the possibility of an individual Jew "hearing" direction from the divine for his or her life.

Divine Guidance in Judaism

In the Hebrew Bible, patriarchs (and occasionally matriarchs) and prophets are said to experience direct visual and auditory contact with God. Of course, biblical interpreters through the ages have differed on how to understand such anthropomorphic descriptions, but the texts clearly describe something akin to person-to-person communication. Since the close of the age of formal prophecy, Rabbinic Judaism teaches that divine guidance is to be discerned through study of Torah, the record of collective revelation from the divine.

In traditional Jewish communities, individuals are to consult a rabbinic authority as to how such general principles are to be applied in their

28. Eisen, *Rethinking Modern Judaism*, 206.

own life situation. Particularly in ultra-Orthodox communities, Jews bring questions about personal life decisions to a rabbi (or "rebbe"), investing the rabbi's answer with divine authority. Most contemporary non-Orthodox Jews rely primarily on their own conscience, the advice of loved ones, mentors, and professional advisors for individual guidance, considering Jewish principles, if so inclined.

For some spiritually minded Jews, prayer and meditation have once again become vehicles for seeking divine direction about a particular life situation. While many consider prayer to be primarily focused on communal needs, others might invoke the concept of *kavvanah* (intention, from the root meaning, "direction"), classically used to describe an individual's attitude of piety and attentiveness in prayer. Ancient sources use this term in the sense of "directing the heart towards heaven" in prayer.[29] Prayer in this spirit—deriving from the desires and needs of the heart rather than from formal liturgy—can be used as part of a process of discerning guidance about a personal life decision.

Living Out a Calling

The Hebrew Bible contains a genre of call narratives, in which individuals are summoned by God for a particular task, usually a position of community leadership or prophecy. For example, Abram (with Sarai) is called to leave his native land and lead a great people; Abraham is summoned to sacrifice his son Isaac; and several literary prophets (among them, Isaiah, Jeremiah, and Ezekiel) are called to bring God's word to the people in particular historical situations. Intriguingly, several of these stories include expressions of resistance on the part of the chosen one who feels inadequate to the task, or, in the case of Jonah, who is opposed to God's desires.

As contemporary Jews reflect on how to make life decisions in accord with a sense of meaning or even divine guidance, very few would identify with biblical characters who were literally called by God to perform a particular task. Identifying oneself with such a character would, in a contemporary Jewish context, seem arrogant at best. But these call stories exemplify elements of a process that can guide contemporary Jews in crafting a meaningful life.

For this purpose, the best example to consider may be the call of Mo-

---

29. E.g., Babylonian Talmud *Berachot* 31a.

ses. As the book of Exodus tells his story, he is saved from death by Pharaoh's decree when his mother courageously places him in a basket and leaves him at the river, where he is miraculously rescued by the Pharaoh's own daughter. A child of Israelite slaves, he is raised in the royal family, the oppressors of his own people.

But as the text tells the story, it is not this remarkable personal background that causes God to choose Moses as the leader of his people, but rather an apparently ordinary act on Moses's own part in a nondescript place in the wilderness. In the third chapter of Exodus, we are told that Moses, keeping the flocks for his father-in-law Jethro, noticed a small bush on fire. There would be nothing unusual about such a sight in a parched Middle Eastern landscape. What was unusual was that the bush, aflame, was not consumed (Exod. 3:2).

Rabbi Lawrence Kushner has observed that Moses could only have noticed this peculiar feature of the bush by stopping and choosing to pay close attention to the scene over a period of time.[30] Only by pausing in the midst of his workday and deeply observing what was before him was he able to see that the bush was not growing smaller as the fire consumed it. His focused and faithful attention allowed him to recognize that this bush was a wondrous sight, an invitation into the presence of God. It was only when God saw that Moses had "turned aside," bringing his full awareness to what was before him, with readiness to perceive the extraordinary, that God called to Moses, in the characteristic language of call narratives, "Moses, Moses." And Moses replied, "*Hineini*, Here I am" (Exod. 3:4). God then made explicit what Moses already knew, that the place where he stood was holy ground.

The text then details a remarkably protracted negotiation between God and Moses, who protests that he is inadequate to the task to which God calls him. Moses is hesitant and afraid, doubting his own capacity for leadership, frightened that the Israelites will not follow him, and concerned that he lacks the oratorical skill required for the task. God must respond at length (first patiently and then angrily) to Moses's apprehensions before Moses accepts the call.

This complex story contains many of the key features of a process of discernment of call: attentiveness, wonder, communal consciousness, and humility. I will briefly explore each of these in turn.

---

30. Lawrence Kushner, *God Was in This Place and I, I Did Not Know* (Woodstock, VT: Jewish Lights, 1991), 25.

First is attentiveness. As indicated above, the essential feature of the story of Moses's call is his willingness to turn his full attention to how life is addressing him at that moment. Moses, engaged in his daily responsibilities, might have rushed on by the small brushfire, entirely missing the sacred opportunity that awaited him. The text indicates that God did not call out to Moses until God saw that Moses had "turned aside to see" (Exod. 3:4), revealing that Moses possessed the essential capacity for deep attentiveness that would be required for his sacred assignment.

Second is wonder. The sacred moment at the bush would not have unfolded had skepticism kept Moses from seeing deeply what was transpiring before him. Had Moses responded to the reality of the miracle in the wilderness with doubt or distrust, the divine would not have revealed itself. Moses might have lived out his life without ever finding the great work that was his to do, and the Israelites' suffering would have continued as God sought an appropriate human partner.

Third is communal consciousness. Prior to the story of the burning bush, the Torah had described two formative occurrences in Moses's early life: his killing an Egyptian taskmaster (Exod. 2:11–12) and his rebuke of two Hebrew slaves struggling violently with one another (Exod. 2:13–15). The first indicated Moses's recognition of the persecution suffered by his people, and his willingness to act boldly on their behalf. The second revealed Moses's readiness to act as a leader, chastising his countrymen for attacking one another. These two incidents established that Moses, despite his sojourn in Pharaoh's house, felt deep empathy for his people's predicament, and could embody the imperative to lead them out of their physical, moral, and spiritual degradation, even if they would frequently resist his leadership.

Fourth is humility. Moses, consumed by burdens of fear and self-doubt, struggled mightily against God's assignment for him. This characteristic is a common motif in the calling of prophets—most strikingly in the call of the prophet Isaiah, whom God leads through a ritual of healing and atonement to transform his "unclean lips," which made him feel unqualified to serve God (Isa. 6:6–7). Moses conjured one image of failure after another, doubting both himself and his people in the process, eventually wearing out God's patience in the negotiation. One might find the scene humorous or pathetic were it not such a telling window into the soul of the prospective leader.

The descriptions of the biblical prophets frequently include this element of humility and self-doubt, all the more so for us, who must discern our callings without hearing God's voice directly. A project born of arrogance and hyper-certainty more likely derives from personal ambition or impulsiveness than from the voice of the holy. While ambition certainly has a place in a life of purposeful action, self-aggrandizement easily crowds out the still small voice of the divine.

Moses's experience, as described in the text, then, is not a tale of self-actualization alone. Rather, all of the circumstances of his life converged, so that the circumstances of his birth, his personal characteristics, and his deep desire to combat injustice made him the right person to lead his people out of slavery. Paraphrasing Buechner's renowned definition of calling,[31] Moses's personal anguish over injustice met his people's "deep hunger" for liberation. This confluence of factors was powerful enough to overcome his doubt and lead him to accept the work assigned to him.

This story illustrates a number of suggestions that contemporary Jews—both those who cultivate a relationship with the divine in their lives and those who do not—can use to discover a path in work and life that accords with their own deepest sense of meaning, purpose, and righteousness. The first is paying deep and reverent attention to one's life over a period of time, seeking responses to the question, "What am I called to do?" Second, the process of listening for guidance, while it may include rational analysis, is nourished primarily by an attitude of wonder, an openness to guidance that may come from beyond the self or from deep within. Third, a sense of calling arises out of our deep-rooted understanding of the needs of our community or our world, and the way in which our own gifts and experiences may allow us to address those needs. Finally, the process requires humility, including willingness to set aside more self-centered preferences in order to accept a call to serve.

Many contemporary Jews engage the qualities of attentiveness and communal consciousness, particularly in the course of choosing a career path. While they may or may not think of this as an explicitly spiritual process, they think deeply about their unique blend of gifts, passions, life experience, and the needs of their community and the world, as they make choices about how to invest their time and efforts. Many would also do well to engage the qualities of wonder and humility as they discern a life path. This kind of contemplation would likely direct Jews away from decisions

---

31. "The place God calls you to is the place where your deep gladness and the world's deep need meet." Frederick Buechner, at Frederick Buechner Center, accessed June 30, 2015, http://www.frederickbuechner.com/content/vocation-1.

based on self-serving, materialistic, or purely rational analysis and toward choices more in alignment with who they are meant to be.

Jewish Spiritual Practices

"Simon the Just said: The world rests upon three things: Torah, worship, and deeds of lovingkindness."[32] In this classic early Rabbinic formulation, Simon the Just[33] describes Judaism as a religious system that rests on three legs: study of Jewish sacred text, worship, and the regular practice of interpersonal and communal acts of kindness, particularly to those in need.[34] While faith in a personal God is the defining characteristic of religious life in most forms of Christianity, Judaism is built on three equally important religious practices: study, prayer, and action.

While all Jews are considered bound to engage in all of these religious obligations, some Jews are temperamentally drawn to one more than to another. Some contemporary Jewish thinkers have observed that there are "head Jews, heart Jews, and hand Jews."[35] Some Jews are naturally drawn— perhaps called, by virtue of temperament or preference, to the "head"—the intellectual work of encountering sacred texts; to the "heart"—the way of prayer, meditation, and cultivation of connection to the divine; or to the "hand"—serving others through acts of care and kindness and the work of social justice.

By this logic, some contemporary Jewish leaders (particularly the non-Orthodox) embrace the plurality of ways in which Jews may plumb the resources of the tradition, construct a richly meaningful life, and do good in the world, as in this evocative description by Rabbi Lawrence Kushner:

32. Mishnah *Avot* 1:2.

33. Temple priest and scholar, third century BCE.

34. Intriguingly for our purposes, the word translated as "worship" literally means "work," which could be taken to mean that devotion to (presumably meaningful) work is a key ingredient of religious life. This teaching was first offered at a time when the Temple stood, when the word *avodah* referred to sacrificial worship. Later, it came to mean prayer, observance of *mitzvot* (commandments), and relationship with God. However, some commentators understand it literally, suggesting that in work, human beings partner with God, whose work created the universe.

35. This coinage is so widely used that it is difficult to isolate a source. I suspect that it originates with Rabbi Lawrence Kushner, *I'm God, You're Not: Observations on Organized Religion and Other Disguises of the Ego* (Woodstock, VT: Jewish Lights, 2010), 23.

There are many ways we reach for the Holy One(ness). We can attain self-transcendence through our mind in study, through our heart in prayer, or with our hands in sacred deed. We say, in effect, that through becoming God's agent, through voluntarily setting God's will above our own, we literally lose ourselves and become one with the One whom we serve.[36]

For "head Jews," the way to integrate time-honored sources of meaning is through encounter with sacred texts. The way to find guidance with a life decision is to look to the ancient texts and apply collective truths expressed there to one's personal situation.

For "heart Jews," the "seekers," the way to get beyond the self is through prayer, meditation, and reflective introspection. For such people, contemplative practice, spiritual teachers, and community are central resources, including, for some, the help of a Jewish spiritual director.

"Hand Jews" find their personal meaning in service, whether to those suffering illness and bereavement, for example, or to social justice work. It is this group that has enthusiastically revived the ancient Jewish idea of *tikkun olam,* repair of the world, providing ancient Jewish language for the pursuit of justice and compassion in the world. Remarkably, the newly refashioned term *tikkun olam,* disconnected from its original moorings in Rabbinic and Kabbalistic Judaism in which God was central, has served to provide many secular Jews with a way to name a sense of transcendent meaning without a belief in a personal God.

Jews seeking to align their lives and life choices with Jewish wisdom and meaning have all of these practices, as articulated in the tradition, to support and enrich their way of living. For some, engaging in regular study of Jewish sacred texts is the way to stay grounded, to continue to grow spiritually, and to find answers to real-life questions with which they struggle. For other Jews, the primary source of Jewish spiritual support is the life of prayer, including daily prayer and observance of the Shabbat and other sacred holy days. For many Jews, especially those of a secular orientation, the best source of nourishment and meaning is in the interpersonal realm: engaging in acts of kindness, tending treasured relationships with loved ones, active involvement in Jewish community, and working for justice in the broader society.

Shabbat practice is particularly significant for this exploration of Jew-

36. Lawrence Kushner, *The Book of Words: Talking Spiritual Life, Living Spiritual Talk* (Woodstock, VT: Jewish Lights, 1993), 15–16.

ish practices of call and vocation. In Shabbat observance, one enacts a weekly cycle of alternating between times of work and active engagement with the world, on the one hand, and Shabbat—a time of intentional withdrawal from work in the world, on the other. The Torah commands, "Six days you shall labor and do all your work, but the seventh day is a sabbath of Adonai your God; you shall do no manner of work . . ." (Exod. 20:9–10). The Torah honors and even requires days of work—engagement with the world, creative activity by which humans help to complete God's work of creation. But the work days must be punctuated by Sabbath—a time of pause and replenishment, prayer, reflection, and appreciation—living in the sphere of being rather than doing. On the Sabbath we cease our efforts to put our mark upon the world, and turn our attention instead to the beauty of the world as it is, as God gave it to us.

Searching for God in Contemporary Judaism

The Pew Research Center's recent authoritative study, "A Portrait of Jewish Americans," confirms what has long been clear to observers of American Jewish life:

> Secularism has a long tradition in Jewish life in America, and most U.S. Jews seem to recognize this: 62% say being Jewish is mainly a matter of ancestry and culture, while just 15% say it is mainly a matter of religion. Even among Jews by religion,[37] more than half (55%) say being Jewish is mainly a matter of ancestry and culture, and two-thirds say it is not necessary to believe in God to be Jewish.[38]

> Most Jews see no conflict between being Jewish and not believing in God; two-thirds say that a person can be Jewish even if he or she does not believe in God.[39]

---

37. The Pew Study distinguished between "Jews by religion," for whom Jewish identity is primarily experienced as a matter of religion, and "Jews of no religion," who self-identify as Jews based on ancestry, culture, or social networks.

38. "A Portrait of Jewish Americans: Overview," Pew Research Center, 10/1/2013, accessed March 2, 2015, http://www.pewforum.org/2013/10/01/jewish-american-beliefs-attitudes-culture-survey/.

39. "A Portrait of Jewish Americans: Full Report," accessed March 2, 2015, http://www.pewforum.org/files/2013/10/jewish-american-full-report-for-web.pdf, 74.

To put it starkly, a substantial majority of American Jews, even those who observe an active Jewish religious life, are basically secular in their attitudes. Such people generally do not think of God as a reality in their lives, or affirm a belief in God in any but the most general terms.[40]

Strange as this may sound from a Christian perspective, it is entirely possible to be profoundly connected to Jewish religious life—attending synagogue regularly, participating in a range of home-oriented rituals, constructing one's life around the Jewish sacred calendar, and engaging in regular study of Jewish sacred text—and not believe that "God" (at least the anthropomorphic version of God described in most Jewish sacred texts) has anything to do with it. In a widely told joke with a ring of truth, Mr. Cohen speaks to a fellow synagogue member about their common friend, an unusually pious Jew named Mr. Schwartz. "He (Mr. Schwartz) comes to synagogue to talk to God. I come to talk to Schwartz!" North American synagogues have many people like the mythical Cohen and relatively few Schwartzes.

Without God-belief, the notion of a life of holiness is difficult to grasp, much less a personal relationship with the One. For such Jews, it seems far more reasonable to construct one's life around a set of choices carefully chosen on rational terms than to seek elusive connection with the supernatural realm.

Generally speaking, Jews tend to treasure Western ideals of individual autonomy and rationalism, since these ideas were fruits of the European Enlightenment that liberated Jews from a life in the ghetto. Even Jews who yearn for a deeper spiritual life can find it exceedingly difficult to transcend the typically secular thought patterns of skepticism, materialism, and consumerism that pervade North American Jewish life. This leaves such Jews without a familiar place to turn to in times of personal tragedy, loss, or confusion.

A corollary to this secular outlook is a particular construction of Jewish identity in the post-Holocaust era. Since the Nazi Holocaust, great numbers of Jews (especially the non-Orthodox) have built their religious lives around what Jacob Neusner has called the "American Judaism of Holocaust and Redemption," drawing semi-religious meaning from the abyss of the Holocaust and messianic faith in the rise of the State of Israel as

---

40. "Seven-in-ten U.S. Jews believe in God or a universal spirit (72%), including one-third (34%) who say they are 'absolutely certain' about this belief." "A Portrait of Jewish Americans: Full Report," 74.

evidence of redemption.[41] A form of "religious" life focused on Holocaust memory, defense of the State of Israel and endangered Jews around the world, and participation in Jewish communal organizations has for a remarkable number of American Jews replaced the traditional beliefs and practices prescribed in Jewish tradition.

This construction of Jewish life powerfully impacts the individual identity of many American Jews, enriching personal life with a deeply felt sense of connection to Jews throughout the ages and around the world. It also provides individuals with a set of powerful and orienting imperatives for their lives, including working to build and nurture local Jewish communities, defending Jews in peril around the world, standing as a witness to the nature of evil as embodied in the Nazi Holocaust, and a passion for protecting the State of Israel against real and feared assaults. This form of "Jewishness" imbues individual lives with collective connection and commitment. However, it does not enrich personal life in the ways that traditional religious categories of sacred wisdom, practice, commandment, or religious community can.

All of that said, North American Jewry has in recent decades seen a resurgence of interest in the spiritual dimensions of Judaism. An entire library of books on Jewish spirituality, a large community of spiritually minded rabbis and Jewish educators, and a cottage industry of Jewish retreat programs have emerged to respond to the spiritual hunger of contemporary Jews. For many, the political, intellectual, and consumerist convictions that seemed so compelling in the modern era have not fulfilled the existential needs that religion once did. The new Jewish spiritual resources offer possibilities for accessing ancient Jewish texts and practices and experiences of community that can offer dimensions of a life of meaning, purpose, and attunement to the Ultimate, even without traditional God-belief. In these ways, even secular Jews can draw on authentic Jewish texts and practices as they construct moral lives of significance and connection.

Starting Points

William C. Placher asks poignantly, "Can there be a calling without someone who calls?"[42] This question parallels a key question for modern Judaism: how

---

41. Jacob Neusner, *The Way of Torah: An Introduction to Judaism,* 6th ed. (Belmont, CA: Wadsworth, 1997), 225–34.

42. William C. Placher, ed., *Callings: Twenty Centuries of Christian Wisdom on Vocation* (Grand Rapids: Eerdmans, 2005), 2.

to inculcate a sense of *mitzvah* (commandment) for those who no longer believe in a Commander or a divine Author of Torah. How can we construct a basis for a sense of obligation to others, to community, and to the divine without the traditional theological scaffolding? How are we to nurture commitment to community, to ethical living, and to the continuity of Jewish life, without a belief in a commanding God? This is perhaps the key question that has engaged Jewish leaders since the dawn of the Enlightenment, heightened as postmodern sensibilities have led many young people to distance themselves from traditional and communal structures of any kind.

Spiritually minded rabbis and educators work to encourage contemporary Jews to question how well their dogmatically individualist and materialist convictions serve them in the creation of a life infused with meaning. The tradition is full of starting points for the gradual transformation of a secular life into a way of living characterized by God-awareness, humility, awe, gratitude, and commitment to service. Once seekers allow themselves to encounter Jewish sacred texts with the heart rather than with the prized skeptical mind, models and directions for reorienting one's life are everywhere. Jewish sources—from the Bible to the voluminous contemporary literature on Jewish spirituality and everything in between—are filled with suggestions of how individuals can and do encounter the divine. There are countless avenues for developing a personal practice of prayer and contemplation, even without a belief in an anthropomorphic version of God.

It is essential to recognize that many of the treasures of Jewish tradition are still accessible, even to liberal and secular Jews, as long as their leaders are cognizant of the work needed to bridge the gaps between ancient imagery and contemporary lives. Large numbers of Jews cannot relate to the God described in classical texts: a God described in human terms, who prefers one people over another, a deity who commands and punishes at will. But this anthropomorphic imagery is only the surface meaning of these classical texts. Jews and Jewish leaders together can continue the process of creative exegesis, unearthing the deeper meanings of the texts and practices so that they can reach contemporary Jews, who are so much in need of sources of guidance and meaning in their lives.

Conclusion

In closing, I am reminded of a beloved prayer in the Shabbat and holiday liturgy, *"Vetaher libeinu l'ovdecha be'emet,"* "Purify my heart to serve You in truth." This brief prayer can serve as a concise summary of Jewish beliefs about the path to a life of meaning, righteousness, and God-awareness. The prayer is based on an assumption that the human heart contains all the goodness (even the divine essence) needed for any human life. When, in the course of living, accretions of impurity and pain gradually clog and cloud the heart's clarity, one must ask for help to restore it to its pure state. This ongoing work of cleansing and refining the heart, the core of religious practice, offers an always-available path to a life of service, connection, and meaning.

Resources

Addison, Rabbi Howard A., and Barbara Breitman. *Jewish Spiritual Direction: An Innovative Guide from Traditional and Contemporary Sources.* Woodstock, VT: Jewish Lights, 2006.

Eilberg, Rabbi Amy. *From Enemy to Friend: Jewish Wisdom and the Pursuit of Peace.* Maryknoll, NY: Orbis, 2014.

Elwell, Sue Levi, and Nancy Fuchs Kreimer, eds. *Chapters of the Heart: Jewish Women Sharing the Torah of Our Lives.* Eugene, OR: Wipf & Stock, 2013.

Fuchs-Kreimer, Nancy. *Parenting as a Spiritual Journey.* Woodstock, VT: Jewish Lights, 1998.

Kushner, Lawrence. *The Book of Words: Talking Spiritual Life, Living Spiritual Talk.* Woodstock, VT: Jewish Lights, 1993.

Green, Arthur. *Judaism's Ten Best Ideas: A Brief Guide for Seekers.* Woodstock, VT: Jewish Lights, 2014.

———. *These Are the Words: A Vocabulary of Jewish Spiritual Life.* Woodstock, VT: Jewish Lights, 2012.

Levy, Naomi. *To Begin Again: The Journey Toward Comfort, Strength, and Faith in Difficult Times.* New York: Ballantine, 1999.

Ochs, Carol. *Our Lives as Torah: Finding God in Our Own Stories.* San Francisco: Jossey-Bass, 2007.

Strassfeld, Rabbi Michael. *A Book of Life: Embracing Judaism as a Spiritual Practice.* Woodstock, VT: Jewish Lights, 2006.

2

Called to Follow

Vocation in the Catholic Tradition

KATHLEEN A. CAHALAN

During the summer after my senior year of high school I volunteered in a six-week service program. I had a sense that God was guiding me to a life of service to the sick or the handicapped, but I wanted to experience something of this before I went off to study for a career in these fields. I was disappointed when I was not assigned to a hospital and ended up in Georgia teaching in a Bible camp for grade-school children. I was pretty sure this was not my calling since I had no gift for teaching children. Over the course of the first few weeks, the situation was not going well between me and the sister who was leading our four-person team—no doubt I was grumbling about my unfair situation. The sister finally told me not to attend the camp for the final two weeks, but to go visit the sick if that's what I wanted to do. With that, the team left me alone to figure it out. I had the list of parishioners but actually little desire to go meet strangers by myself. So, instead of visiting the sick, I hung around our house and slept most of the day.

During one afternoon nap I had a dream in which my name was shouted at me: "Kathleen." Startled, I woke up. Groggy and hot, I struggled to wake up. But then I really woke up, and not just from the nap, but from my own laziness. I heard God shouting at me. I realized I had just one week left and so I grabbed the list and visited everyone in the parish. When I went to college that autumn, I wrote "Kathleen" on the registration form rather than "Kathy," the name with which I had been called since childhood.

My story has several significant features of calling stories in the Catholic tradition. I'm trying to discern what I should do with my life and

26

whether I have certain gifts for a particular kind of work. I'm frustrated when choices don't work out and wonder what God is up to with my life. I received a message in a dream, woke up from my blindness and selfishness, and went out to serve. And, finally, I changed my name.

Discernment, gifts, frustration, feeling lost, a message, service, and a new name. Throughout the Catholic tradition, these elements have been essential to understanding vocation. Take, for example, Iñigo López de Loyola, later known as St. Ignatius of Loyola (1491–1556), the sixteenth-century Spanish noble who created one of the most powerful global religious orders whose purpose was education. He was a young man pursuing the good life but was wounded in battle and bedridden for months. With plenty of good books to read on chivalry and brave knights who won their battles, he also began reading a book about the life of Christ and another about the saints. Initially he liked both sets of books, but was increasingly drawn to the latter. He began to realize that he felt differently when reading about the saints' lives—he experienced great peace and a sense of consolation. He realized the life he had been leading was not worthwhile and that he was seeking his own glory. He wanted to change and be in the service of God and to give God glory through his work.

He became a pilgrim and longed to visit the Holy Land. Along the way, he experienced several significant visions of Christ that offered him reassurance and direction. He went on to study in Paris and, with a few other young men, they vowed together to live a life of chastity, poverty, and obedience, thus forming the Society of Jesus, or the Jesuits, as they are commonly called. During his studies it seems that he adopted the name "Ignatius," after a saint he admired, Ignatius of Antioch (died ca. 107), and his diploma from the University of Paris bears his new name.

The word "catholic" comes from the Greek *katholikos,* meaning "universal," and from the phrase *kath' holou,* "on the whole." It was first used by St. Ignatius of Antioch in a letter in which he is making a case for a bishop's leadership: "Where the bishop is to be seen, there let all his people be; just as wherever Jesus Christ is present, we have the catholic Church."[1] But since the time of the East-West Schism in 1054 CE and the Protestant Reformation in the early 1500s, Christians have tended to use Catholic as a name for one of the Christian churches, which is distinct from Orthodox or Protestant Christians. It is important to note, however, that the term

1. Quoted in Richard P. McBrien, *Catholicism,* new ed. (San Francisco: HarperSanFrancisco, 1994), 3.

"catholic" is used by all Christians who recite the Apostles' Creed: "we believe in one, holy, catholic and apostolic church."

Although we tend to think of the name as the "Roman Catholic Church," Roman is a geographical description—a place that is central for this community because it is the diocese where the Bishop of Rome presides, who is also called the Pope, or *papa*, the leader of the whole worldwide church. A clearer designation of what makes the Catholic church distinct from other Christian churches is the Petrine primacy, the belief that Christ established his church on St. Peter, the rock (Matt. 16:18).

Within Catholicism there have been two dominant interpretations of "catholic," each having deep roots in the tradition, which continue to shape theology and practice today.[2] The first approach defines "catholic" as "universal" and "worldwide," drawing from Ignatius of Antioch and most recently expressed in the Second Vatican Council (1962–1965) pastoral document, *Gaudium et Spes* ("The Church in the Modern World"), which calls for the church to embrace the world as the place of theological engagement. The second approach defines "catholic" as the "fullness of faith, the depository and guarantor" of the faith. The second approach is concerned with the unique life of the church, the defender of the true deposit of faith, as it is expressed in its liturgy and moral teachings. It rests on a neo-Augustinian view of the world that sees the culture as morally corrupt and dangerous and the church as a safe shelter from the world's unethical and evil ways. The church bears a truth that the world does not know.

The Catholic tradition is a living tradition, which means its life, teachings, and practices are rooted in the biblical narrative and have taken shape over the past two millennia. Its practice is rooted in seven sacraments (Baptism, Eucharist, Confirmation, Reconciliation, Marriage, Ordination, Anointing of the Sick), the ordination of celibate men to be priests and bishops, a long tradition of theological writings, especially a body of social teachings, and compelling stories of people called "saints."

Today Catholicism is a worldwide community with about 1.2 billion believers, of which 41 percent live in Latin America, 23 percent in Europe, 15 percent in Africa, 11.7 percent in Asia, 7.3 percent in North America, and 0.8 percent in Oceania.[3] In the US, there are 69 million Catholics,

2. Robert Schreiter, CPPS, "Pastoral Theology as Contextual: Forms of Catholic Pastoral Theology Today," in *Keeping Faith in Practice: Aspects of Catholic Pastoral Theology*, ed. James Sweeney, Gemma Simmonds, and David Lonsdale (London: SCM Press, 2010), 64–79.

3. See "How Many Roman Catholics Are There in the World?" BBC News World,

about 22 percent of the population; of these about 52,000 are bishops and priests, 52,000 sisters, 18,000 deacons, 4,400 brothers. Catholics gather in local churches (17,900 parishes) for worship, education, and service; they also sponsor many schools and hospitals (e.g., 542 hospitals, 3,300 social service agencies, 232 colleges and universities, 1,300 high schools, 5,600 grade schools, and 165,000 lay teachers).[4]

The God Who Calls and the Catholic Response

In addition to the key characteristics of a call experience noted above, there is a major difference between my story and that of St. Ignatius of Loyola. The Catholic tradition has for many centuries used the language of vocation to refer to a call to the priesthood or religious life, meaning a life in which a person joins a community and takes the vows of poverty, obedience (to the superior of the community), and celibacy. Max Weber, a sociologist of religion, calls these "heroic" or "virtuoso" people who a community deemed unique and special in the way they strove to pursue a life completely focused on their religious commitments. As distinct from Protestantism, but not unlike some other traditions discussed in this book, religious virtuosos in the Catholic community created a "status stratification" between the spiritual elite and the ordinary believer, or layperson. Catholics have not generally used the term "vocation" to refer to married or single life, or to work, as in the Protestant tradition, though this has been changing over the past sixty years, as I discuss later in the chapter.

In the first four hundred years of the Christian church, what is often referred to as the patristic age because of the number of writings by church fathers, vocation had two primary meanings: the call to become a Christian and the call to a special, holy life set apart from others. The call to become a Christian begins in the New Testament accounts of the first disciples who follow Jesus of Nazareth. As the Gospel writers portray, Jesus invited people to "Follow me" (Matt. 4:19).

In the Gospel of Mark, the first disciples ("disciple" means "follower")

March 14, 2013, accessed February 20, 2015, http://www.bbc.com/news/world-21443313. See also Bryan T. Froehle and Mary L. Gautier, *Global Catholicism: Portrait of a World Church* (Maryknoll, NY: Orbis, 2003).

4. *The Official Catholic Directory 2013* (New Providence, NJ: P. J. Kenedy & Sons, 2013), 2046. See also Bryan T. Froehle and Mary L. Gautier, *Catholicism USA: A Portrait of the Catholic Church in the United States* (Maryknoll, NY: Orbis, 2000).

drop everything and follow "immediately." The Gospel is constructed around two main narratives: the initial excitement of crowds of people following during Jesus's ministry in Galilee, which consists of his teaching, primarily through parables, and healing the sick. In the middle of Mark's Gospel is an interesting set of stories that contain the phrase "on the way" six times, thus reinforcing the idea that discipleship is a path one follows to learn the ways of Jesus. The second main narrative is the account of Jesus's journey to Jerusalem in which many of the initial disciples fall away, some reject him, and the government and religious leaders begin to plot against him. In this part of the narrative, those disciples who stay with Jesus have a difficult path to follow—in fact "the way" is leading to Jesus's crucifixion. Mark tells of a "certain young man" who is present at Jesus's arrest in the Garden of Gethsemane. "A certain young man was following him, wearing nothing but a linen cloth. They caught hold of him, but he left the linen cloth and ran off naked" (Mark 14:51–52). Biblical scholars believe this is a symbol of the baptized Christian in Mark's community who faced the challenge of holding on to his or her faith. The call to be a disciple of Jesus is indeed difficult and early Christians often denied following him.

There are many other call narratives in the Bible that have influenced Catholics. The call of Moses (Exod. 3:1–6), Samuel (1 Sam. 3:1–9), the prophets, and certainly St. Paul's dramatic conversion (Acts 9:1–9) all point to a God who summons people to heed God's ways and follow in the path of righteousness. Most people who became Christian in the early church were baptized as adults, in an initiation ritual that included being washed with water and blessed with oil. Christianity faced sporadic persecution in its first three hundred years, until the conversion of the emperor Constantine (312 CE), a call story not unlike that of St. Paul's.[5]

A brief sketch of the history of religious communities in the Catholic tradition demonstrates the importance of the second understanding of calling to emerge in the early church. As sociologist Patricia Wittberg notes, Catholic religious orders have gone through periods of growth, in which there were strong personal incentives (social, economic, and spiritual) to join an order, and periods of decline and stagnation, when groups shrink or become extinct, usually in response to social and political factors that

5. Paul's story is recounted in several places in the New Testament (Gal. 1:11–17; 1 Cor. 15:3–8; Acts 9:1–9). He was a Jewish Pharisee, set on persecuting Christians for their claims about Jesus. In Acts 9:1–19, Luke tells of how Paul was struck by light on the road to Damascus, heard a voice, "I am Jesus, whom you are persecuting," and was blinded for three days, upon which he was healed and baptized a Christian.

impact personal incentives. As social movements, she contends, most periods of growth and expansion last about 200 years before decline emerges.[6]

Once Christianity became the official religion of the Roman Empire in 380 CE and Christians did not face the possibility of a martyr's death, some felt called to a different kind of spiritual life and practice, and they withdrew from the cities of the great empire into the Egyptian desert. *The Life of Antony* is one of the first recorded stories of an early Christian ascetic. The author recounts Antony's birth into a wealthy family, but his parents died when he was eighteen, leaving him to figure out what he should do with his life. "He went into the church pondering these things, and just then it happened that the Gospel was being read, and he heard the Lord saying to the rich man, 'If you would be perfect, go, sell what you possess and give it to the poor, and you will have treasure in heaven.'" He followed this command and "immediately" sold everything he owned. He went back to the church and heard these words, "Do not be anxious about tomorrow."[7] With that, Antony moved out into the desert where he had heard other Christians were pursuing a life of simplicity and complete devotion to God. Here they learned to "pray without ceasing" through memorization of the scripture text, especially the Psalms, fasted from food, relinquished material goods, and gave up sex. They were called "monks," from the Greek word *monos*, meaning "single," "alone." Two forms of monastic life developed, the anchorites who lived alone (from a Greek word meaning "one who withdraws"), and the cenobites, those who lived in community.

The movement into the desert is the beginning of what is called monasticism, a form of religious life in which people vow to live according to a set of rules. The goal of this life, for early Christians, was purity of heart, to rid oneself of all sinful inclinations and to imitate Christ in all ways, especially through love of God and neighbor. In the beginning of the Age of the Desert (200–500 CE) the "Doctrine of the Two Ways" developed, which "held that life of perpetual virginity removed from the world was superior to the daily round of married Christians." By 400 CE, some 5,000 male monks lived in Egypt; some women, identified as virgins and widows, found their way to the desert, but most lived within homes or local churches. They outnumbered men about two to one.[8]

6. Patricia Wittberg, *The Rise and Fall of Catholic Religious Orders: A Social Movement Perspective* (Albany: State University of New York Press, 1994), 4.

7. *Athanasius: The Life of Antony and The Letter to Marcellinus*, trans. Robert C. Gregg (Mahwah, NJ: Paulist, 1980), 31.

8. Wittberg, *The Rise and Fall*, 32–33.

In early developments there were different models of community life and rules that people followed, but by the sixth century one rule—the Rule of St. Benedict—emerged and would dominate Christian religious life for the next thousand years. St. Benedict understands that some people receive a calling from God to live this way of life. The monastery is the "school of the Lord's service." He writes in the Prologue of the Rule,

> Seeking workers in a multitude of people, God calls out and says again: "Is there anyone here who yearns for life and desires to see good days?" (Ps. 34:13[12]). If you hear this and your answer is "I do," God then directs these words to you: If you desire true and eternal life, "keep your tongue free from vicious talk and your lips from all deceit; turn away from evil and do good; let peace be your quest and aim" (Ps. 34:14–15[13–14]). . . . What is more delightful than this voice of the Holy One calling to us? See how God's love shows us the way of life.[9]

A monastic rule may sound to us like a set of laws or strict disciplines, and the Rule of Benedict does define a set of norms for what time to pray, how to pray, what to eat, and how to sleep. However, we miss the point if we think it is all about rules, when in fact it is part of the wisdom tradition, an ancient set of writings in which persons strive to live fully, question every dimension of human reality, and seek to be wise in their actions and loving toward others.[10] The purpose of following the Rule, as one contemporary Benedictine author notes, is to follow "the call to the center of ourselves where the God we are seeking is seeking us."[11]

During the early Middle Ages (500–1000 CE) a calling did not refer to becoming a Christian, since most Christians were baptized as infants, but to the choice of adult Christians to enter a religious order or become an ordained priest and leader of the community. These two forms of Christian life began to cross over and influence each other, so that by 700 CE, what emerges is the "monasticization of ministry" and the "sacerdotalization of monasticism."[12] The monastic life, lived in community with a set time for prayer and study, consisted primarily of laypeople. But

9. Joan Chittister, *The Rule of Benedict: Insights for the Ages* (New York: Crossroad, 1993), 23.

10. See Valerian John Odermann, OSB, "Interpreting the *Rule of Benedict:* Entering a World of Wisdom," *American Benedictine Review* 35, no. 1 (March 1984): 33–34.

11. Chittister, *The Rule,* 22.

12. Thomas O'Meara, *Theology of Ministry* (Mahwah, NJ: Paulist, 1999), 100–102.

Benedictine monasticism grew to be so large that its way of life began to influence how ordained priests lived: more and more of them began to embrace celibacy and poverty, and to pray at set times of the day. Furthermore, monks started to become priests. St. Benedict envisioned monastic life as one way that ordinary Christians would live in community, but by the 800s most monks were priests and most priests looked more and more like monks.

This one form of religious life dominated the Christian tradition up until the thirteenth century, when two figures, St. Francis and St. Dominic, felt a calling to preach the gospel in the streets, serve the poor, and live in the world rather than cloistered in a monastery. Thus began the Mendicant Era (1200–1500 CE), in which monasticism declined and the mendicant, the beggar or poor man, emerged as the model of vocation. In the Middle Ages, then, a Christian male had the opportunity to follow one of three callings: to be a priest, a monk or a beggar, or a knight. Women had two options, which were largely determined by the men in their lives: to be a wife or to be a nun. During this period, some women, such as Clare of Assisi, an early follower of Francis, preached the gospel in the streets, but most women's orders were controlled by ecclesiastical authorities and kept them safe in a convent, living a monastic life.

When the Protestant reformers challenged the dominant view of vocation, claiming that all Christians have a vocation, not only monks, clerics, and religious, two things happened. The Mendicant Era came to an end with a drastic decline in men and women entering religious orders, especially in Protestant countries, where their houses were closed.[13] The second response came from the Catholic Church, which was not enthusiastic about Luther's view of vocation. In fact, between the Council of Trent (1545–1563) and the Second Vatican Council (1962–1965), the church reinforced the medieval understanding of callings within a hierarchy of "states of life." As one drawing from a catechism illustrates, a married couple are situated on the left, with the caption "good," and a priest and nun on the right side, with the caption "better."[14]

The "better" calling was a catalyst for yet another form of religious life to emerge in what is called the Apostolic Era (1500–1800 CE), which refers to noncloistered communities dedicated to service in renewing the

13. Wittberg, *The Rise and Fall*, 35–36.
14. James Martin, SJ, and Jeremy Langford, *Professions of Faith: Living and Working as a Catholic* (New York: Sheed & Ward, 2002), xiii.

church. The most influential and largest order of the period was the Society of Jesus, committed to ministering "where no one else will."[15]

During the seventeenth century, a particular Catholic theology of calling emerged that influenced callings to religious life and to the priesthood. Based on the medieval distinction between nature and grace, God's grace was viewed as "supernatural," external to human persons, a gift and power that transforms our natural state into a graced state. In this system, vocation was an "actual grace" that God gave to a person; "it became some 'thing' placed in the individual by God, but difficult to determine." A calling was experienced as an "inner call" and a "secret voice" by which God whispered in the depths of the soul; without experiencing the call in this way, a young man was not called to be ordained.[16] The "inner call" approach to vocation fostered a strong sense of the individual's relationship to God and God's power to act on the individual to give one one's calling in such a way that "one can know one's vocation by attending to the inclination or attractions of the soul."[17] However, it also placed serious limitations on how people understood what God was up to. "Thus the voice of God was either restricted to the official channels of revelation and church, on the one hand, or reduced to a mystical illumination or miraculous impulse, on the other."[18]

The Age of the Apostolic Orders came to an end with the French Revolution, which effectively destroyed monasteries and religious houses in France and other European countries. But by 1850, new communities, predominantly female, began to emerge in Europe and the US, and the "Age of the Teaching Congregations" began, the form of religious life most Catholics experienced in their grade schools in the twentieth century. Waves of European missionaries came to the US: in 1805 there were 1,344 sisters; by 1900, 40,340.[19] By 1966, the number of religious in the US hit an all-time high: 181,421 women and 45,300 men.[20]

Catholicism has changed a great deal in the past fifty years. In the

---

15. John O'Malley, "Early Jesuit Spirituality: Spain and Italy," in *Christian Spirituality III: Post Reformation and Modern,* ed. Louis Dupré and Don E. Saliers (New York: Crossroad, 1989), 7.

16. Edward P. Hahnenberg, *Awakening Vocation: A Theology of Christian Call in a Postmodern World* (Collegeville, MN: Liturgical Press, 2010), 84.

17. Hahnenberg, *Awakening Vocation,* 89.

18. Hahnenberg, *Awakening Vocation,* 90.

19. Wittberg, *The Rise and Fall,* 39.

20. Wittberg, *The Rise and Fall,* 224.

US, there has been a significant decline in ordained priests and religious women and men, while at the same time an increase in laypeople answering a "call" to the ministry and the formation of the permanent diaconate, a "calling" for men to be ordained to serve as deacons, who can be married with children and who serve under the leadership of bishops and priests.[21] Three significant social changes have contributed to this shift: the decline in family size (immigrant families in the late nineteenth and early twentieth centuries had large families and were willing to support a son or daughter who had a "vocation" in the church), the rise of opportunities for women to receive advanced education and pursue a variety of professions (women no longer needed religious orders to secure an education and social advancement), and secularization in Western societies (the decline in religious participation). As with other eras in church history, however, there is a resurgence of religious vocations in other parts of the world today.[22]

The traditional view of vocation in the Catholic tradition has had both positive and negative implications. Positively, it validated ways of life that embraced radical countercultural expressions of faith. Not everyone is called to be married or to be single, and religious life provided one avenue for living in community pursuing a common life of prayer and service. Religious were on the front lines of feeding the hungry, visiting the sick and imprisoned, and advocating for justice. This was especially important for women, who had few options for education or social advancement outside the convent. Negatively, the narrow view distorted the idea of vocation as being for only a few, who were special and more holy than the rest. It emphasized a calling as God's plan determined outside of a person's life and given to them through a secret message. This view reinforced negative aspects of human sexuality, family life, and work in the world. It supported the idea that vocation has to do with work in the church, separate from what people do in the world.

Official church views of vocation shifted at Vatican II. In a document on the laity, the bishops write that the apostolate of the laity is part of the whole church's mission and that those who make up the church have distinct roles in that mission.[23] The vocation of the laity is in the temporal

---

21. See David DeLambo, *Lay Parish Ministers: A Study of Emerging Leadership* (New York: National Pastoral Life Center [NPLC], 2005), 45.

22. See, Wittberg, *The Rise and Fall*, 2–3; Froehle and Gautier, *Global Catholicism*, 41–43.

23. "The term laity is here understood to mean all the faithful except those in holy orders and those in the state of religious life specially approved by the Church. These faithful

order, or the world, as distinct from those called to serve in the church. "In this way, their temporal activity openly bears witness to Christ and promotes the salvation of men. Since the laity, in accordance with their state of life, live in the midst of the world and its concerns, they are called by God to exercise their apostolate in the world like leaven, with the ardor of the spirit of Christ."[24]

The vocation of the laity is rooted in the spiritual life, in "union with Christ," through the liturgy and other spiritual practices.

> These are to be used by the laity in such a way that while correctly ful-filling their secular duties in the ordinary conditions of life, they do not separate union with Christ from their life but rather performing their work according to God's will they grow in that union. In this way the laity must make progress in holiness in a happy and ready spirit, trying prudently and patiently to overcome difficulties. Neither family concerns nor other secular affairs should be irrelevant to their spiritual life.

The document acknowledges that the lay vocation can be lived in a variety of ways: "This plan for the spiritual life of the laity should take its particular character from their married or family state or their single or widowed state, from their state of health, and from their professional and social activity."[25] Though Vatican II continues to make a distinction between the laity's calling in the temporal world and the clergy's calling in the church, it also advocates the "universal call to holiness" that is shared by all.[26]

The role of lay Christians who live out their calling in the world is demonstrated in a unique book published in 2002. In *Professions of Faith: Living and Working as a Catholic,* a group of Catholics explore the meaning of their work in professions such as business, architecture, law, journalism, social work, education, medicine, and acting. The book's editors acknowl-

---

are by baptism made one body with Christ and are constituted among the People of God; they are in their own way made sharers in the priestly, prophetical, and kingly functions of Christ; and they carry out for their own part the mission of the whole Christian people in the Church and in the world." *Lumen Gentium,* The Dogmatic Constitution on the Church, in *Vatican Council II: The Conciliar and Post Conciliar Documents,* ed. Austin Flannery (Northport, NY: Costello, 1987), no. 31.

24. *Apostolicam Actuositatem,* The Decree on the Apostolate of the Laity, in Flannery, ed., *Vatican Council II: The Conciliar and Post Conciliar Documents,* no. 2.

25. *Apostolicam Actuositatem,* no. 4.

26. See *Lumen Gentium,* chapter 5.

edge that "[i]f you read between the lines a bit, you'll also notice that the concept of 'vocation' looms large in the experiences of the essayists." Despite the fact that these Catholic laypeople do not use the "word explicitly, each essay conveys a powerful sense of *vocation*." Each feels called to their work and yet the traditional understanding of vocation as pertaining to priests, nuns, and brothers lurks behind the authors, constraining them from using the term. But the editors acknowledge that today vocation applies to everyone. "After all, why wouldn't God call everyone in his or her own way to contribute to the building up of the Kingdom? And, as for 'hearing the call,' it need not be anything more mystical than enjoying your job and feeling that you're in the right place. Or, if you're not enjoying your job, it could be the feeling that you are called to be there anyway, as a sort of 'leaven' at work."[27]

Dreams, Visions, and Messages

Catholics experience God's call through a variety of mediated experiences such as dreams, hearing a voice, seeing a vision, but also through other people, nature, and by identifying their abilities and gifts. Catholic religious experience is built on a sense of sacramentality and mediation. Sacramentality refers to the belief that God is made known to us through visible, human, tangible means. Because God is transcendent, that is, cannot be seen or heard, Catholics believe that God's message is mediated through events, objects, places, and people. Thus, St. Augustine defined a sacrament as a "visible sign of invisible grace," which Catholics have always held as foundational to the seven sacraments, but the belief also describes a sense of seeing the "divine in the human, the infinite in the finite, the spiritual in the material, the transcendent in the immanent, the eternal in the historical."[28] Ignatius of Loyola also embraced this worldview through his teaching on "seeing God in all things." While God is distinct from human reality, a sacramental view of the world holds that the world is God's and God makes the divine will known in and through the world.

A sacramental worldview provides the basis for a theology of calling—the activity by which God communicates with human persons. In biblical stories as well as stories of the saints, Catholics have a strong narrative

27. Martin and Langford, *Professions of Faith*, xiii–xiv.
28. McBrien, *Catholicism*, 9–10.

tradition of stories of God at work in people's lives. Classic calling stories point to three primary ways that God calls people: through dreams, visions (seeing), and messages (hearing).

Dreams can contain both seeing and hearing. My dream, recounted at the beginning of this chapter, was only auditory. I heard, but did not see. Ignatius's experience was visual but not auditory. In the Bible, we find many similar experiences: Abraham is called by God to leave his home and travel to a new place; Moses is told by God to be a leader and speaker; Samuel is called by a voice; in the New Testament, Mary is visited by an angel with a message that she is called to be Jesus's mother, and Joseph is called in a dream to marry Mary and to name Jesus, thus making him his son. (Joseph carries the name of the Old Testament figure, Joseph, who was called the "master dreamer.") Jesus calls out to some fishermen, "Come, and follow me," and Paul experiences the power of God in a vision and a verbal message.

Callings are understood as a message to a particular person about their life. God asks people to change their ways, to turn away from sin and to live in the ways of God. Like Protestants with their concept of "general calling," Catholics too share the notion that the entire people of God are called to live according to God's ways, made known in and through Jesus of Nazareth. To be a disciple of Christ, which means to be a follower, is at the heart of Christian vocation.

God also gives particular directions: go here and do this. Perhaps the most radical calling that Jesus invites his followers to heed is contained in Matthew 25:31–46.[29] In the twentieth century, these patterns of calling continue. People have felt God's urging to build schools and educate the illiterate (St. Katherine Drexel), start hospitals and provide medical services (Catherine McAuley), provide food and shelter for the hungry and homeless (Servant of God Dorothy Day), and live a contemplative life of silence and prayer (Thomas Merton).

Unfolding the Creator's Work: Living Out a Calling

Catholic Social Teaching (CST) refers to a body of theological and ethical reflection about society, economics, and politics. Questions related to

---

29. In this parable, Jesus tells his disciples that at the last judgment they will be separated into those who followed his way and those who did not, the sheep and the goats.

public life have been part of Christian theology since the early church, but CST became a formal body of teaching in the nineteenth century when Pope Leo XIII, in 1891, published an encyclical (meaning "letter"), titled *Rerum Novarum* ("On the Condition of Labor"). In the midst of the European Industrial Revolution, the Pope articulated a set of principles on just wages, private property, limited government involvement, and free trade associations or labor unions. On its one hundredth anniversary in 1991, Pope John Paul II released the encyclical *Centesimus Annus* ("One Hundred Years"), which reviewed the church's teaching on work and labor, emphasizing the way technology shapes work, the need for fair markets, the role of the state in economic life, and a critique of consumerism and environmental degradation. CST, as it has developed over the past century, consists of seven key teachings: the dignity of every human person; participation in the common good (through family and community); human rights and responsibilities; the option for the poor and vulnerable; the dignity and rights of workers; solidarity with all human persons; and care for God's creation.[30]

Because the term "vocation" has been used primarily in regard to "states of life," it does not appear as a central category in CST, though it begins to make an appearance in recent writings. For example, Pope John Paul II claims that human persons are "called to work" because they are created by God and through their work participate in "God's activity." Drawing on the creation stories in Genesis, the Pope states that work is a "fundamental dimension of man's existence on earth" since it appears before the Fall (when persons sinned against God in the Garden of Eden), but it is also marked by toil and difficulty after the Fall (Gen. 1:26–31; 3:19). The Pope places a strong emphasis on the connection between God's work in creation and the purposes of human work: "By our labor we are unfolding the Creator's work and contributing to the realization of God's plan on earth."[31] Because we are created in the image of God, and work is integral to God's creation of the world, work is fundamental to being human. Thus, a part of upholding the human dignity of each person is honoring and recognizing the importance of work in their lives.

30. United States Catholic Conference of Bishops, "Seven Themes of Catholic Social Teaching," accessed May 8, 2015, http://www.usccb.org/beliefs-and-teachings/what-we -believe/catholic-social-teaching/seven-themes-of-catholic-social-teaching.cfm.

31. John Paul II, *Laborem Exercens,* "On Human Work," 1981, no. 25, accessed May 13, 2015, http://w2.vatican.va/content/john-paul-ii/en/encyclicals/documents/hf_jp-ii_enc _14091981_laborem-exercens.html.

John Paul II makes a further point about work: it is both objective insofar as it produces something external to us but it is also subjective in that work shapes who we are. Work as formative means it shapes the moral character of persons.[32] He states: "*As a person, man is therefore the subject of work.* As a person he works, he performs various actions belonging to the work process; independently of their objective content, these actions must all serve to realize his humanity, to fulfil the calling to be a person that is his by reason of his very humanity."[33] Because the subjective nature of work is "the ultimate purpose of work" it can never, for the Pope, be "subordinated to the objective output of the work done."[34]

Obviously CST and in this case John Paul II are interested in the dignity of work, especially for workers who are exploited and impoverished. Catholic business ethicist Michael Naughton notes that work as a calling is "inherent in CST," meaning it is consistent with notions of work that link the individual's sense of calling to the larger public and common good.[35] Naughton is one of two contemporary Catholic theologians who are making explicit connections between CST on work and a theology of vocation.

Naughton was the coordinator of the 2012 project "Vocation of the Business Leader" for the Pontifical Council for Justice and Peace. The document notes that "the vocation of the businessperson is a genuine human and Christian calling" because business leaders "are called to conceive of and develop goods and services for customers and communities through a form of market economy," which serves the common good of all. The challenges of responding to this calling, the document notes, are many: the pressure to lead "a divided life" between one's faith and the "damage done by businesses"; the idolatry of the "maximization of profit" for personal wealth; and an overreliance on worldly success.[36] In leading a business with a sense of Christian calling, leaders are asked to develop three capac-

---

32. See Michael Naughton and Gene R. Laczniak, "A Theological Context of Work from the Catholic Social Encyclical Tradition," *Journal of Business Ethics* 12 (1993): 982.

33. John Paul II, *Laborem Exercens,* no. 6.

34. Daniel Finn, "Human Work in Catholic Social Thought," *American Journal of Economics and Sociology* 71, no. 4 (October 2012): 876. See also Naughton and Laczniak, "A Theological Context of Work," 981–94.

35. Naughton and Laczniak, "A Theological Context of Work," 983.

36. Pontifical Council for Justice and Peace, "Vocation of the Business Leader: A Reflection," 2012, nos. 10, 11, 12, accessed May 13, 2015, http://www.iustitiaetpax.va/content/dam/giustiziaepace/VBL/Vocation_ENGLISH_4th%20edition.pdf.

ities: "seeing" the "signs of the times" that are impacting business today; "judging" their choices and decisions based on the principles of human dignity and service to the common good; and "acting" to integrate their "spiritual life, the virtues and ethical social principles into their life and work."[37]

A second perspective on work and vocation is developed by Claire E. Wolfteich in *Navigating New Terrain: Work and Women's Spiritual Lives*. Lay Catholic women steadily moved into the workforce in the twentieth century, but in so doing they clashed with two prevailing notions of women's vocation. An ideal of "True Womanhood" developed during the Industrial Revolution stressed the "cult of domesticity" as the domain of women's work. This prevailing cultural view of women was linked to church and religion, which also reinforced the notion that the home is the proper place for women's influence. In *Rerum Novarum,* Pope Leo XIII states: "Women, again, are not suited for certain occupations; a woman is by nature fitted for home-work, and it is that which is best adapted at once to preserve her modesty, and to promote the good bringing up of children and the well-being of the family."[38]

According to Wolfteich, "Employment provokes questions about women's vocation."[39] She examines this dilemma in relationship to three issues: working both inside and outside the home, developing particular gifts, and juggling multiple commitments and identities.[40] Many Catholic women struggled in the twentieth century to embrace work outside of the home since they were leaving the place both society and the church deemed to be their true calling and entering the secular world. However, many had to for economic reasons, and many wanted to for educational reasons, but they did not have the language of vocation to support their work in the world. She advocates that today we can embrace both "do-

37. Pontifical Council for Justice and Peace, "Vocation of the Business Leader," 3.

38. Pope Leo XII, *Rerum Novarum,* "On Capital and Labor," 1891, no. 42, accessed May 13, 2015, http://w2.vatican.va/content/leo-xiii/en/encyclicals/documents/hf_l-xiii_enc _15051891_rerum-novarum.html. John Paul II, a hundred years later, in *Mulieris Dignitatem,* "On the Dignity and Vocation of Women," 1988, focuses on women's calling to motherhood and virginity, but has little to say about work, accessed July 3, 2015, http://w2.vatican.va/content/john-paul-ii/en/apost_letters/1988/documents/hf_jp-ii_apl_19880815_mulieris -dignitatem.html.

39. Claire E. Wolfteich, *Navigating New Terrain: Work and Women's Spiritual Lives* (Mahwah, NJ: Paulist, 2002), 15.

40. Wolfteich, *Navigating New Terrain,* 82.

mestic vocation" and "other forms of work" as a calling because they each serve society and the common good. We do not have to equate "women's spirituality, nature, or virtue" with the former or pit one against the other. Rather, a sense of calling arises from discerning one's gifts and passions, which for some women do not involve childrearing, but for others they do. "Gifts point in vocational directions. . . . One cannot walk down all of those paths, and so the range of vocations must be weighed in light of the deep passions of the individual, the potential for service in a given context, and practical circumstances."[41] A contemporary theology of vocation must, for Wolfteich, account for a sense of identity and human dignity that are grounded in "God's purposes for human life."[42] Our general vocation is lived out in the concrete particular situations of our lives and reaches out toward the good of others.

Though Catholics have not always thought about work as a calling, there is more evidence that some people do. Ron Hansen, for example, felt called to be a writer since the time he could read. "I may have been five or so when I first noticed that calling." It emerged at church when the priest read the gospel and Hansen recognized it as a story he knew. He realized that his vocation as a writer was formed both by "Catholicism's feast for the senses, its ethical concerns, its insistence on seeing God in all things, and the high status it gave to scripture, drama, and art" and by "something unnamable that I can only associate with a yen to live out, in my imagination, other lives and possibilities, a craving that . . . made storytelling necessary to me."[43] David Armitage recounts how his calling to be an architect and to build affordable housing for the poor was born in hearing the story of Genesis, God's work as the architect of the world.[44] John Eterno has discovered in his work as a New York City police officer the challenge of living out the church's teaching on the human dignity of all persons.[45]

At times a calling can be dangerous, demanding not just long hours of service but death. Jim Foley, raised as a Catholic and educated by Jesuits, was a young photojournalist who was tortured and executed by ISIS in

41. Wolfteich, *Navigating New Terrain,* 90.

42. Wolfteich, *Navigating New Terrain,* 104.

43. Ron Hansen, "Hotly in Pursuit of the Real: On Being a Catholic Writer," in Martin and Langford, *Professions of Faith,* 1–3.

44. David H. Armitage, "A World to Live In: On Being a Catholic Architect," in Martin and Langford, *Professions of Faith,* 27.

45. John A. Eterno, "Justice from a Higher Power: On Being a Catholic Police Officer," in Martin and Langford, *Professions of Faith,* 41–54.

Syria in August 2014 after being held captive for twenty-one months. He graduated from college in 1996, worked as an inner-city teacher with Teach for America and later in the jail system. He earned a master's degree and became a photojournalist, with the desire to be a "conflict journalist" and report from war zones. He sought to tell the stories of those suffering from war by taking pictures of people's faces. He covered the wars in Afghanistan and Libya, and the ongoing war in Syria, where over 190,000 have been killed in three years and over three million people have had to flee their homes. Jim's mother reported that she had tried to talk him out of going back to Syria after a trip home and he responded: "But *Mom,* I've found *my passion,* I've found *my vocation.*" Foley was certain he had to go back to take those pictures and tell the stories of what people were going through.[46]

Community, Prayer, and Discernment

In addition to sacramentality and mediation, communion is a key aspect of Catholic identity and belief. The Latin term *communio* means "sharing in common." But communion is not merely sharing what people possess but of participating together in a common life in God. Catholicism is first and foremost a community of faith, what St. Paul calls the "Body of Christ" and the "Temple of the Holy Spirit," a mystical body that is joined to God through Jesus Christ. By being one Body, Christians share in Jesus's suffering as well as his resurrection to new life, what Catholics refer to as the paschal mystery. The "mystical Body of Christ" refers to the profound mystery of God's love for humanity that comes through Christ and redeems us all as one.

Furthermore, the belief in the communion of saints teaches that both the living and the dead are joined together as one body. In the Catholic tradition, the category of "saints" has several different meanings, both broad (those justified by grace through Christ who are living and those who have died and entered eternal life) and specific (people who exemplify holiness and the church has canonized or publicly recognized for their lives and thus referred to as "saints").[47]

---

46. Foley attended Marquette University, a Jesuit school in Milwaukee. This quote comes from an interview with Foley's parents, "James Foley's Parents: 'Jim Had a Big Heart,'" accessed July 3, 2015, at https://www.youtube.com/watch?v=jo3Som8cTSo&feature.

47. McBrien, *Catholicism,* 1109–10.

The community, then, is a primary way in which people practice their faith and discern their callings. Public worship through the seven sacraments, in particular the Eucharist, is the primary way in which Catholics gather together and worship God. In the context of public prayer, Catholics hear the Word of God proclaimed and participate in the celebration of the Eucharist, eating the Body of Christ and drinking the cup of salvation.

In addition to public worship, personal or individual prayer practices are engaged in four primary forms: praise, thanksgiving, petition, and contrition. Prayer is both personal and communal in the Catholic tradition. "Grounded in both individual attentiveness and communal reflection, vocational discernment as a Christian practice invites us to notice where and how we are experiencing God in our daily lives."[48]

Discernment is a key prayer practice related to vocation. It involves deciding, making a decision, judgment, and sorting out one's motivations to determine what is from God and what is not from God. Discernment is about listening to "the many voices that act like crosscurrents, overwhelming the deeper current of vocation and calling"—the voices of parental expectation, professional success, wealth, fame and glory, and doubt and fear.

Ignatius of Loyola taught a practice of discernment that is used widely today. He was a young man from a wealthy family who served the King of Spain as a soldier, but a battle injury left him bedridden. Through his reading, he found that his mind was attracted to two different daydreams: Ignatius the courageous hero in battle and Ignatius the servant of God, who, like the saints he read about, was devoted to service of others. He also noticed something else: the way he felt in response to these two self-images. The first, while initially exciting, eventually left him cold and empty, but the second, while initially difficult, brought him a sense of joy and fulfillment. "I learned from experience that one kind of thought left me sad and the other cheerful. Thus, step-by-step I came to recognize the difference between these two . . . the one being from my own sinfulness and vanity and the other from God."[49]

From this experience, Ignatius brought into Catholic spiritual practice

48. Jennifer Grant Haworth, "Discerning God's Call," in *On Our Way: Christian Practices for Living a Whole Life,* ed. Dorothy C. Bass and Susan R. Briehl (Nashville: Upper Room Books, 2010), 38.

49. Haworth, "Discerning God's Call," 43.

an emphasis on the imagination and on paying attention to the feelings of desolation and consolation that arise from our discernments. These emphases form the core of the spiritual practice he developed called the *Spiritual Exercises*. "Motivated by the love he experienced in his daydreams, Ignatius discerned that what *really, truly, authentically* had a hold on his heart was God."[50]

Ignatius developed two prayer practices of discernment. The first is called the Examen, a daily practice to be done at nighttime. It is a practice of examining one's conscience, to see where one is attentive to God and where one is not. The prayer consists of three parts: asking for the Spirit of illumination: "For what am I most grateful today?" or "When did I feel most alive today?" The pray-er offers a prayer of thanksgiving. The second question is: "For what moment today am I least grateful?" or "When did I most feel life draining out of me?" The pray-er offers a prayer of forgiveness. The third part is to notice feelings during the examination: Where is there desolation (low energy, evil) or consolation (a sense of well-being in God, a sense of peace, energy)? From this daily practice, Ignatius taught his followers that one would learn to discern which desires, actions, and forms of life are of God and which are not of God. A clear sense of calling begins to emerge through this daily exercise.

The second prayer form is a thirty-day retreat under the guidance of a spiritual director, usually a Jesuit priest, called the Spiritual Exercises. This is a structured experience through which a retreatant is led through the life of Christ. In the first week the retreatant contemplates his or her sin and God's grace and mercy, in the second week, Jesus's incarnation and ministry, in the third week, Jesus's passion and death, and in the fourth week, Jesus's resurrection. Through the thirty days, the retreatant notices "emotions, affects, thoughts, images, and yearnings that encourage or dishearten you, including those that you recognize as temptations to sin." Many practitioners today use the Exercises as a way to help them discern a decision, whether a major life commitment, such as getting married or joining a religious order, or whether to take a new job or leave work and retire, or for spiritual growth and maturity. In the Jesuit approach to vocation, the Christian is actively seeking to understand God's calling, and God's call is communicated to the person through the Scripture stories, symbols, and rituals of the faith.

---

50. Haworth, "Discerning God's Call," 43.

Called in Suffering, Called to Suffer With

How can a man from Burkina Faso in West Africa, with a master's degree in sociology, find work in the US?[51] How can a couple face the devastating news that the husband has Alzheimer's disease? How can an immigrant from Mexico who struggles to find work support herself and her children on wages below the poverty level? Many aspects of contemporary social, economic, and political circumstances challenge how we think about vocation. What happens when people cannot use their gifts in meaningful work? What happens when serious illness cuts short the dreams of late adulthood? What does calling mean to those in desperate poverty who can barely sustain themselves? Do these people have a calling?

Such situations also challenge how we think about Catholic teachings on human dignity and the common good. If each person is made in the image of God, then it follows that God loves and calls each person regardless of their life circumstances. Catholic theologians today emphasize the ways in which God finds and accompanies people in their suffering. John Neafsey, author of *A Sacred Voice Is Calling,* states that "painful life experiences have the potential to deepen and mature us, to make us wiser and more compassionate,"[52] but he notes that this is not always the case. We can become bitter and angry. It matters how we look at innocent suffering: What is our attitude toward the circumstance? "How we see our problems has a profound impact upon how they are experienced, including the degree to which they are felt to be either meaningful opportunities for growth or meaningless obstacles that are better avoided."[53] In his work as a psychologist with torture victims, Neafsey has seen how people can experience the redemptive power of God through their suffering.

> They get the idea that it is worth "hanging in there" a little longer until the meaning of the issue or problem, the message in the symptom, can be discerned. This almost always involves allowing the suffering or pain to reveal and clarify the truth of *who they are*—a process that seems to be inherently healing and redemptive.[54]

---

51. To see a video interview, accessed July 3, 2015, http://collegevilleinstitute.org/the-seminars/resources-for-congregations/lives-explored/.

52. John Neafsey, *A Sacred Voice Is Calling: Personal Vocation and Social Conscience* (Maryknoll, NY: Orbis, 2006), 126.

53. Neafsey, *A Sacred Voice Is Calling,* 123.

54. Neafsey, *A Sacred Voice Is Calling,* 125.

Suffering is also an "occasion for deepened loving connection with God or other human beings."[55] When Ken was diagnosed with Alzheimer's, both he and Mary Margaret had to figure out where God was in all this pain. She realized that "Alzheimer's is not a blessing, it's not a curse, but many blessings have come" from it, one being that she has heard God's call to be a caregiver. "The diagnosis of Alzheimer's was extremely painful, it took a while for me to process, it took a while to see that there was any joy in the world. . . . When Ken was diagnosed, I realized I had a choice to make, either I could continue to be in pain or in suffering, or I could find the joy in the pain, become an advocate, educator, and an ambassador." Ken too realizes that in his diagnosis God has never left him and he has found a calling, for as long as he is able, to educate others with Alzheimer's and their families. "My hope is that people will look and see a person first and treat them with dignity and respect."[56]

Jesus's suffering on the cross is a symbol of "God's love and compassion for suffering humanity"; it also points to our calling to be compassionate to those who God suffers with, the "crucified peoples" of the world.[57] Neafsey points out how "Christian spirituality is not about suffering for its own sake. It is about the redemptive breakthrough of love and compassion *through* suffering, or in the midst of it, or in spite of it." Catholics can find in their suffering a calling to find meaning and hope and a calling to be compassionate to others who suffer. Suffering leads to compassion, and compassion leads to service.

In addition to compassion, the Catholic tradition has a strong commitment to social justice. Jesus preached that our service to the hungry, the thirsty, the naked, the homeless, and the prisoner is service to him (Matt. 25:31–46). This story is the basis for the CST on the preferential option for the poor, a teaching that emphasizes that "[t]he obligation to provide justice for all means that the poor have the single most urgent economic claim on the conscience of the nation."[58] Catholic theologian Edward Hahnenberg links the language of vocation to social justice as well:

55. Neafsey, *A Sacred Voice Is Calling*, 125.

56. See an online interview with Mary Margaret and Ken, accessed July 3, 2015, http://collegevilleinstitute.org/the-seminars/resources-for-congregations/lives-explored/. They are Episcopalians and not Catholic.

57. Neafsey, *A Sacred Voice Is Calling*, 129.

58. United States Catholic Bishops, *Economic Justice for All: Pastoral Letter on Catholic Social Teaching and the U.S. Economy* (Washington, DC: United States Catholic Conference, 1997), no. 86.

"Ultimately, the call to be *for* others is always a call to be *with* others, particularly those who suffer unjustly. For it is in the sad but sacred darkness of solidarity with the poor that our senses are heightened, and we come to hear more clearly the voice of God."[59]

Expanding Vocation to Include Everyone and Everything

Based on the principles of sacramentality, mediation, communion, human dignity, and the common good, Catholic theology has a strong foundation to expand its understanding of vocation. Based on these principles, Catholic theologians have been embracing the idea that calling relates to every Christian life and to everything about the Christian life. Thus it does relate to our state in life, not only to celibacy and religious life, but also to marriage and single life. But it is broader than our state in life—it also includes work and service in the world as well as the whole lifespan from children to the elderly.

The Catholic understanding of vocation, prior to the Second Vatican Council, focused on the calling to religious life and to the priesthood. At its best, these notions of calling provided three helpful ways of thinking about vocation for Catholics today. First, religious life provided a model of calling in community, through community, and for community. Much of the way we think about vocation today is about *my* calling to be or to do something. Second, these callings entailed living a celibate life and taking vows of poverty. The lives of many sisters, brothers, and priests embodied a life of simplicity, not worldly fame or riches, and a life of radical love, giving up everything to follow the way of Christ. Their callings pointed to countercultural ways of embodying the gospel. Many embraced the "little way" articulated by Ste. Thérèse of Lisieux, a French woman who died at age twenty-four, after living a quiet life devoted to finding God in the ordinary places of her life. Third, these commitments combined a whole life into one calling: what one did (teach, preach, administer the sacraments) and how one lived (taking vows in community) were joined together in one integrated life for one purpose (who one is): to serve God by serving the neighbor.[60] As the Jesuit and peace-activist Daniel Berrigan said, "The

---

59. Hahnenberg, *Awakening Vocation*, 195.
60. See Marie Theresa Coombs and Francis Kelly Nemeck, *Called by God: A Theology of Vocation and Lifelong Commitment* (Collegeville, MN: Liturgical Press, 1992), 2.

term 'vocation' is not to be confused, as it commonly is, with a successful outcome."[61]

The teaching at the Second Vatican Council recognized the impoverishment of the church's understanding of vocation that slighted the laity, placing them lower on the ladder of spiritual ascent. This teaching shifted in two ways. First, the church proclaimed that "all Christians in whatever state or walk of life are called to the fullness of Christian life and to the perfection of charity."[62] The call to holiness became the basis for exploring the vocation to marriage and, further, to the single life. The US bishops note that

> [t]he call to marriage is a particular way of living the universal call to holiness given to every Christian in the Sacrament of Baptism. The calls to priesthood, or to the vowed religious life, or to the single life are other Christian vocations. Along with marriage, all of them equally though in different ways are a response to the Lord who says, "Follow me."[63]

A second shift has been the turn to Martin Luther's understanding of vocation, which many Catholic leaders and theologians embrace. The US bishops state, "We also have much to learn from the strong emphasis in Protestant traditions on the vocation of lay people in the world and from ecumenical efforts to develop an economic ethic that addresses newly emergent problems."[64] In addition to the call to holiness, the church embraced Luther's emphasis on the priesthood of all believers, teaching that all are baptized priest, prophet, and king, participating in Christ's threefold mission to be messengers of the good news, mediators through worship and prayer, and servants to all.

In my work as a Catholic theologian on vocation, I have retrieved Luther's idea of general calling and particular calling. I see the general vocation shared by all Christians as shaped by seven features of discipleship: follower, worshiper, witness, neighbor, forgiver, prophet, and steward.[65]

---

61. Neafsey, *A Sacred Voice Is Calling*, 162.

62. *Lumen Gentium*, no. 40.

63. United States Catholic Conference of Bishops, "The Vocation of Marriage," accessed May 13, 2015, http://www.foryourmarriage.org/the-vocation-of-marriage/.

64. United States Catholic Bishops, *Economic Justice for All*, no. 59.

65. See Kathleen A. Cahalan, *Introducing the Practice of Ministry* (Collegeville, MN: Liturgical Press, 2010), chapter 1, and Kathleen A. Cahalan and Laura Kelly Fanucci, *A Living Discipleship: Called on the Way* (New London, CT: Twenty-Third Publications, 2015).

I also understand vocation as particular. We are called as unique individuals within the contexts of our lives (race, ethnicity, class, gender) and our age (experiences of call as children, teens, adults, and older adults). I also retrieve Luther's idea of being called in our station of life to understand how we experience God's callings in situations not of our own choosing, such as illness, unemployment, and caregiving.[66]

As the Catholic tradition broadened its understanding of vocation to include marriage and single life and to consider work in the world as a calling, it has also faced several thorny issues related to its own teaching on the ministry: Can women be priests? Can priests be married? These two questions have been widely debated, but the challenge to a contemporary theology of vocation comes when a woman declares that she is called by God to ordination or when a priest says that God is calling him to marriage. Can a community block God's calling? And if they do, what are the consequences?

The Catholic tradition's understanding of vocation is both ancient and new, involving religious virtuosos and ordinary people alike. It focuses on how God, through Jesus Christ, by the power of the Holy Spirit, calls people to follow in the ways of Jesus, discern their gifts, and give their lives in service to others for the sake of the common good. Even through frustration, failure, and suffering, Catholic Christians experience God as one who calls them in whatever situation they find themselves. The experience is so great, according to this tradition, that many followers mark their calling with a new name.

Resources

Allegretti, Joseph G. *Loving Your Job, Finding Your Passion: Work and the Spiritual Life*. Mahwah, NJ: Paulist Press, 2000.

Cahalan, Kathleen A. *Introducing the Practice of Ministry*. Collegeville, MN: Liturgical Press, 2010.

Cahalan, Kathleen A., and Laura Kelly Fanucci. *A Living Discipleship: Called on the Way*. New London, CT: Twenty-Third Publications, 2015.

Coombs, Marie Theresa, and Francis Kelly Nemeck. *Called by God: A Theology of Vocation and Lifelong Commitment*. Collegeville, MN: Liturgical Press, 1992.

66. See my book tentatively titled *Call It What It Is* (Grand Rapids: Eerdmans, forthcoming 2017).

Hahnenberg, Edward. *Awakening Vocation: A Theology of Christian Call in a Postmodern World.* Collegeville, MN: Liturgical Press, 2010.

Haughey, John C., SJ. *Revisiting the Idea of Vocation: Theological Explorations.* Washington, DC: Catholic University of America Press, 2004.

Langford, Jeremy, and James Martin, SJ. *Professions of Faith: Living and Working as a Catholic.* New York: Sheed & Ward, 2002.

Naughton, Michael. *The Good Stewards: Practical Applications of the Papal Social Vision of Work.* Lanham, MD: University Press of America, 1992.

Neafsey, John. *A Sacred Voice Is Calling: Personal Vocation and Social Conscience.* Maryknoll, NY: Orbis, 2006.

Wolfteich, Claire E. *Navigating New Terrain: Work and Women's Spiritual Lives.* Mahwah, NJ: Paulist Press, 2002.

3

To Follow Christ, to Live in the World

Calling in a Protestant Key

DOUGLAS J. SCHUURMAN

Dietrich Bonhoeffer (1906–1945) was one of the first German Lutheran pastors and theologians publicly to oppose Adolf Hitler's anti-Semitic legislation, known as the Aryan Clause, promulgated on April 7, 1933.[1] Hitler had formed a Reich church to control Protestant churches and their leadership. The leader of the Reich church demanded a loyalty oath from all German Protestants who held church offices. Officers either signed the oath or were dismissed. Bonhoeffer refused and became a leader in the alternative, Confessing Church movement. He helped Jews escape Germany and established educational communities to train and support leaders of the Confessing Church. The seminaries he established in Finkenwalde and Zingst trained pastors for nearly two years before the Gestapo shut them down. After this, Bonhoeffer continued to train church leaders as an itinerant mentor of several pastors in various churches. It was risky to do what Bonhoeffer was doing. Martin Niemöller, fellow pastor and Confessing Church leader, was arrested and imprisoned in Sachsenhausen where he remained until his death.

Already in 1939 Bonhoeffer was directly involved in subversive political activity against Hitler and the Reich. Perhaps weary of his nomadic life and anxious about his imminent conscription, in June of 1939 Bonhoeffer accepted Reinhold Niebuhr's invitation to come to America. He had studied with Niebuhr and others at Union Theological Seminary in New York City from 1930 to 1931. Niebuhr and his friends worried about Bonhoeffer's

---

1. See Bonhoeffer's "The Church and the Jewish Question," in *Dietrich Bonhoeffer: Witness to Jesus Christ,* ed. John de Gruchy (San Francisco: Collins, 1988), 124–33.

safety, and wanted him to come to the US to fill an office in the newly formed Federal Council of Churches, work with the Student Christian Movement, and lecture at Union Seminary and other educational institutions in the US. His friend and biographer, Eberhard Bethge, identifies questions Bonhoeffer was having about his calling that led him to accept Niebuhr's invitation:

> Must he really wear himself out over church and national affairs in Germany? For what, really, were his life's ambitions to be sacrificed? Couldn't he pursue theology, the most important thing to him, in more conducive surroundings? Would not the universal church and its theology benefit more if he could develop these gifts freely elsewhere? Might there not be a call waiting for him outside, and wasn't it necessary to leave in order to hear this clearly? Moreover, didn't his own church view a refusal of military service as a destructive and isolated course?[2]

But from the beginning of his voyage to the US Bonhoeffer felt plagued by concern for the people left behind. While at sea he says in his journal entry dated June 9, 1939: "[W]e ought to be found only where God is" rather than where "great programs" bring us. "Whether it is you working over there [in Germany] or I working in America, we are all only where he is. Or have I, after all, avoided the place where he is? The place where he is for me? No, God says, you are my servant."[3] His arrival in New York did not relieve, but rather intensified his agonized misgivings. Eventually he also learned that his new position resettling German refugees for the Federal Council of Churches mandated that he not return to Germany. Since he had from the start planned to stay in America for only one year, this restriction distressed him greatly. On June 15 he wrote, "I have not been able to stop thinking about Germany. I would not have thought it possible that at my age, after so many years abroad, one could get so dreadfully homesick. . . . This inactivity, or rather activity in unimportant things, is quite intolerable when one thinks of the brothers and of how precious time is."[4] On June 20 Bonhoeffer decided he would return to Germany. Though his decision is clear, his motives are not.

2. Eberhard Bethge, *Dietrich Bonhoeffer: A Biography,* revised edition, rev. and ed. Victoria J. Barnett (Minneapolis: Augsburg Fortress, 2000), 636.

3. Bethge, *Dietrich Bonhoeffer,* 636.

4. Bethge, *Dietrich Bonhoeffer,* 652.

The decision has been made. . . . It is remarkable how I am never quite clear about the motives for any of my decisions. Is that a sign of confusion, of inner dishonesty, or is it a sign that we are guided without our knowing, or is it both? . . . [God] certainly sees how much personal feeling, how much anxiety, there is in today's decisions, however brave it may seem. The reasons one gives for an action to others and to one's self are certainly inadequate. . . . In the last resort one acts from a level which remains hidden from us. So we can only ask God to judge and forgive us. . . . It is now in his hands.[5]

Bethge suggests that Bonhoeffer's decision "was simply his readiness to recognize that he was and would have to remain a German, fully accepting of guilt and responsibility."[6] He put his case most clearly in his letter to Reinhold Niebuhr:

I have made a mistake in coming to America. I must live through this difficult period of our national history with the Christian people of Germany. I will have no right to participate in the reconstruction of Christian life in Germany if I do not share the trials of this time with my people. . . . Christians in Germany will face the terrible alternative of either willing the defeat of their nation in order that Christian civilization may survive, or willing the victory of their nation and thereby destroying our civilization. I know which of these alternatives I must choose; but I cannot make that choice in security.[7]

On July 9, 1939, Bonhoeffer began his voyage back to Germany. He resumed his efforts to resist Hitler and the Reich. Among his resistance activities was his plotting to assassinate Hitler. On April 5, 1943, while he was staying at his parents' home in Berlin, he was arrested for his activity in the underground resistance movement. He spent two years in several German concentration camps. He was executed by special order at Flossenburg on April 9, 1945, a few days before the Allies liberated the prison camp.

Bonhoeffer's experience of God's calling reflects several features of Protestant, and Lutheran, understandings of vocation. First, God's call was not away from family, friends, and country. God's call was to stay in his

---

5. Bethge, *Dietrich Bonhoeffer*, 653.
6. Bethge, *Dietrich Bonhoeffer*, 654.
7. Bethge, *Dietrich Bonhoeffer*, 655.

home country, working with family and churches to resist Hitler. Second, Bonhoeffer is not entirely clear or certain about his own motives in deciding to leave America and return to Germany. Third, Bonhoeffer's discernment of his calling was an intensely personal matter. Fourth is that his call was not to self-actualization or career-advancement but to the costly path of discipleship that demanded self-sacrifice of his freedom and his very life. Fifth, his call made distinctive use of Bonhoeffer's particular identity and social relations. In many ways Bonhoeffer's calling was to a project that "had his name on it."[8] Sixth, living out his calling did not involve conservative conformity to the status quo; it required resistance to the corrupt powers that then ruled Germany. This chapter elaborates these and other elements of calling central to Protestant Christianity.

Historians often mark the start of this tradition on October 31, 1517, when Martin Luther (1483–1546), an Augustinian monk and theology professor at Wittenberg, posted for public discussion on the door of the Wittenberg cathedral ninety-five theses protesting against many Roman Catholic teachings and practices. Luther's "protest" was especially against the teaching that one earns salvation by doing good works, particularly through the practice of selling indulgences. Originally indulgences were deeds of mercy that reduced one's temporal punishment for sins that had been forgiven. By the sixteenth century it referred to a treasury of merit from which the pope could draw and assign to people who gave monetary donations to the Catholic Church. The indulgences could then be used to reduce deceased loved ones' time in purgatory. In northern Germany a Dominican friar, Johann Tetzel, sold many indulgences for the dead, saying "When a penny in the coffer rings, / A soul from Purgatory springs."[9]

There was widespread discontent with the Roman Catholic Church throughout Europe, due in part to famine and poverty among the peasants, resurgent nationalism, and resentment of papal power on the part of the secular nobility. Others, such as John Huss (1368–1415) and John Wycliff (1331–1384), had made similar protests, but were executed by the Catholic Church. Luther's protests caught fire and soon there were numerous

---

8. Robert M. Adams discusses Bonhoeffer's decision to return to Germany in his chapter, "Vocation," in *Finite and Infinite Goods: A Framework for Ethics* (Oxford: Oxford University Press, 1999), 292–317.

9. For more on indulgences see Lawrence G. Duggan, "Indulgence," in Encyclopaedia Britannica, accessed May 21, 2015, http://www.britannica.com/topic/indulgence.

groups of protesters throughout Europe and in England.[10] Protesters held forth a common argument: a return to biblical sources, and a rejection of church traditions that could not be supported by the Bible. Three themes sum up the heart of the Protestant Reformation. First, Scripture alone (and not tradition and the papacy) is authoritative in matters of faith and good works. Second, faith alone (not good works) makes one right with God, which is a gift of grace rather than a meritorious good work. Third, love for neighbors by being faithful in one's varied callings (and not the separated, monastic life) is the Christian way to express love for God.

Many taxonomies of Christianity begin by distinguishing three groups: Roman Catholic, Eastern Orthodox, and Protestant. Today there are approximately 670 million Protestants. As the Protestant movement grew, it divided into many different subgroups. In the US the main groups are Anabaptist, Anglican, Baptist, Congregational, Lutheran, Methodist, Pentecostal, Quaker, and Reformed/Calvinist.[11]

This chapter focuses on Lutheran and Calvinist strands of Protestantism, two[12] forms of Protestantism sometimes called "magisterial," which distinguishes them from the radical reformers, especially the Anabaptists. One key issue dividing Luther and Calvin from the Anabaptists was whether God calls Christians to coercive political offices, such as being a

10. Two reasons were particularly important for Luther's success where others failed. The first was the invention of the printing press, which spread his ideas to tens and hundreds of thousands of readers. The second was the strong support of Frederick the Wise (1463–1525), Elector of Saxony, a major principality in Germany.

11. Numbers and denominational breakdowns vary. These groupings are from "Major World Denominations," accessed May 22, 2015, http://www.888c.com/worldChristian Denominations.htm.

12. In addition to the writings of Luther and Calvin, the understanding of callings developed here is shaped by Puritans and by twentieth-century writers such as Dietrich Bonhoeffer, Karl Barth, Emil Brunner, and Abraham Kuyper. Some of the more influential sources are Martin Luther, "To the Christian Nobility of the German Nation," "Trade and Usury," "Whether Soldiers Too Can Be Saved," "The Estate of Marriage," and "A Sermon on Keeping Children in School"; John Calvin, *Institutes of the Christian Religion*, ed. J. T. McNeill, trans. F. L. Battles, vols. 20 and 21 in The Library of Christian Classics (Philadelphia: Westminster, 1960), 3.7.1–5; 3.10.2, 5, 6; 3.24.8–9; 4.20; and *John Calvin: Treatises against the Anabaptists and the Libertines,* ed. and trans. B. W. Farley (Grand Rapids: Baker, 1988); William Perkins, "A Treatise of the Vocations," in *The Works of William Perkins,* ed. Ian Breward (Abingdon, UK: Sutton Courtenay Press, 1970); Dietrich Bonhoeffer, *The Cost of Discipleship,* trans. R. H. Fuller with some revisions by Irmgard Booth (New York: Simon & Schuster, 1995); Karl Barth, *Church Dogmatics* III/4: *The Doctrine of Creation,* ed. G. W. Bromiley and T. F. Torrance, trans. G. W. Bromiley (Edinburgh: T. & T. Clark, 1961).

soldier, prince, or king. Luther and Calvin said yes; the Anabaptists, following their pacifist interpretation of Jesus's example and teaching, said no. For Luther and Calvin those who hold political power are servants of their neighbors. As such they have their offices as callings from God.

There are a variety of biblical and theological sources for Protestant understandings of callings. In addition to the "call stories" in the Bible, the biblical accounts of creation, of God's covenant with Israel, of the formation of the church, and of the Christian in society shape this approach.[13] The Creator's blessing on humanity is also a "mandate" or calling. "God blessed them and said 'Be fruitful and multiply, and fill the earth and subdue it; and have dominion over the fish of the sea and over the birds of the air and over every living thing that moves upon the earth'" (Gen. 1:28). God's blessing connects all of human life to divine creative activity, including marriage and family, culture and the arts, science and technology, and more. God's creative work continues today through human beings who bear God's image. As Luther says, God milks the cows through the milkmaid.

Because many call stories require leaving parents and one's work in society (e.g., Abraham, Gen. 12:1–3; Peter and the disciples, Mark 1:16–20), some emphasize the "other-worldly" dynamic of God's callings. This dynamic is embodied in monastic callings. Luther and Calvin stress the "this-worldly" dynamic of God's callings. Luther advises the celibate monks and priests of his day to break their vows, get married, and have children.[14] He criticizes those who abandoned family to go on a religious pilgrimage or to become nuns and monks. God does not call Christians away from society and family, but rather to serve God in and through their roles in the family, economy, the state, and in all "worldly" occupations.[15]

---

13. Some of the prominent call stories in the Christian Bible are the following: Genesis 12:1–3, call of Abram; Exodus 3:1–22, call of Moses; Judges 4:4–10, call of Deborah; 1 Samuel 3:1–4:1, call of Samuel; Isaiah 6:1–8, call of Isaiah; Jeremiah 1:4–10, call of Jeremiah; Matthew 4:8–22, call of Peter, Andrew, James, and John; Acts 1:21–26, call of Matthias (to replace Judas); Acts 6:1–6, call of first deacons; Acts 9:1–19, call of Saul of Tarsus on the road to Damascus; and Acts 13:2–3, call of Paul and Barnabas to first missionary journey. For a more complete account of the Bible on vocation, see Douglas J. Schuurman, *Vocation: Discerning Our Vocations in Life* (Grand Rapids: Eerdmans, 2004), chapter 2.

14. See Luther, "On Monastic Vows," in *Luther's Works,* vol. 44: *The Christian in Society I,* ed. J. Atkinson, gen. ed. H. T. Lehmann (Philadelphia: Fortress, 1966), 243–400; and Luther, "The Estate of Marriage," in *Luther's Works,* vol. 45: *The Christian in Society II,* ed. W. I. Brandt and H. T. Lehmann (Philadelphia: Fortress, 1962), 11–50.

15. A key biblical support for Luther's approach is 1 Corinthians 7:17–24. Paul advises Christians not to abandon spouse and occupation when God calls them to faith in Christ. The

Concepts of Calling

There are two distinct types of call, and they are discovered or discerned in different ways. First is the "spiritual" or "general" calling to become a Christian, be baptized, and take up the duties of the Christian life. All Christians share this calling. It is this call to faith and discipleship that is prominent in the New Testament.

Second is "particular" or "external" callings. Though all Christians share the same spiritual calling, their particular callings vary. God calls some to be married, others to the single life. God calls some to be pastors, others to be carpenters. Particular callings, then, constitute the complex and distinctive social matrix of an individual's life. Christians are to live out their spiritual calling concretely and specifically in all the social spheres in which they live, offering each and every part of life as a sacrifice of thanksgiving to God.

God is the Caller, the one who summons, invites, and guides people away from sin and back to Godself. God then calls people back into the world to express God's continuing love and care for all people and for all creation. The language of "call" and "callings" is metaphorical; those called do not actually hear a voice from God with their physical ears. The auditory imagery points to the prominence of the Word of God in Christian texts and traditions, and the importance of hearing or listening for the "voice of God" in the Bible and in Creation.

Three other theological ideas are central to Protestant understandings of calling. First is the doctrine of justification by faith. The works of love undertaken in and through one's callings do not cause salvation; rather, they are the result of receiving God's salvation through faith. Faith trusts the promises of God given in Jesus Christ, that God is full of mercy and eager to give new spiritual life to all who believe the good news about God in Christ. Salvation is a gift of God's grace to be received, not earned.

---

passage reads, "[L]et each of you lead the life that the Lord has assigned, to which God called you. . . . Was anyone at the time of his call already circumcised? Let him not seek to remove the marks of circumcision. Was anyone at the time of his call uncircumcised? Let him not seek circumcision. . . . Let each of you remain in the condition [*klesei*] in which you were called. Were you a slave when called? Do not be concerned about it. . . . For whoever was called in the Lord as a slave is a freed person belonging to the Lord, just as whoever was free when called is a slave of Christ. You were bought with a price; do not become slaves of human masters. In whatever condition you were called, brothers and sisters, there remain with God." Unless otherwise noted, biblical quotations are from the NRSV.

Faith in Christ brings about a new identity, one that no longer strives to earn God's favor through good works but rather spontaneously expresses love for God by loving one's neighbors. Later Protestants, especially the Puritans, shifted the doctrine of calling. They viewed success in one's life as a sign of being elected by God and therefore destined to salvation, but their view was not shared by Luther or Calvin.[16]

I touched on the second theological idea earlier, namely, the doctrine of creation and providence.[17] Creation is unfinished, and God continues to nourish what God creates and to bring all things to their appointed purposes. As individuals, our genetic makeup, our parents and family members, our aptitudes and senses of priority, our time in history, our citizenship, and our entire socially situated life have been shaped by God's providence and continuing creation. This is not solely the result of chance, fate, or human freedom; it is shaped by God's will and providence. Especially for particular callings, this brings a profound religious sensibility to daily life and its opportunities for service to God and others.

Third is the incarnation. Those with a sense of calling believe that Jesus Christ is incarnate in human need and that in serving others through their callings they are serving Christ. Luther advises fathers to look upon the tedious tasks of early childcare through the eyes of faith, and so to imagine they are holding the baby Jesus in their hands while they are changing dirty diapers.[18] A central biblical passage is the parable of the final judgment in which Christ returns to judge the nations and separate the sheep from the goats. He will put the sheep at his right hand, bless them, and welcome them to inherit the kingdom prepared for them from the foundations of the world. The basis for their being welcomed into the kingdom is giving Christ food, drink, welcome, clothing, and visitation in prison.

> Then the righteous will answer him, "Lord, when was it that we saw you hungry and gave you food, or thirsty and gave you something to

---

16. See Max Weber, *The Protestant Ethic and the Spirit of Capitalism,* trans. Talcott Parsons, foreword by R. H. Tawney (New York: Charles Scribner's Sons, 1958).

17. See Miroslav Volf, *Work in the Spirit: Toward a Theology of Work* (New York: Oxford University Press, 1991), for developing an eschatological vision, where calling is based on hope for the new creation rather than upon providence and creation. For an exchange between Schuurman and Wolf on this point, see "Eschaton, Creation, and Social Ethics" and "Creation, Eschaton, and Social Ethics," *The Calvin Theological Journal* 30, no. 1 (April 1995): 130–58.

18. "The Estate of Marriage," in *Luther's Works,* 45:41.

drink? And when was it that we saw you a stranger and welcomed you, or naked and gave you clothing? And when was it that we saw you sick or in prison and visited you?" And the king will answer them, "Truly I tell you, just as you did it unto the least of these who are members of my family, you did it to me." (Matt. 25:35–40)

Christ then will put the goats at his left hand and will say they are accursed along with the devil and his minions because they did not aid Christ in his need. They too ask when they ever saw Christ hungry, thirsty, a stranger, naked, sick, or in prison and failed to help him. He will reply, "[T]ruly I tell you, just as you did not do it to one of the least of these, you did not do it to me" (Matt. 25:45).

Because of their conviction that Christ is incarnate in neighbors' needs, Luther and other early reformers were critical of the monastic practice of abandoning home and society in favor of a higher spiritual life apart from this world. For Luther and Calvin, our callings offer opportunities to serve our neighbors. Whether it is changing diapers or working for an employer, all "secular" work is infused with religious meaning as spiritual service or worship of God. Rather than divert a person away from the world to a monastery, Protestant calling becomes a lens of faith that perceives God in all of life, and especially in the needs of the neighbors who are served.

In addition to seeing Christ incarnate in the needs of the neighbor, the Protestant vision of calling perceives Christ in the actions of those helping others in and through their callings. When people feed the hungry, support the lonely, they are incarnating Christ for their neighbors. Christ is present in acts of justice, love, and mercy.

Receiving a Calling

How do human beings come to know what God is calling them to be and to do? God does not speak audibly or appear visually to people. With very few exceptions, God's callings come through mediators, such as angels, dreams, visions, prophets, priests, apostles, sacred texts, friends, parents, and the wisdom and the beauty of creation.[19]

---

19. In some of the most remarkable call stories in the Bible, God speaks directly to the one called. God told Abram to leave his country and kin and go to a land God would show him (Gen. 12:1). God spoke to Moses from a burning bush (Exod. 2:23–4:17). God

Discernment is important for how people come to know both the general call and particular callings, but there are also some important differences between how people become aware of each type of call. The shared *spiritual call* to become a Christian comes mainly through hearing the proclamation of the gospel, the good news about Jesus Christ. The Bible uses a variety of metaphors for how God calls, but the biblical stress on the "word" of God leads to a prominence of auditory imagery for God's activity, and of listening for human receptivity to God's call. Jesus audibly called his disciples to "follow me." One "hears" the voice of God and obeys it.

The core promises of the gospel are also communicated through participation in the practices of the church community, and especially through the sacraments of Baptism and the Eucharist. These sacraments are "visible words" and their ritual celebration helps make the promises given in the gospel experientially meaningful in a person's life. Here very tangible, sensual media convey the call to become and remain a Christian. In the case of Baptism it is water; in the Eucharist it is bread and wine. Touch and taste, in the context of the church's liturgy and practices, mediate God's call and make it a felt reality in a Christian's life. Faith in the proclaimed word and participation in the sacraments are the means by which one receives one's spiritual calling.

We become aware of our *particular callings* in a variety of ways. God not only calls us to faith and new life in Christ, God also calls us to specific tasks, roles in our family, and forms of paid work. Here it may be helpful to distinguish between how a vision of callings affects "pivotal decisions" and how it affects our interpretation of our central social locations. "Pivotal decisions" are decisions to enter a form of paid work, to marry or remain unmarried, to have or not have children, or to take on a particular task. I call these decisions "pivotal" because they determine the larger institutional and relational contexts of our subsequent actions. Luther and Calvin were concerned with how callings can become a lens enabling us to see loving participation in all our relational settings as sacred service to God.

---

called Samuel's name (1 Sam. 3:4). The voice of the Lord said to Isaiah, "Whom shall I send, and who will go for us?" (Isa. 6:8). The Lord came to Amos and told him to prophesy to Israel (Amos 7:15). In God's freedom, God may or may not use mediators, but by far the prevalent pattern is making use of some part of creation to mediate God's call. It is also possible that even in these exceptional call stories, the terse phrases about the Lord speaking could be a kind of shorthand for what in fact was a process in which mediating elements were present.

They said little about how callings shape pivotal decisions. Since this is an important area today, at least for those whose economic and social position allows greater freedom, I will extend the trajectory of what they do say about callings to pivotal decisions.[20]

Experience of God's callings in relation to pivotal decisions in biblical call stories is more dramatic than in our experience. For most of us, the pattern is more like the one found in the book of Acts than the one depicted in the dramatic call stories. As the church grew and complaints arose because Hellenic Christian widows' needs were being neglected, "the twelve called together the whole community" and directed them to "select from among yourselves seven men of good standing, full of the Spirit and of wisdom, whom we may appoint to the task" of daily distribution of food (Acts 6:1–4). The seven were selected and stood before the apostles, "who prayed and laid their hands on them" (6:6). With some exceptions, the process in Acts is communal, flexible, and dynamic.[21] As new needs and gifts are recognized, the Spirit—most often through the Christian community—selects and commissions individual Christians in their callings. Though the New Testament does not provide a formula for discerning God's callings in relation to pivotal decisions, it does indicate key elements often present in this process. They include gifts, needs, obligations, communal discussion, and prayer.

Drawing from these biblical accounts, and from stories of how people came to experience their lives as callings, we can identify some practical

---

20. At the time of Luther and Calvin there was little freedom to choose spouse and career; one's lot in life was "ascribed" to one based largely on one's location in the social hierarchy. It is often noted that today we have much greater freedom. Although many readers of this volume enjoy social positions allowing greater freedom, most of the human population does not. Even for those who do have social positions enabling greater freedom, that freedom may be more a myth than a reality. For further thoughts on this issue, see Schuurman, *Vocation,* 118–22.

21. After the church formally resolved the controversy about whether to accept Gentiles into the Christian community, the apostles and elders "with the consent of the whole church" selected Judas and Silas and sent them to Antioch, where Paul and Barnabas were working, to deliver a letter spelling out the conclusions of the first church council (Acts 15:22–35). The core of the letter said "it seemed good to the Holy Spirit and to us" not to impose the burden of Jewish law upon believing Gentles. Paul and Barnabas parted ways over a disagreement about whether Mark should go with them on their second missionary journey. Barnabas took Mark with him to Cyprus, and Paul took Silas with him to Syria and Cilicia and beyond (Acts 15:36–41), indicating that the Spirit's callings are effectual even through sharp controversy among the leaders of the churches.

guidelines for how we should discern God's callings as we make pivotal decisions.

The first guideline is need. Because callings are directed in service to the care and redemption of all that God has made, attentiveness to the needs of the world guides pivotal decisions relating to our callings. These needs are diverse. The nonhuman world needs tending, healing, and stewarding. Agriculture, forestry, care of local, state, and national parks, veterinary services, for example, include a wide variety of needs. People have spiritual needs, and for Christian believers this need is met through the gospel of Jesus Christ and the power of the Holy Spirit in the Christian community. People also need food, physical and emotional health, recreation, clothing and shelter, education, music, scientific knowledge, the arts, just political order, and more. Because God's shalom includes human flourishing in all its fullness, human needs go beyond what is necessary for survival.

Some needs are objectively more pressing than others, in general or at a given time. Acute awareness of spiritual need causes some to choose paid work in offices contributing directly to the spiritual needs of religious communities. In church communities they become pastors, teachers, church musicians, and church office assistants. Others are acutely aware of the need of many people for the basic necessities of life. This awareness leads some to become social workers, human rights activists, and employees of organizations devoted directly to meeting the needs of the poorest of the poor for clean water, food, clothing, and shelter.

Because the needs of the human and nonhuman communities are diverse, God does not call everyone into forms of paid work whose specific focus is preaching or advocacy, but rather God calls some to be carpenters, engineers, lawyers, or investment bankers. To the extent that these people are able, they should bend their occupations and skills in ways that help those most in need. Many law firms, for example, encourage pro bono work. Doctors Without Borders enables doctors to spend at least some of their time providing medical services where they are most needed. Carpenters can also help with Habitat for Humanity on occasion.

Some needs may be objectively more pressing, not in general, but at a given time and place. A professional may give up an advancement opportunity, for example, to enable her to stay closer to a needy parent, or to provide better communal resources for a special-needs child.

There is also an important subjective factor relevant to need and pivotal decisions. Bonhoeffer felt the needs were greater in his home country than in the US. Despite the need for good theology, and his love of writing theology, Bonhoeffer felt God's call through the dire need for resistance to the Nazi regime. God has so shaped us that we are attentive to different needs. Some Evangelical Christians use the language of having a "burden" for this or that need. For some the burden is the need for health; for others it is the need for education. Some see needs for beauty and music; others see needs for buildings and houses. Some Christians feel so strongly about the needs they see that they devalue the needs others see. Those who stress the need of the lost to hear the gospel, for example, sometimes fail to see the importance of food, shelter, clothing, and the arts. Develop passionately your vocation to address the needs you believe most pressing, but do not judge another who is passionate about a different set of needs.

The second guideline is gifts. God has given each person a particular constellation of gifts to be identified and exercised for the good of the whole. In Bonhoeffer's case his gifts included not only his extraordinary ability to teach and preach, but also his contacts within the German and English churches that enabled him to be a strong leader in the resistance movement. He also came from a very prominent family that had numerous personal and political connections that put him in a unique position to oppose Hitler.

The New Testament associates gifts with callings (Rom. 12; 1 Cor. 12; Eph. 4). In sovereign freedom, the Holy Spirit distributes gifts, which are in turn to be used to build up the body of Christ. Gifts differ rather strikingly; some are intellectual, artistic, administrative, mechanical, emotional, biological, and social. God's callings take account of these aptitudes. Discovering and developing our aptitudes are important for discerning what God is calling us to be and to do. It is unlikely that God is calling someone to become a philosopher if that person has little love of or aptitude for ideas and contemplative wonder. Tone-deaf people are unlikely candidates for musical callings. People who are all thumbs are not usually called to become mechanics, or surgeons. People who are "unmusical" spiritually—who cannot feel the rhythms of God's grace amid the hopes and fears, presumption and despair, the wonder and the agony of life—are not likely candidates for callings as leaders in their religious communities. There are exceptions. In many of the "call" stories of the Hebrew Bible (e.g., Moses, David, Isaiah) the inadequacy of the one called is highlighted. Some have concluded from this that God calls people to positions they do not enjoy and for which they have little or no aptitude. The older Pietists had an adage, "What we take ill, will be God's will." Thus, an element of duty and a sense of inadequacy can be present in the way that some experience God's callings.[22] But God usually works with, and not against, the abilities and aptitudes of people. The biblical stories that seem to suggest otherwise only prove the rule by their exceptional character. They finally underscore the basic truths that all gifts and callings depend upon God's grace and good will, and that God delights to take what is weak in the eyes of the world to shame the strong. Some people, like humanitarian and Nobel Prize awardee Albert Schweitzer (1875–1965), have so much aptitude and opportunity that they find it almost impossible to know which direction to pursue. He had successful careers as a musician, theologian, and medical doctor.[23] People with multiple gifts should feel free to choose among paths, so long as their aim is to be of service to God and neighbor.

A person's gifts form one important indicator of directions in which God may be calling that person. Although the rapid pace of change in today's society creates stress, it also provides opportunities for aptitudes to shape one's callings. Only a generation ago, for example, mothers stayed at home with children and fathers went out to a paid job, even if in a particular marriage the father had greater parental aptitude and the mother had greater work aptitude. Today there is more freedom for parents to take on particular tasks suited to their abilities and interests. Increasingly women

22. Although popular conceptions of calling downplay the role of duty, it is central to biblical and classic Protestant views. For examples that resist this popular view, see J. Stuart Bunderson and Jeffrey A. Thompson, "The Call of the Wild: Zookeepers, Callings, and the Double-edged Sword of Deeply Meaningful Work," *Administrative Science Quarterly* 54 (2009): 32–57, and Kathleen Cahalan's tentatively titled book *Call It What It Is* (Grand Rapids: Eerdmans, forthcoming 2017), chap. 7.

23. By the ripe age of thirty, he had already firmly established himself as one of Europe's leading organists, had written a definitive study of Bach that transformed the way musicians performed Bach all over the world and was soon translated from French into German and English (844 pages in the German), was Principal of the Theological College of St. Thomas, lectured regularly on New Testament studies, had written all but the final chapter in his book *Quest for the Historical Jesus,* a book that redirected the course of New Testament scholarship, and had also mapped out the rough lines of Pauline theology that were to be later published as *The Mysticism of Paul.* In his early twenties, Schweitzer felt the need for a "more direct" form of service and resolved to make a "career move" when he became thirty years old. True to his earlier resolve, when he was thirty, after achieving the sort of acclaim in three fields that most only hope to achieve in one field and after an entire lifetime, Schweitzer began his seven years of medical studies in order to become a medical doctor in Africa. Schweitzer is, of course, extraordinary in aptitude and in the opportunities he found to express this aptitude. See Schweitzer, *Out of My Life and Thought: An Autobiography,* trans. C. T. Campion, with postscript (New York: Henry Holt and Co., 1933).

have more freedom to explore their gifts for particular callings, rather than being arbitrarily kept out of occupations.

The third practical guideline is opportunity and limit. Twentieth-century Reformed theologian Karl Barth (1886–1968) offers some useful guidelines to help people discern the special spheres of responsibility in which God calls them to freedom of obedience.[24] Barth advises Christians to consider three aspects of their lives in order to discern God's command, which is not chosen as much as discovered. He identifies each as a "limit of obedience" that shapes what I have called pivotal choices. As such they both open and close possibilities for God's callings. One aspect is aptitude, or gifts, which I have already treated above. The others are place in the life cycle and our place in history.

God calls us to different possibilities and tendencies depending upon our stage in life. *Youth* is the time of stepping into freedom from the past for new opportunity; it is the time of preparation, hope, and planning. The young are called to explore new possibilities and to be diligent in hope of a full harvest. *Middle age* is the time for maturity of obedience. Now we are called to harvest what we have sown. It is no longer too early for many activities, and it is not yet too late for others. We are no longer inexperienced, but we are not yet exhausted. We are young enough to be open and to shape our future in definite ways. *Old age* is the special time to see life in the light of all eternity, to see the future as gift more so than as task. God calls us, then, to basic directions depending on our time in the life cycle. The time of each stage has its own special opportunities, many of which can never be recovered, and its special limits. Barth's interpretations of life's stages are debatable, but his insight is helpful. There are limits and possibilities constituting the range of what God might be calling us to at a given time in our lives.

The second aspect, our place in history, includes citizenship, the century in which we live, family history, political structures, economic class, and religious communities. Barth's first word to us about our place in history is to "accept and keep your place." Barth says that God's providence controls the general and particular sway of historical forces that constitute our historical location. Bonhoeffer's decision to return to Germany offers a dramatic example of Barth's general guideline. He "accepted" his place in Germany. He returned to his country, his family, and his church. God's call now was not "other-worldly" but "this-worldly," embedded in a particular history that directed him to hear God's call, not in Niebuhr's advice, but in the needs of family and country.

24. My discussion of these guidelines follows Barth, *Church Dogmatics* III/4, 607–47.

Barth's second word about our historical situation is to "grapple" with it and to bring it into obedience to God's will. Our country, century, family, class, race—and the particular institutions mediating these to us—are not only expressive of God's sustaining providence; they also express human sin, and so must be transformed. Bonhoeffer's Germany was notoriously corrupt under Hitler, so much so that Bonhoeffer and others sought to destroy that regime before building a new one. Not all situations are so corrupt; some can be reformed and improved through constructive participation. The historical situation, Barth says, is "one's cradle, not one's grave." We cannot assume that the demands of our contexts are expressions of God's command; we must determine anew, in each context, what God is requiring us to be and to do. Insofar as it is possible, we must bring our situation into line with God. Because of the deeply flawed nature of culture and society, we cannot merely "accept" our social-historical contexts. These contexts do not measure up to the standards of God's will and Word; they must be grappled with, and transformed. Properly understood, the doctrine of callings leads to participation in our contexts with a view to transforming them to express God's shalom.

In addition to the general limits of place in the life cycle and in history, there must be a concrete opportunity. The job I applied for and hope to receive must be offered; the one you choose to marry must say, "I will marry you." A person may have identified the need of higher education and gained the necessary credentials for teaching in a college, but being a professor is not your calling unless and until you get a concrete offer to teach at this or that university. You may feel called to serve as a US senator, but that is not your calling unless and until you get elected. You may think Jane is the one whom God is calling you to marry, but if she does not concur then God is not calling you to marry Jane. However, there may be other concrete opportunities for paid work, such as seeking a job in another country, or pursuing related fields. Likewise, a new relationship may develop with potential for a lifelong, exclusive mutual commitment.

It is often difficult to know how long to persist, whether in seeking a job offer in the area of one's choice or in pursuing a prospective but reluctant potential spouse. The oxymoronic "creative destruction" of capitalist economies plunges people into unemployment and requires retooling for new jobs. A sense of call can be a bulwark in such anxious times. God's call and callings are far broader than one's marriage or one's paid work. We are freer to be patient during adversity if we believe that our life belongs to God in Christ, who gave his life for us. If the point of our whole existence is to serve Christ in and through all our lives, then our existence finds its ultimate meaning and worth elsewhere than in our nationality or status at work and in the family. God's call will find avenues of concrete expression, even if not in the ways we anticipated. Adversity often becomes a spur for creative change and discovery of new places to which God is calling one to serve.

The fourth guideline is communal discernment. There are profoundly personal and individual dimensions to making pivotal decisions. Often it is in the dark nights of the soul, or in the brightness of an experience of God's presence, that we perceive God's callings. Prayer, honest self-examination, clarifying one's motives and intentions are difficult personal work that should accompany pivotal decisions. Bonhoeffer confesses that he did not fully know his motives in deciding to return to Germany. Only God finally knows. As in the case of responding to God's call to be a Christian, responding to God's particular callings requires individual decision in the sanctuary of God's presence.

But there are also important communal elements in the process of discerning God's callings. Traditionally those who felt called to the ministry of word and sacrament must have their internal sense of call confirmed by the external confirmation of the Christian community. For other occupations there are exams to pass, job qualifications to meet, interviews, and finally the offer of a job. The community plays an important role in the process of discerning one's callings. A Christian should consult with those who know them well when they are deliberating about job and marriage. Often God's direction comes through parents, coaches, friends, pastors, teachers, spiritual directors, and other authorities in our lives.

Though God's callings often come through the community, they do not always do so. Communities, like individuals, are plagued by sinful corruptions such as racism, patriarchy, and classism. A friend of mine strongly felt called to become a pastor, but when she applied to seminary she was told that God does not call women to church ordination as pastors. Institutionalized sexism and racism have for centuries been unjust, barring women and racial minorities from holding public offices and from the more prestigious and lucrative forms of paid work. Pervasive injustices like these should remind us that the Spirit distributes gifts and callings "as the Spirit chooses" (1 Cor. 12:11) and not by race, class, and gender. An incredibly strong sense of calling is required to swim against the stream. But, by God's power and grace, it is at times necessary and possible to do so. With this important qualification, the community can be a very important source of guidance for discerning God's callings.

Living Out a Calling

The Protestant vision of calling has had two major impacts on how Christians understand their lives and how they live and act in daily life.

The first is that calling infuses daily life with profound spiritual meaning. The lens of calling sees self, others, and the social locations of one's life in relation to God's presence. Doing one's paid work is more than "just a job." It is a sacrifice of thanksgiving to God. Tending to the needs of one's children, spouse, parents, and family members is serving Christ. In the same way that color-tinged glasses enable one to see otherwise invisible patterns in a picture, so too viewing one's life through the lens of faith and calling causes new patterns of meaning to appear.

Second, this vision impacts how believers understand their lives and how they live and act as *moral*. Because they are serving God in all they do and are called to love God and neighbor in and through all the social spheres they occupy, Christians ought to strive to resist evil and do what is morally good and right in and through their callings. Although the doctrine of vocation has been often misused to support obeying unjust authorities and passive tolerance of abuse and other evils, its original impulses form a catalyst for challenging injustice and advancing justice, peace, healing, and the well-being of all creation.[25] Shalom is much more than the absence of hostility; it includes joy and delight. Shalom is a condition of wholeness, of health and flourishing to the fullest extent. Shalom includes, but goes beyond, justice. Shalom expresses God's original will for life in creation, and God's ultimate goal for life in the New Creation.[26]

Practices to Sustain Callings

In an increasingly secular pluralistic society, there are fewer overtly Christian institutional supports for the Protestant sense of vocation and the faith

25. For examples of abuses of the doctrine of vocation see Schuurman, *Vocation*, 76–116.

26. In *Not the Way It's Supposed to Be: A Breviary of Sin* (Grand Rapids: Eerdmans, 1995), theologian Cornelius Plantinga Jr. describes shalom as follows: "The webbing together of God, humans, and all creation in justice, fulfillment, and delight is what the Hebrew prophets call *shalom*. We call it peace, but it means far more than mere peace of mind or a cease-fire between enemies. In the Bible, shalom means *universal flourishing, wholeness, and delight*—a rich state of affairs in which natural needs are satisfied and natural gifts fruitfully employed, a state of affairs that inspires joyful wonder as its Creator and Savior opens doors and welcomes the creatures in whom he delights. Shalom, in other words, is the way things ought to be" (10).

that affirms God's presence and providence working in, through, and under all things. A central task of the church is to inspire a piety that sees all of life in relation to God. Word and sacrament, prayer and liturgy, fellowship and music revive and sustain the sense that God is present in and through our world. With St. Augustine we ask "the whole mass of the universe" about God and hear it reply, "'I am not God. God is he who made me.'"[27] Creation is a gift of the Spirit, who blows wherever she wills.

There are, however, some institutions and disciplines that may help people sense God's callings in their lives. The Spirit uses certain "helps" to spark, confirm, strengthen, and redirect our sense of call. Because so much of our culture and institutional life either neglects or opposes a vital sense of calling, renewed attention to strategies for preserving a "spirituality" for daily life that can help maintain a sense of call is needed.[28]

Prayer and meditation help spark and sustain a sense of calling. According to one survey, 73 percent of respondents who reported feeling God's calling in their paid work also said they regularly engaged in devotional reading of the Bible.[29] Many hospitals still contain chapels that once were regularly occupied by the staff for prayer and meditation. Many business offices likewise included prayers in daily routines. Participation in worship services reinforces daily prayer and meditation. As society becomes more and more secular, Christians must become more intentional

27. Augustine, *Confessions* 10.6, trans. and intro. by R. S. Pine-Coffin (London: Penguin, 1961), 212.

28. A recent study about the explosion of interest in spirituality in the workplace, on the one hand, and the bureaucratization of churches, on the other, argues that while "religious authority" of clerics is declining, spirituality is growing. See Don Grant, Kathleen M. O'Neil, and Laura S. Stephens, "Neosecularization and Craft versus Professional Religious Authority in a Nonreligious Organization," *Journal for the Scientific Study of Religion* 42, no. 3 (2003): 479-87. Researchers sent questionnaires asking whether nurses were willing to perform functions of the displaced chaplains. The results showed that where religious professionals are absent, "craft versions of religious authority may still develop" (480). Eighty-five percent of the nurses surveyed say there is "something spiritual" about the care they provide (483). Nearly a fourth, 24 percent, say they feel "more spiritual at work than elsewhere" (483). Forty-two percent of the nurses say they are "spiritual but not religious" (482), and one-quarter of them use the term "calling" to describe their work. Twenty-eight percent of the "spiritual only" nurses were willing to provide chaplains' services if given time for training. Thirty-seven percent of self-identified "religious" nurses were willing to do so. In all, 30.4 percent said they "would provide the same services as chaplains if given the time and training" (481).

29. William E. Diehl, *In Search of Faithfulness: Lessons from the Christian Community* (Philadelphia: Fortress, 1982), 38.

and disciplined in prayer and meditation. Family-based practices, so important for Hindu and Jewish religious life, must complement church-based practices to evoke and sustain a sense of call.

The Christian tradition is vastly rich in resources for anyone who wants help in prayer and meditation. The Psalms, the challenging words of the prophets, the stories of the Bible, proverbs and parables, and apostolic letters—the whole biblical canon is rich with resources. The liturgies of Eastern and Western churches, the writings of Christian mystics, and the theology and sermons of past church leaders contain an inexhaustible reservoir for anyone who wants to come and drink. Prayer and meditation can spark and sustain a sense of life as calling.

Exemplary individuals and groups can and often do inspire a sense of calling. The biblical stories about Abraham, Sarah, Jacob, Joseph, the midwives, Moses, the kings, the prophets, Jesus, and the apostles are an instructive and at times inspirational legacy for believers today. The genius and extraordinary accomplishments of Catholic exemplars like Mother Teresa and Dorothy Day, and Protestants like Dietrich Bonhoeffer, Albert Schweitzer, and Martin Luther King Jr., remind us of God's grace and power working in this world.

In our warranted admiration for such noteworthy service, Christians must not forget the "ordinary saints" God has blessed.[30] Grandmothers and mothers whose loving care sustains the lives of their dependents; grandfathers and fathers who faithfully and loyally give of themselves to their children; children who care for their aged parents; honest politicians, businesspeople, and mechanics; friends whose constancy and care sustained us in our hour of need; predecessors whose honest work and generosity created and developed the institutions on which we depend, can provoke a sense of vocation in others.

Often the choices of paid work, and its ethical tenor, are greatly influenced by a saint who formed an influential example. As a professor I write many letters of recommendation, sometimes years after a student has left St. Olaf College. I am especially diligent in this task because I continue to be grateful to my former teachers, particularly Richard J. Mouw and James M. Gustafson, who were faithful and diligent in recommending me when I was a student. I cannot repay them, but I can show my gratitude

---

30. Robert Benne, drawing from his Lutheran heritage, emphasizes this point very fruitfully in his book *Ordinary Saints: An Introduction to the Christian Life* (Minneapolis: Fortress, 1988).

by being faithful and diligent in this part of my work. Exemplars function in similar ways in other occupations. By reflecting on especially exemplary mothers, friends, fathers, husbands, wives, carpenters, mechanics, pastors, businesspeople, or executives, our sense of call can be sparked and deepened.

Christians reflect upon those times in their lives during which God's grace and calling were more deeply and clearly sensed than at other times. The Greek word *kairos* refers to times especially full of God's purpose and presence. The New Testament refers to the time of God's sending Christ into the world as a time of *kairos* (Eph. 1:10), the time of the inbreaking of God's kingdom (Mark 1:15), and the time of decision (2 Cor. 6:2). Unlike *chronos,* which merely marks the passage of hours, days, and years, *kairos* is time as it is filled with meaning and sets the basic direction of individual and communal history.

Each Christian has times of personal *kairos,* times of decision and insight, times that set the basic stance of life. These may be more dramatic and more definite for some Christians than for others, but to some degree nearly all Christians eventually have some experiences like these. Remembering these times, meditating upon them, and sharing them with others can renew a sense of calling.

Often we seem to need extraordinary examples and experiences to shake us out of our unbelieving stupors. Flannery O'Connor used the grotesque and the extreme in her novels because in our secular culture "you have to make your vision apparent by shock—to the hard of hearing you shout, and for the almost-blind you draw large and startling figures."[31] The problem with extraordinary examples and experiences is that they can as easily conceal as reveal the sacred, sacramental character of the ordinary. So we must beware that our reflection upon *kairos* experiences does not result in further distancing God from mundane life but rather leads to a faith that perceives God behind, before, and within all circumstances of life.

One example of a *kairos* experience in my own life occurred during my last year of doctoral study, the seventh year of full-time, post-college study. My wife and I had two children, ages one and three, and were expecting our third. We lived in an undergraduate dorm at the University of Chicago, as Resident Directors, to earn our food and rooms. Prospects for employment as a faculty member were bleak, partly because of a glutted market

---

31. Flannery O'Connor, *Mystery and Manners: Occasional Prose,* ed. Sally and Robert Fitzgerald (New York: Farrar, Straus & Giroux, 1957), 34.

and partly because I had not written a page of my dissertation, usually the death-knell for job prospects in college teaching. Too proud to apply for food stamps, for which we would have easily qualified, we struggled along economically. Then the car radiator broke. Three hundred fifty dollars might as well have been $350,000. We simply did not have it. Burdened, and finally broken, by a load of care that had never been heavier, I phoned Starnella Johnson, deaconess of the small African-Dutch-American church where we worshiped, and begged for money.

Starnella expressed gratitude and joy that I had asked for help. "Many people," she said, "really need help but they're too proud to ask." I exhaled in relief. She, with a few discerning words of grace, put me at ease. She asked how much money I needed. I told her. She said not to worry about paying it back. "If you ever do run into some money," she said, "send us a check."

In a day or two Starnella Johnson came to our dorm-room apartment to deliver the check. Our building had once been one of the more impressive ones on Chicago's south side; Al Capone had rented an entire floor for himself. During "white flight" from south Chicago to the suburbs, the building became dilapidated. The University of Chicago refurbished it, and used it as a dorm.

Starnella entered our rather impressive, marble-floored entryway and handed me the check. She said to me: "You know, Doug, when I was a little girl, I used to swing on the swing set in the park across the street. I used to watch all the rich, well-dressed white people go in and out of the building. And I used to wish and pray that someday I could enter this building to see what it was like inside. And today my wish came true!"

It was one of those times when class, race, and gender all became sacramental realities of God's baffling presence. There I was, surrounded by the symbols of economic and cultural power that have been the privilege of white males like me in this society, but yet a needy and very broken man. God met me that evening, in the form of an African American deaconess, offering me her gift in God's name.

I heard the song of Mary, Jesus's mother, and before her of Hannah, echoing down the corridors of time, into the ears of my soul: "[T]he mighty one has done great things for me, and holy is his name. . . . He has brought down the powerful from their thrones, and lifted up the lowly; he has filled the hungry with good things, and sent the rich away empty" (Luke 1:49, 52–53). For me this was a *kairos* experience, one that shapes and will continue to shape my view of myself, of God, and God's ways with us. Meditating on this, and other experiences of God's grace, can help kindle and maintain a piety that brings a person back to the living roots of Christian calling.

Modern Challenges and Opportunities, Retrieving and Reforming Traditions

Throughout this chapter I have been identifying and developing aspects of Protestant understandings of calling that I believe will help Christians live faithfully in contemporary society. In so doing I have been "retrieving" and "reforming" one major wing of the Protestant tradition. Two areas that were neglected by the early reformers, and by the Protestant tradition in general, are calling and the natural environment, and calling and the arts. In recent years there has been renewed interest in these topics.[32] In addition to work needed in these areas, large social and cultural dynamics have changed political and social life in ways that the early reformers could not have seen and so did not address. Central among these dynamics are secularism, capitalism, and pluralism.[33] Space limits only allow me to mention these dynamics, and note that they provide both opportunities and deep challenges to the Protestant vision of callings.

In this closing section I focus on two crucial tensions, or even conflicts, between modern understandings of calling and those of the Protestant tradition: a hierarchical versus an egalitarian view of social order, and the respective roles of self-sacrifice and self-fulfillment in one's callings. On these two tensions there must be mutually critical relations; that is, the Protestant tradition must critically challenge modernity and modernity must critically challenge the Protestant tradition.

Luther and Calvin understood callings within the context of a social hierarchy they believed to be grounded in God's creation and providence, and so expressive of the will of God. The "estates" or "orders of creation"

---

32. For a start on these topics see Deborah J. Haynes, *The Vocation of the Artist* (New York: Cambridge University Press, 1997); Steven Bouma-Prediger, *For the Beauty of the Earth: A Christian Vision for Creation Care,* 2nd ed. (Grand Rapids: Baker Academic, 2010); and Larry L. Rasmussen, *Earth-honoring Faith: Religious Ethics in a New Key* (New York: Oxford University Press, 2015).

33. For a concise expansion of vocation in relation to some of these concerns, see Programs for Theological Exploration of Vocation, "Douglas J. Schuurman Interview," accessed June 16, 2015, http://www.ptev.org/interview.aspx?iid=5.

(marriage and family, temporal powers, and the church) mediate God's care for the world. Superordinate persons (husbands, fathers, princes, etc.) are to rule subordinate persons (wives, children, subjects, etc.) with wisdom and love. Subordinate persons are to obey the will of superiors, even when they may be harsh or unreasonable. Only when a superior requires subordinates to violate the will of God should they disobey authority. In their disobedience to authority, Christians are not to rebel but to be subordinate, enduring the sufferings caused by their refusals to obey superiors even as Christ endured the cross. Luther and Calvin thus confer theological legitimacy upon the offices of persons occupying positions of power within the social order. Parents, princes, employers, teachers, pastors, and judges represent in their offices, not themselves, but God. Though relativized by the supreme authority of the Word of God, this structuring of obligations and freedoms in terms of one's place amid varied authorities is deeply bound up with the early reformers' idea of calling and continues into the twentieth century.

While some Americans act and speak as though differences in social power do not exist, variations in social powers do exist and should be acknowledged. God's will and callings are mediated through parents, teachers, employers, coaches, and others whose positions give them social power over us. That said, the modern emphasis upon equality, freedom, and social mobility rightly resists the hierarchical frame that marks much of the Protestant tradition. The spiritual equality experienced in Christ should transform social inequality in the church, family, and society. Systemic distortions of social institutions, and not merely the individuals occupying positions of power, must be challenged and reformed. The will of God must be heard "from below" in the voices of the oppressed and the suffering.

In his interpretation of Romans 13, the New Testament passage about the state, Bonhoeffer rejects the common interpretation that gives divine sanction to rulers and their projects.[34] At best, he says, rulers should find

---

34. "Let every person be subject to the governing authorities; for there is no authority except from God, and those authorities that exist have been instituted by God. Therefore whoever resists authority resists what God has appointed, and those who resist will incur judgment. For rulers are not a terror to good conduct but to bad. Do you wish to have no fear of the authority? Then do what is good and you will receive its approval; for it is God's servant for your good. But if you do what is wrong, you should be afraid, for the authority does not bear the sword in vain! It is the servant of God to execute wrath on the wrongdoer. Therefore one must be subject, not only because of wrath but also because of conscience"

in this passage a "mandate" to protect innocent life.[35] It is dangerous, both for those who hold social power and for those subject to it, to equate divine agency with official use of social power, whether in the home, workplace, or state. Though God's callings do come through those in authority, they come also and perhaps more clearly through weakness and need. Perceiving God's call within the need of the neighbor must be reemphasized in light of feminist and other liberationist theological perspectives.

Luther's emphasis upon the incarnational is to the point. He wanted parents to see the infant Jesus in their babies' need for food, clothing, and care. Calvin's ideas of the "image of God" in the neighbor, and of nature as a "mirror" of God, hold similar incarnational impulses. God's call is often not heard in the form of a "summons" of a Divine Commander, or of a demanding Ruler's "dictate." It is often heard as a still small voice beckoning us to meet our neighbors' needs and so express love for God and neighbor. God's will is that in all our callings we serve the least of these, and in serving them we serve Christ.[36]

Today Protestants must lift up aspects of the doctrine of callings that undermine hierarchalism—whether based on gender, race, or class—and that point to mutuality between men and women, and among all people. At least three aspects merit retrieval from the writings of Luther and Calvin. First is the calling to resist and reform authority. Resistance implies that institutions and orders, and officials working in them, though expressive of

---

(Rom. 13:1–5). For a discussion of the abuse of this passage by church leaders and politicians in apartheid South Africa see *The South African Kairos Document 1985,* especially 2.1 and 2.4, accessed on June 1, 2015, https://kairossouthernafrica.wordpress.com/2011/05/08/the-south-africa-kairos-document-1985/. See also the *Confession of Belhar,* which became a rallying point for anti-apartheid Christians in South Africa, accessed June 1, 2015, https://www.rca.org/resources/confession-belhar.

35. Dietrich Bonhoeffer, *The Cost of Discipleship,* trans. R. H. Fuller, with some revision by Irmgard Booth (New York: Simon & Schuster, 1995), 260–64. *The Barmen Confession* limited and defined the authority of the state as a protest to Hitler, Nazism, and the Reich church, accessed June 1, 2015, http://www.sacred-texts.com/chr/barmen.htm.

36. The difficulty here is how to combine God's sovereign transcendence with God's immanence. Richard Mouw in *The God Who Commands: A Study in Divine Command Ethics* (Notre Dame: University of Notre Dame Press, 1990) tries to "make room" for feminist immanental themes within a basically hierarchical view of the God-human relation. He also stresses the Reformed teaching that the Spirit internalizes God's law, so that Christian obedience is spontaneous and joyful rather than grudging submission to the arbitrary will of a potentate. Calvin distinguished "servile" obedience—that given by a slave to a master—from "filial" obedience—that given by a loyal son to a loving father—and insisted that Christian obedience is the latter and not the former (*Institutes* 3.2.26–27).

God the Creator, also express human corruption.[37] They can and must be changed, reformed, brought into line with God's creative and redemptive purposes.

Luther did not "submit" to papal authority or quietly endure the penalties imposed by the pope. Based on his own calling as a pastor and theologian, he wrote and spoke in ways nothing short of revolutionary, and in ways that advanced far-reaching political and social change. When criticizing parents for forbidding their children to marry, Luther limits parental authority and advises children to disobey parents. Since marriage is a divine ordinance, willed by God and structured into the very fabric of creation, it is contrary to God's will to forbid one's child from entering into the callings of marriage and family. Parents contradicting these bounds "are to be regarded as if they were not parents at all, or were dead; their child is free to become engaged and to marry whomsoever he fancies."[38]

Similarly, Bonhoeffer not only publicly refuted the Nazis; he also was part of a group of conspirators who attempted to assassinate Hitler.

There are, then, solid grounds for disobedience and even resistance to authority. What is unclear, especially in the writings of Luther and Calvin, is (a) how the mutuality brought about by baptism and expressed in the priesthood of all believers relates to the inequality implied by a subordinationist and hierarchical social structure, (b) how the basis of resistance relates to directives to obey or submit even to abusive authorities, and (c) how to determine when such demands do require or permit resistance rather than submission to authority.

A second aspect of Protestant calling that can lead to criticism of hierarchalism, especially its patriarchal forms, is its positive vision of domestic roles and general revaluation of mundane roles and relations. Though

37. See Nicholas Wolterstorff, *Until Justice and Peace Embrace* (Grand Rapids: Eerdmans, 1983), 16.

38. "That Parents Should Neither Compel nor Hinder the Marriage of Their Children, and That Children Should Not Become Engaged without Their Parents' Consent," in *Luther's Works* 45:390. Earlier in this treatise Luther advises children to submit obediently to parents who force them to marry a specific person, even against the child's wishes, though Luther says it is wrong for parents to force such a choice. Luther directs children to Matthew 5 and the duty not to resist evil, to "let your cloak go with your coat, and turn the other cheek also. From this it would follow that a child should and must obey, and accept the injustice which such a tyrannical and unpaternal father forces upon him" (388). It appears, then, that for Luther authorities ought not to be disobeyed for any and all immoral demands, but only for those demands that force the subordinate party to disobey a clear command or ordinance of God.

Luther did not work out the implications of the priesthood of all believers for restructuring gender relations, a trajectory is present. The doctrine of callings creates equality and mutuality between women and men. Christ no more defined men by their careers than he defined women by their families; rather, he judged women and men based on whether they heard and believed his word. A wife whose husband refuses to recognize her calling to develop professionally would be on solid Protestant ground were she to appeal to her calling as a basis to resist, and hopefully to change, her husband's wishes. By considering domestic roles as callings, the early reformers elevated the status of the activities of women, which, if not ecclesial, were almost exclusively domestic.[39] The effect of this elevated spiritual status is to incline asymmetric relations between husband and wife toward mutuality and symmetry.[40] Spiritual equality expressed in Protestant views of faith and the priesthood of all believers must permeate and transform gender relations in all significant social contexts.

A third aspect of Protestant vocation holding much potential for transforming hierarchical relations is opposition to subordinationism and affirmation of authority as service, which overlaps with the other two. The doctrines of calling and the priesthood of all believers can work to transform asymmetric relations. The social expression of equality and mutuality created by faith and baptism is service to the neighbor. Subordinationism is perpetual and influential discrepancies in social power based merely on race, class, or gender.

Calling ought to transform asymmetric relations in at least four ways: (a) It should ground the authority of the more powerful party upon God's calling and gifts, not exclusively upon race, class, or gender; (b) it should require that the goal of authority be service to others, not being served; (c) it should demand that authorities respect the status of the one served as created and potentially redeemed by God; and (d) it should view the imbalance of power as temporary and dynamic, moving toward symmetry and mutuality. Parental authority, for example, is distorted when it falls into a stifling parentalism that never lets children mature. Positively, authority is based on God's gift and calling to care for children, to serve

---

39. We should keep in mind that the domestic sphere was much larger than now. There was much less separation of "public" and "private" life, since most occupations (farming, artisans, etc.) had their "paid work" right in or near their own homes. Luther's wife, Katherine, even ran a brewery, with Luther's full approval.

40. On this point, see Steven Ozment's book, *When Fathers Ruled: Family Life in Reformation Europe* (Cambridge, MA: Harvard University Press, 1983).

them, and to bring the child to the status of equality with the parent. A teacher using authority to encourage students to depend too much or too little on the teacher likewise abuses authority. In a similar way all authority is tempered by the ideal of service to the neighbor and aims at symmetry.[41]

The expectation that one's calling brings self-fulfillment and self-actualization is central to popular conceptions of calling. However, it clashes with both the biblical and Protestant insistence that one's callings bring self-denial and self-sacrifice, not self-actualization or self-discovery. The heart of one's callings is to meet the needs of one's neighbors, even if doing so involves work that is tedious, routine, and distasteful. Luther and Calvin also note that even in highly prized callings, such as being a prince, there is a great deal of self-sacrifice. Luther writes,

> A man is to live, speak, act, hear, suffer and die for the good of his wife and child, the wife for the husband, the children for the parents, the servants for their masters, the masters for their servants, the government for its subjects, the subjects for the government, each one for his fellowman, even for his enemies, so that one is the other's hand, mouth, eye, foot, even heart and mind.[42]

In a similar vein Calvin writes,

> We are not our own: in so far as we can, let us therefore forget ourselves and all that is ours. Conversely, we are God's: let us therefore live for him and die for him. We are God's: let his wisdom and will therefore rule all our actions. We are God's: let all the parts of our life accordingly strive toward him as our only lawful goal. . . . For, as consulting our self-interest is the pestilence that most effectively leads to our destruction, so the sole haven of salvation is to be wise in nothing and to will nothing through ourselves but to follow the leading of the Lord alone.[43]

---

41. The movement toward symmetry and equality is not always obvious or evident. The authority of a judge, for example, over a criminal about to be sentenced does not directly aim at making the sentenced criminal an equal with that judge. But, in aiming to lead the criminal to a respect for the law, which would in turn liberate the criminal from the punitive powers of the judge, it does indirectly aim at a kind of symmetry.

42. *Luther's Church Postil: Gospels: Advent, Christmas and Epiphany Sermons,* vol. 1 in *The Precious and Sacred Writings of Martin Luther,* ed. John Nicholas Lenker (Minneapolis: Lutherans in All Lands Co., 1905), 37.

43. Calvin, *Institutes* 3.7.1.

Having callings is not to seek one's self, even one's "authentic" self. The point is to love God and neighbor by taking up the cross in the self-sacrificial paths defined by one's callings.

The Protestant idea of callings echoes Jesus's ironic words, "If any want to become my followers, let them deny themselves and take up their cross and follow me. For those who want to save their life will lose it, and those who lose their life for my sake . . . will find it" (Mark 8:34–35). For Luther, one experiences the cross and despair amid one's callings, and calling out to God in prayer for help is the main way Christians are made more holy.[44] Losing one's life is also a central theme of Bonhoeffer's book *The Cost of Discipleship,* a theme he embodied in his own life.

Self-sacrifice is intrinsic and essential to agape, the New Testament term for God's love for the world and for Christians' love for God and others.[45] Agape need not support a self-abnegating attitude toward the self. Presumably Jesus had a healthy self-concept even though he "set his face" toward Jerusalem (Luke 9:51), his betrayal and arrest, his unjust trial, brutal scourging, and death on a cross (Luke 22:47–23:49). Few have callings that will require such suffering, but all callings involve difficult times of yielding one's own interests to the well-being of others, self-denial, and discipline.

It is also the case that there is much joy in serving others in and through one's callings. The saying of Jesus affirms that, ironically, those who lose their lives for his sake will find them. Self-fulfillment is like happiness: you fail to experience it if you aim directly at it. It is a byproduct of giving your life in service to others. Perhaps Calvin and the Puritans were too negative in their view of the Christian life. The freedom that comes from a life of faith brings genuine fulfillment of the deepest desires of human hearts.

---

44. Gustaf Wingren sums up Luther on this point as follows: "The cross is not to be chosen by us; it is laid upon us by God, i.e. the cross comes to us uninvited in our vocation." Wingren, *Luther on Vocation,* trans. C. C. Rasmussen (Philadelphia: Muhlenberg, 1957), 53.

45. Gene Outka and most feminists have argued that self-sacrifice is an extrinsic and instrumental aspect of agape. They hold that, in a sinful world, self-sacrifice is needed to restore love as mutual giving and receiving, or love as equal regard. See Gene Outka, *Agape: An Ethical Analysis* (New Haven and London: Yale University Press, 1972), 274, and Barbara Hilkert-Anderson, "Agape in Feminist Ethics," *Journal of Religious Ethics* 9 (Spring 1981): 69–83. Edmund Santurri argues that self-sacrifice is essential for agape in "Agape as Self-Sacrifice: An Internalist View," in *Love and Christian Ethics: Engagements with Tradition, Theory, and Society* (Washington, DC: Georgetown University Press, forthcoming). For a recent and provocative feminist argument that self-sacrifice can be subversive and resistant to unjust power see Anna Mercedes, *Power For: Feminism and Christ's Self-Giving* (London and New York: Bloomsbury T&T Clark, 2011).

Beyond the ironic result of self-sacrifice, joy and self-fulfillment usually do accompany using our gifts to contribute to the well-being of others and the world. Faith enables us to experience even the difficulty and drudgery of our callings as worshipful service to God, giving them meaning beyond any intrinsically satisfying aspects of our activities.

These revisions form but a small beginning for the much larger task of retrieving and reforming the Protestant concept of callings for modern times. This deep and rich tradition has much to offer contemporary Protestants, and also Catholic and Orthodox Christians. I also hope that members of other major world religions who read about Protestant callings will revisit their own sacred texts and traditions, and draw from their deep wisdom insights to help transform all of life into meaningful service to God, humanity, and creation.

Resources

Brunner, Emil. *The Divine Imperative.* Translated by Olive Wyon. Philadelphia: Westminster, 1937.

Hardy, Lee. *The Fabric of This World: Inquiries into Calling, Career, and the Design of Human Work.* Grand Rapids: Eerdmans, 1990.

Marshall, Paul. *A Kind of Life Imposed on Man: Vocation and Social Order from Tyndale to Locke.* Toronto: University of Toronto Press, 1996.

Miller-McLemore, Bonnie J. *Also a Mother: Work and Family as Theological Dilemma.* Nashville: Abingdon, 1994.

Minear, Paul S. "Work and Vocation in Scripture." In *Work and Vocation: A Christian Discussion,* ed. John O. Nelson. New York: Harper & Brothers, 1954.

Mouw, Richard J. *Called to Holy Worldliness.* Laity Exchange Books. Philadelphia: Fortress, 1980.

Placher, William C., ed. *Callings: Twenty Centuries of Christian Wisdom on Vocation.* Grand Rapids: Eerdmans, 2005.

Schuurman, Douglas J. *Vocation: Discerning Our Callings in Life.* Grand Rapids: Eerdmans, 2004.

Van Leeuwen, Mary Stewart. *Gender and Grace: Love, Work, and Parenting in a Changing World.* Leicester, UK, and Downers Grove, IL: InterVarsity, 1990.

Wingren, Gustaf. *Luther on Vocation.* Translated by C. C. Rasmussen. Philadelphia: Muhlenberg, 1957.

4

Divine Summons, Human Submission

The Idea of Calling in Islam

JOHN KELSAY

The idea of calling is central in Islamic tradition, first in the sense of God's call to human beings, and second in the sense of the human response. The Arabic *al-islam,* "the submission," begins with God's call to human beings. To be a Muslim—that is, to be "one who submits"—involves saying to God "Here I am, at your service"—a statement that opens up to a life of prayer (that is, calling upon God) and good works (including calling other human beings to serve God).[1] From the beginning of the Islamic movement in the seventh century to its modern status as a global religion claiming about 1.6 billion adherents, believers have sought to fulfill this ideal.

In this chapter I make use of three stories to illustrate the intersection between God's call and the human response. I begin with the life of Muhammad, the Prophet of God. While Muhammad's story is set in the sixth and seventh centuries CE, it provides a model for Muslims in all places and times.[2] Al-Ghazali's testimony concerning his quest for faith in the late eleventh and early twelfth centuries exemplifies a way of answering God's

---

1. The phrase "Here I am, O Allah, here I am at your service" is a translation of the Arabic uttered by Muslims during the performance of the *hajj* or pilgrimage to Mecca. I have adopted it here and throughout this essay in order to emphasize that answering God's call is fundamental to Muslim practice. It should be noted that making this pilgrimage is one of the five "pillars" of such practice. The others are pronouncing the *shahada* ("I bear witness that there is no god but God, and that Muhammad is God's prophet"), *salat* or ritual prayer, fasting during the month of Ramadan, and charitable giving (*zakat*).

2. Here and throughout, dates are to indicate the CE or "common era" calendar. From the Muslim point of view, 622 CE equals year 1 in the AH or "after hijra" calendar, dating from the emigration of the community to Medina (see below).

call adopted by many during the period of the great Islamic empires. And the story told by Malcolm X serves to indicate the connection between Muslim practice and the struggle for justice in mid-twentieth-century America.

At the Beginning

Abu Ja'far Muhammad b. Jarir al-Tabari (839–923 CE) was one of the greatest scholars of his time. His *History of Prophets and Kings* tells the story of humankind from creation to his own time from an Islamic point of view. In that work, we read the following account of what could be termed Muhammad's "call" story.

> The Messenger of God used to spend [the month of Ramadan] in every year in religious retreat, feeding the poor who came to him. When he had completed his month of retreat the first thing which he would do on leaving, even before going home, was to circumambulate the Ka'-bah seven times, or however many times God willed, then he would go home. When the month came in which God willed to ennoble him, in the year in which God made [Muhammad] His Messenger, this being the month of Ramadan, the Messenger of God went out as usual . . . accompanied by his family. When the night came on which God ennobled him by making [Muhammad] His Messenger and thereby showed mercy to his servants, Gabriel brought him the command of God. The Messenger of God said, "Gabriel came to me as I was sleeping with a brocade cloth in which was writing. He said, 'Recite!' and I said, 'I cannot recite.' He pressed me tight and almost stifled me, until I thought that I should die. Then he let me go, and said 'Recite!' I said, 'What shall I recite?' only saying that in order to free myself from him, fearing that he might repeat what he had done to me. He said: 'Recite in the name of your Lord who creates! He creates [the human creature] from a clot of blood. Recite: And your Lord is the Most Bountiful, He who teaches by the pen, teaches [human beings] what [they] did not know.'" (Qur'an 96:1–5)[3]

3. Here I am quoting from the translation by W. Montgomery Watt and M. V. McDonald, *The History of al-Tabari* (Albany: State University of New York Press, 1988), 6:70–71. The insertions marked by brackets are my own and are intended to make it easier to follow the story.

Muhammad ibn Abdullah, the Prophet or Messenger of God, was born in 569 or 570. The incident related above took place in 610, when he was forty years old. Our sources suggest that by this time Muhammad had built a considerable reputation among the inhabitants of his home city. Mecca, a city presently located in Saudi Arabia, was not a very large place in the late sixth and early seventh centuries. Among the Arabs living in the area, it was known as the province of the Quraysh, a tribe whose members claimed a special role as guardians of the Ka'ba or "cube." This structure, which Muslims trace to the biblical Abraham, was regarded by the Quraysh as part of the general heritage of the Arabs. By the time of Muhammad's birth, the tribes gathered annually to perform religious ceremonies that included circumambulation or "walking around" the building. Hence Muhammad's actions were not strange or out of place.

In addition to religious ceremonies, these annual gatherings provided an opportunity for commerce. As Muhammad entered adulthood, Mecca was enjoying a period of economic growth, with leading families among the Quraysh compiling considerable fortunes. Their primary vehicle involved providing capital to support caravans. Goods were picked up in Damascus and other great cities to the north; once the cargo had been transported through the Arabian Peninsula to Mecca or other cities, it was loaded onto ships in the Red Sea for passage to markets in India and other eastern ports. The original goods were then traded for others; when the ships returned (hopefully) laden with items to be sold, the original investors hoped to earn a substantial profit. Despite considerable risks, the evidence suggests that at least some people succeeded.

A good part of Muhammad's reputation had to do with such endeavors. Working for his uncle, the young man came to be known as *al-amin,* "the trustworthy one," suggesting reliability and honesty. Eventually, he came to the attention of Khadija, a well-to-do widow some years older, who hired Muhammad to manage some of her own interests; in short order, they married, cementing their alliance. By the time of his encounter with the angel Gabriel, Muhammad was thus a relatively secure, successful, and well-regarded businessman.

He was also what we might call a "seeker." The tribes gathering at the Ka'ba each year brought a variety of religious perspectives. Most thought of religion as a matter of offering worship to a pantheon of gods and goddesses, some tied to the powers of nature, others with power over sickness, death, or other issues of import for human well-being. At the top of the pantheon was the Creator. Known simply as *al-lah* or "the god," this deity's obvious significance in the great scheme of things seems not to have translated into everyday living. Arab worshipers paid more attention to more proximate beings: *al-lat,* "the goddess" whose sphere was fertility, or *al-manat,* whose name suggests control of the time and manner of death.

The practice of the Arab tribes thus seems polytheistic. And yet, there were other tendencies. Those who traveled with caravans became acquainted with Christianity. Arabs also knew something of that faith by way of longstanding interactions with political and military forces from Abyssinia (Ethiopia) in Yemen, at the southern edge of the Peninsula. Jewish tribes also had an ancient presence in Yemen and elsewhere in the region. From what we can tell, Arabs identifying as Jews or Christians came to the Ka'ba along with others; perhaps they considered *al-lah* the equivalent of the Lord or of God the Father, while choosing to ignore the other deities honored by their neighbors.

Muhammad's practice of an annual retreat suggests he was looking for something. Al-Tabari and other Muslim scholars understood this as God's preparation—that is, Muhammad's quest was actually (and unbeknownst to him) a work of grace by which the Creator and Ruler of the universe made this humble merchant ready for the great task before him. And so, in the fullness of time, Gabriel delivered God's call. The order "recite!" or "read!" points to Muhammad's role as a recipient of revelation. As with other prophets, he would bring a "book" or a "scripture" by which the Divine Word might be communicated to a group of people in terms they would understand. In this case, the Arab tribes would learn to think of God in connection with the Qur'an or "recitation" delivered to Muhammad over the next twenty-two years.

From a Muslim perspective, as in biblical religion generally, God's call comes first. Human beings are summoned—some to do particular tasks, others more generally to a life of service. Human action is a response to the divine initiative. One says "here I am, ready to serve." From there, one moves forward to carry out God's plan.

Sometimes responding takes time, however. In the story recounted above, Muhammad at first resists Gabriel's charge to recite. To say "I am not a reciter" is a way of indicating one's sense that somehow God has gotten things wrong—has chosen the wrong person. Here, Muhammad's demurral is reminiscent of the story of Moses, who in Exodus 3 responds to the directive "Go to Pharaoh, and tell him to let my people go" by suggesting that someone more eloquent might be found. Indeed, as al-Tabari's account continues, we learn that the Prophet was uncertain about his experience and feared for his sanity. Encouragement from his wife and from a relative who was a Christian helped Muhammad to overcome these doubts.

> [Khadijah] rose up, gathered her garments around her, and went to Waraqah b. Nawfal b. Asad, who was her paternal cousin. He had become a Christian, read the Scriptures, and learned from the people of the Torah and the Gospel. She told him what the Messenger of God had told her that he had seen and heard. Waraqah said "Holy, holy! By him in whose hand is the soul of Waraqah, if what you say is true, there has come to [Muhammad . . . the one who] came to Moses. [That means that] Muhammad is the prophet of this community. Tell him to stand firm."[4]

Other people, then, play an important role in the confirmation of God's call. And, once Muhammad accepted Gabriel's charge—said, in effect, "here I am"—he would soon find more "companions" ready to join him in affirming God's word. A small community gathered around him, to hear the verses of the Qur'an and join in prayer.

At the same time, the Prophet met opposition. The interplay between positive and negative responses helps us to follow the next developments in the story.

In the early going, Muhammad's charge was to proclaim the message of Islam. In this regard, the following passage is instructive.

> One of God's signs is that He created you from dust and—lo and behold!—you became human and scattered far and wide.
> Another of God's signs is that He created spouses from among yourselves for you to live with in tranquility: He ordained love and kindness between you.
> There truly are signs in this for those who reflect.
> Another of God's signs is that He created the heavens and the earth, the diversity of your languages and colors.
> There truly are signs in this for those who know.
> Among His signs are your sleep, by night and by day, and your seeking God's bounty. There truly are signs in this for those who can hear.
> Among His signs, too, are that God shows you the lightning that terrifies

4. Watt and McDonald, *The History of al-Tabari*, 6:72.

and inspires hope; that God sends water down from the sky to restore the earth to life after death.

There truly are signs in this for those who use their reason. Among God's signs, too, is the fact that the heavens and the earth stand firm by His command.

In the end, you will all emerge when He calls you from the earth.

Everyone in the heavens and the earth belongs to Him, and all are obedient to Him. He is the one who originates creation and will do it again—this is even easier for Him.

God is above all comparison in the heavens and the earth; God is the Almighty, the all wise. (Qur'an 30:20–27)[5]

One of the great themes of the Qur'an involves pointing to God's "bounty" or generosity. There are many things human beings experience as good: life itself, the blessings of family life, the beauty of creation. There are other things we experience as cause for wonder or even fear: the ways of nature provide an example. All these are "signs" to human beings. In a sense, they are means by which God calls people to faith. The references to "those who use their reason" and "those who reflect" suggest that everyone has the capacity to grasp this—in effect, to read the signs that point to God. As the references to "those who can hear" and "those who know" suggest, however, not everyone exercises this capacity. Prophets come to remind human beings of God's gifts, to make them aware or conscious of the fact that God is calling, and that they are to say "Here I am, Lord."

Prophets also warn human beings that actions have consequences. "In the end, you will all emerge when He calls you from the earth." All things come from God, and all things return to their Creator. Judgment is a divine reality, along with power, goodness, beauty, and love. To this, the first response is, or ought to be, prayer. And so, the first thing Muhammad taught—that is, after proclaiming the message of God's goodness and power—was the mode of worship Muslims call *salat*, the ritual of ablutions, prostration, and verbal expressions appropriate in responding to God.[6] It is interesting to note that the general word for prayer in Arabic, *du'a*, itself means "calling," so that one responds to God's call, in effect, by calling upon God. The opening chapter of the Qur'an provides a fine example.

5. Here and throughout, I cite the translation by Muhammad A. S. Abdel Haleem, *The Qur'an* (Oxford: Oxford University Press, 2004).

6. Watt and McDonald, *The History of al-Tabari,* 6:77–78.

In the name of God, the Lord of Mercy, the Giver of Mercy!
Praise belongs to God, Lord of the Worlds,
The Lord of Mercy, the Giver of Mercy,
Master of the Day of Judgment.
It is You we worship; it is You we ask for help.
Guide us to the straight path:
The path of those you have blessed, those who incur no anger and who
have not gone astray. (Qur'an 1)

As Muhammad proclaimed the message of the Qur'an, and along with his companions began the practice of calling upon God through prayer, the citizens of Mecca took note. The evidence suggests they did not like what they saw. A few lines from the account of a meeting between Muhammad's uncle and the great men of Quraysh are instructive.

O Abu Talib, your nephew has cursed our gods, insulted our religion, mocked our way of life and accused our forefathers of error. Either you must stop him or you must let us get at him. . . . [Muhammad is one who] brought a message by which he separates a man from his father, or from his brother, or from his wife, or from his family.[7]

To understand this complaint, one must recall the polytheistic aspect of Arab religion. The tribes acknowledged a pantheon of deities, and gathered at the Ka'ba in recognition of this fact. Now, Muhammad described this way as false, proclaiming Allah as the only God rather than as one of many. The Quraysh interpreted Islam as a challenge to their way of life. To insist, as the Muslims did, that there really is a distinction between true and false religiosity would be to sow strife among the various tribes.

In addition, it appears that some found parts of the message ridiculous. What did it mean, they asked, to say that God would call people from their graves on a Day of Judgment? How could people live again after they died? The Qur'anic answer was simple, as above: God "is the one who originates creation and will do it again—this is even easier for Him." Nevertheless, many did not accept Muhammad's claims. And, as feelings of distrust built, expressions of hostility began: discrimination against the Muslims, an economic boycott by which their business in-

7. A. Guillaume, trans., *The Life of Muhammad* (Oxford: Oxford University Press, 1955), 11.

terests were affected, persecution, torture, and threats on the life of the Prophet all form a part of the story. In the face of such opposition, some asked Muhammad to authorize them to use their weapons in defense of the community; but he refused, saying that God's order thus far was to preach and bear witness.

By 619, however, the situation became so dire that the Prophet began to explore alternatives, and in 622 he reached an agreement with the tribes in Medina. The Muslims made this city their new home, and the community moved into a new phase of mission. The verses at Qur'an 22:39–40 were revealed around this time:

> Those who have been attacked are permitted to take up arms because they have been wronged.
> God has the power to help them; those who have been driven unjustly from their homes only for saying "Our Lord is God."
> If God did not repel some people by means of others, many monasteries, churches, synagogues, and mosques, where God's name is much invoked, would have been destroyed.

For the next ten years, until his death in 632, Muhammad functioned not only as a prophet, proclaiming the message and providing instruction for worship. Now he became a statesman, directing policies designed to make the community secure. Sometimes this involved military action against the Quraysh and other tribes; at other times, the Prophet preferred diplomacy and building alliances. As the story concludes, he was ultimately successful, so that before his death Muhammad proclaimed that "Arabia is solidly for Islam"—a secure space in which believers could respond to God's call, calling upon God through prayer and calling others to the practice of Islam.

The Faith and Practice of al-Ghazali

Muhammad's death presented the Muslim community with a critical challenge. Whether the movement would continue, and if so, what would be the form of its mission?

With respect to the first, the answer was not long in coming. As Abu Bakr, one of the earliest to join the Prophet in the practice of Islam, put it, Muhammad's death could not be the end of the matter. God lives, and as long as that remains true, the call to serve endures.[8] Here it is important to recall that Muhammad and his companions did not understand themselves to be doing anything particularly new. Rather, their response to the divine initiative was simply the latest chapter in the long story of God's dealings with the human race. According to Qur'an 7:171–72, that story begins with creation.

> [W]hen your Lord took out the offspring from the loins of the Children of Adam and made them bear witness about themselves, He said, "Am I not your Lord?" and they replied, "Yes, we bear witness." So you cannot say on the Day of Resurrection, "We were not aware of this."

There is a primordial covenant between God and humanity, so that the latter are without excuse. No one can say that he or she did not know of the duty to serve God.

As indicated in our discussion of Qur'an 30:20–27, God fills the world with signs "for those who reflect" or "for those who use their reason." The suggestion is that anyone who spends the time to think about the world around him or her will come to the conclusion that there is something behind it all, and to seek further understanding. Qur'an 6:74–82 provides a fine example, relating the story of the prophet Abraham's religious quest. The accounts begin with wonder at the appearance of a star, when the seeker exclaims "This is my Lord." As the moon rises, the star grows dim, however; even so, Abraham's estimation of its power and wonder fades, and he now proclaims the lordship of the moon. The same thing happens with the sun, at which point we read: "My people, I disown all that you worship besides God. I have turned my face as a true believer towards Him who created the heavens and the earth." One might say that Abraham's reflection on the "signs" of the heavens leads finally to the conclusion that nothing he actually sees, feels, or touches can possibly be the source from which all creation comes. Rather, all things point to something beyond and unlike themselves. *Al-lah*, "the God," is unique in power and wisdom and is thus the Lord, worthy of worship.

As noted, however, the Qur'an's judgment is that "most do not reflect." In order to remedy this, a merciful God sends prophets to remind human beings of their obligations. At various places and times, these messengers

---

8. See the account in Ismail K. Poonawala, trans., *The History of al-Tabari* (Albany: State University of New York Press, 1990), 9:185.

proclaimed the basic message: there is one God; there is a moral law; there will be a Day of Reckoning, at which time God will ask each and every person "What did you do with the life given to you?" Muhammad stands in the long line of prophets, speaking first to his own people, in their language; then, by extension to people of all places and times.

The second question—the form of the Muslim mission—proved a bit more difficult to answer. Abu Bakr became the first *khalifa,* a term that suggests "following in the way" of the Prophet. He and his successors did not claim status as prophets themselves. Instead, they allowed Muhammad's example to lead them. As they understood it, this involved political and military activity aimed at creating space for the Prophet's message. Within a generation, the Muslims became the dominant political and military power in the Middle East and North Africa. The patterns of governance they developed mirrored that of the great empires of the time—the Byzantines, representing the eastern portion of the old Roman Empire, and the Sassanids, who inherited the mantle of the ancient Persian kings. In the Muslim version, the established religion of the empire was Islam, and before long the majority of people in the "liberated" areas came to identify with the new faith.

All this is prelude to the story of al-Ghazali's response to God's call. Born in 1058 in Tus (present-day Iran), al-Ghazali became one of the greatest of the "men of religion," that is, Muslims whose work focused on providing guidance with respect to religious practice. Muslim political leaders needed advice, and they also needed scholars able to teach the people. To achieve this goal, Muslim rulers supported institutions for training religious experts in *kalam* (theology), *falsafa* (philosophy), and *fiqh* (jurisprudence), which formed the standard curriculum for those who would serve in mosques and religious schools throughout the territory of Islam.

Al-Ghazali entered one of these institutions at an early age; by all accounts, he excelled in every aspect of scholarly training. It is no surprise, then, that he came to occupy a leading role at the center of "official" Islam, the Nizamiyya *madrasa* or religious school in Baghdad, the capital city of the Abbasid caliphs.[9] In this position, he could advise political leaders, affect policy, and influence other scholars' interpretation of the faith across the empire.

---

9. The Abbasids are one of the great dynasties of Islam. Having come to power as a result of a civil war in the 740s, they held sway until the Mongol invasion of 1258. Below I speak briefly about their successors.

Al-Ghazali's move to Baghdad took place in 1091. As he later put it, assuming this post was a great honor as well as a great responsibility. And yet, he would soon leave. In 1095, the great scholar gave up teaching and spent nearly ten years in solitude. When he returned to public life in 1106, he took an appointment in Nishapur, in Iran; al-Ghazali died in 1111, having never returned to Baghdad.

What happened? Late in his life, al-Ghazali produced an account of the matter, reflecting on the way a life of study provided him with the tools to point out the weaknesses of various arguments, yet did not satisfy his spiritual needs. His comments tell us a great deal about the notion of calling in the context of the high caliphate:

> You should first of all know . . . that the diversity of men in religions and creeds, plus the disagreement of the Community of Islam about doctrines, given the multiplicity of sects and the divergency of methods, is a deep sea in which most men founder and from which only a few are saved. Each group alleges that it is the one saved, and "each faction is happy about its own beliefs." This is the state of affairs which the truthful and most trustworthy Chief of God's envoys . . . ominously promised us when he said: "My community will split into seventy-odd sects, of which one will be saved." And what he promised has indeed come to pass.
>
> In the bloom of my youth and the prime of my life, from the time I reached puberty before I was twenty until now, when I am over fifty, I have constantly been diving daringly into the depths of this profound sea and wading into its deep water like a bold man, not like a cautious coward. I would penetrate far into every murky mystery, pounce upon every problem, and dash into every mazy difficulty. I would scrutinize the creed of every sect and seek to lay bare the secrets of each faction's teaching with the aim of discriminating between the proponent of truth and the advocate of error, and between the faithful follower of tradition and the heterodox innovator.[10]

Al-Ghazali describes this "thirst for the real meaning of things" as something God "placed" in him, as part of his personality. He realized that the aim of such inquiry was, or at least ought to have been, knowledge

---

10. Richard Joseph McCarthy, *Deliverance from Error: An Annotated Translation of al-Munqidh min al Dalal and Other Relevant Works of Al-Ghazali* (Louisville: Fons Vitae, 2004), 54.

of the truth. Al-Ghazali was an expert in pointing out the weaknesses of various arguments, but he became increasingly uneasy with his pursuit. Developing one's intellect is an important part of one's calling to be a Muslim; the Prophet said "Seek knowledge, even though it be in China," and also "The acquisition of knowledge is compulsory for every Muslim, whether male or female."[11] But true faith, in the sense of a settled disposition of trust in and reliance upon God, is not only intellectual. Al-Ghazali realized that he was

> a skeptic in fact, but not in utterance and doctrine. At length, God Most High cured me of that sickness. My soul regained its health and equilibrium. . . . But that was not achieved by constructing a proof or putting together an argument. On the contrary, it was the effect of a light which God Most High cast into my breast. And that light is the key to most knowledge.[12]

At this point, we might expect al-Ghazali to turn back to theology, and in particular to the relation between a human being's natural capacity for reflection and the role that prophets play in reminding people that all things belong to God. But instead, he focuses on spiritual discipline. Al-Ghazali found his calling among the Sufis. Usually described as the "mystics" of Islam, Sufis encouraged people to take up practices designed to foster awareness of God in daily life. Over the centuries, Sufi "masters" organized groups that provided a structured spirituality by which ordinary Muslims—merchants, weavers, soldiers, political leaders, and scholars— might find a way to remember God in the midst of their worldly activities. Typically, those involved in these orders were assigned a particular text—say, a verse of the Qur'an—that would become the focus of their attention for a designated period. For most people, this meant reciting the text throughout the day, in conjunction with other activities; at a set time, those engaged in the practice returned for a consultation with the master, who would assess their progress and, if it seemed proper, assign another text or perhaps suggest the addition of fasting or works of charity as a means of promoting attachment to God, rather than to the things of the world.

---

11. See the discussion by Ibrahim b. Syed, "The Pleasures of Seeking Knowledge," accessed May 18, 2015, http://www.islamicity.org/6580/the-pleasures-of-seeking-knowledge/.
12. McCarthy, *Deliverance from Error,* 57.

Al-Ghazali's ten-year hiatus from teaching thus seems a little extreme. Perhaps it suggests the depths of his personal crisis. That certainly seems to be his view. He describes the Sufis as "masters of states," meaning that they focused on faith as a matter of the heart, and on attachment to worldly things as an obstacle to spiritual progress. Al-Ghazali understood both.

> It had already become clear to me that my only hope of attaining beatitude in the afterlife lay in piety and restraining my soul from passion. The beginning of all that, I knew, was to sever my heart's attachment to the world by withdrawing from this abode of delusion and turning to the mansion of immortality and devoting myself with total ardor to God Most High. That, I knew, could be achieved only by shunning fame and fortune and fleeing from my preoccupations and attachments.[13]

Teaching at the most prestigious school in the empire might in fact not be a blessing, but a source of temptation. At a critical point, Al-Ghazali judged that his intention "was not directed purely to God, but rather was instigated and motivated by the quest for fame and widespread prestige." In short, if he was to be ready to say "Here I am, O Allah," this great scholar needed to attend to matters of faith and character. By way of an extended retreat, he focused on freeing himself from worldly attachments. When he did return to teaching, al-Ghazali described his work as a fulfillment of an obligation to contribute to society, rather than as an expression of ambition.

For some, al-Ghazali's path seems a bit extreme. But for Muslims, as for other people of faith, responding to God's call involves the development of good character, in the sense of doing the right things for the right reasons. Al-Ghazali's long retreat involved an attempt to achieve this ideal. When he resumed the life of a scholar and teacher, he did so with a renewed sense of calling as a service to God.

Right conduct, heartfelt trust, and excellence in character are all important in answering God's call. The pursuit of these is compatible with any number of forms of worldly work. Performed with right intention, these constitute a service to God and to the human community. Performed out of a desire for personal gain or other, less noble motives, worldly vocations may constitute an obstacle to responding to the divine summons. That is the lesson of the faith and practice of al-Ghazali.

13. McCarthy, *Deliverance from Error,* 78.

Malcolm X and the Pursuit of Justice

The Sufi practices lauded by al-Ghazali helped many people through the centuries, particularly with respect to balancing the demands of everyday life with the need for a disciplined spirituality. Sufi orders flourished throughout the medieval and early modern periods, in conjunction with a succession of imperial states. As the power of the Abbasid rulers familiar to al-Ghazali diminished, new dynasties arose, all claiming legitimacy in connection with the establishment of Islam as the state religion. From their base in Turkey, the Ottomans (1299–1919) controlled much of southern and central Europe, in addition to most of North Africa and the Middle East. For them, al-Ghazali's combination of standard Sunni theology and jurisprudence with Sufism represented official Islam. By contrast, the Safavids (1501–1722) established Twelver Shi'ism in Iran. In this, they would be followed by their successors, the Qajars (1785–1925). The doctrinal and, to some extent, the legal structures of this form of Islam made for important differences between these regimes and their Sunni rivals. Interestingly, though, the Sufis made their presence felt in Shi'i circles, as well as among the Sunnis. Finally, in the Indian subcontinent, the Moghuls (1526–1857), like the Ottomans, established a form of Sunni practice; but the presence of significant Shi'i communities as well as the vast array of non-Muslim practices in this region influenced the religious policy of many rulers. One way to address these issues involved support for Sufi orders.[14]

---

14. The term "Sunni" comes from a longer phrase that may be translated as "the people who follow the example of the Prophet and who adhere to the consensus of the community." Sunni Islam is preferred by the majority of Muslims; while estimates vary, most scholars would put this at 80–85 percent of Muslims around the world. The term "Shi'i" comes from a phrase for which the translation would be "the partisans of 'Ali." Here, the basic claim is that Muhammad appointed 'Ali b. 'Abi Talib, his cousin and son-in-law, as the one who would be the leader of the Muslim community whenever he died. The fact that Abu Bakr became the first *khalifa,* followed by 'Umar b. al-Khattab and then by 'Uthman, means that, from the Shi'i perspective, the majority disobeyed the Prophet and thus that the community has been in a problematic state for centuries. The "twelvers" are the largest of the various Shi'i groups. The name stems from their belief that 'Ali was the first of twelve divinely appointed leaders, most of them dying as a result of conspiracies intended to save power for illegitimate rulers. The last of these, known as Muhammad al-Mahdi, the "rightly guided," was taken into hiding by God in 873 or 874. He will appear at the appointed time and will establish the rule of justice and equity for a thousand years. Aside from Iran, there are significant Shi'i populations in Iraq and Lebanon, as well as in south Asia and parts of Africa.

Thus, al-Ghazali's emphasis on a religion of the heart, with a focus on personal renewal and a certain detachment from the goods of this world, achieved the status of a kind of popular Islam. Indeed, the influence of Sufism extended beyond the territories associated with the empires. Beginning in the fifteenth and sixteenth centuries, we can identify Muslim communities in the areas we know as Indonesia, Malaysia, and the Philippines. About the same time, Islam began to advance from the northern African territories of Algeria, Morocco, and Tunisia into the interior of Africa. In almost every case, these developments can be traced to Sufi missionaries, usually combining their preaching with an interest in trade.

Sufism thus contributed much to the development of Islam as the global phenomenon we know today, to which slightly less than a quarter of the world's population professes allegiance, with a presence in almost every country. The demise of the great empires created a context in which many came to think that al-Ghazali's emphasis on nonattachment might not be the right message for the times—Sufism might place too little value on matters of public life. In the twentieth and twenty-first centuries, Muslims, holding a variety of perspectives, stress the notion that while responding to God begins with prayer, it also involves witnessing or calling people to Islam and action aimed at promoting justice.

This brings us to the story of Malcolm X. Born in 1925 in Detroit, Michigan, Malcolm Little changed his name in a manner consistent with the practice of the Nation of Islam, a specifically African American expression of faith in which aspects of Muslim tradition were combined with activities intended to liberate people of color from racial oppression. As he put it,

> My application [i.e., for membership in the Nation of Islam] had, of course, been made and during this time I received from Chicago my "X." The Muslim's "X" symbolized the true African family name that he would never know. For me, my "X" replaced the white slavemaster name of "Little" which some blue-eyed devil named Little had imposed upon my paternal forebears. The receipt of my "X" meant that forever after in the Nation of Islam, I would be known as Malcolm X. Mr. Muhammad taught us that we would keep this "X" until God Himself returned and gave us a Holy Name from His own mouth.[15]

15. *The Autobiography of Malcolm X,* with the assistance of Alex Haley (New York: Ballantine Books, 1992), 229.

For those familiar with Muslim tradition, even this brief passage will suggest that the version of Islam taught by the Nation and by its leader, Elijah Muhammad, was not quite "orthodox." Historic Islam does not distinguish between people on the basis of race—a fact that Malcolm X would eventually come to understand.

For now, though, let us stay with Malcolm's story. It tells us something very important about the history of Islam in the United States. Most Americans today associate Islam with the Middle East or with South and Southeast Asia. There is good reason for this, since these are regions where Islam developed, and from which Islam spread through the efforts of Sufi missionaries. It is also true that changes in US immigration policies in the late 1960s made it possible and attractive for people from these historically Muslim regions to make America their home—in particular, US policy favored those with professional or technical skills in medicine, engineering, and other fields. While not all of those taking advantage of this opportunity were Muslims—many were in fact Christians—some were. Their migration helps to explain the current numbers of Muslims in the US, which are, according to the best estimates, about 2.6 million (slightly less than 1 percent of Americans).

Malcolm's account of receiving his "X" reminds us that Islam has a longer history with America, however. Whenever one begins to tell that story, it needs to begin with an acknowledgment: when Islam first came to America, it came in chains.[16] We do not know how many of the Africans captured and shipped to the New World were Muslims. But we know that some were. In addition to the evidence provided by historians of the slave trade, that is, with respect to the presence of Islam in the regions from which people were taken, one finds reports of what might be called "remnants" of Muslim practice—say, of slaves who would not eat pork or drink alcohol, or who passed on Arabic words to their children. Following emancipation, a diverse assortment of religious associations grew up, offering African Americans an eclectic mix of Christian, Islamic, and other traditions.

The Nation of Islam provides an important example. Elijah Muhammad (1897–1975) claimed to be the successor of W. D. Fard (dates uncertain), the "messenger" who presented himself as called to preach to the "lost-found nation of Islam" in America—that is, to African Americans

16. Manning Marable and Hishaam D. Aidi, eds., *Black Routes to Islam* (New York: Palgrave Macmillan, 2009).

in need of recovering a forgotten identity. In Chicago, Detroit, and other northern cities, members of the Nation organized congregations, sponsored business ventures, built educational institutions, and above all, spread their message: African Americans, and by extension all people of color, have a special place in God's plan. The experience of slavery and of ongoing racial discrimination encouraged a mindset by which many had accepted their status as helpless victims. Recovery of Islam, with its emphasis on personal discipline and service for the good of one's community, would build pride, self-determination, and strength.

Such a message came with a warning, however. In order to fulfill their destiny, members of the Nation of Islam must separate themselves from their oppressors. Elijah Muhammad's rhetoric, like that of Malcolm in explaining his "X," was tinged with warnings about the white "devils," the dangers of collaboration between the races, and predictions of the coming judgment by which the white race would pay for its sins.

As a young man, Malcolm received little in the way of formal education; he did not progress past the eighth grade. Moving to Boston, then later to New York, he worked a variety of jobs. His main business, though, involved "hustling"—trading in drugs, gambling, and other vices, supplemented by petty theft. Running afoul of the law, Malcolm went to prison in 1946, at the age of twenty, where things began to change.

> One day in 1948, after I had been transferred to Concord Prison, my brother Philbert, who was forever joining something, wrote me this time that he had discovered "the natural religion for the black man." He belonged now, he said, to something called "the Nation of Islam." He said I should "pray to Allah for deliverance." I wrote Philbert a letter which . . . was worse than my earlier reply to his news that I was being prayed for by his "holiness" church.[17]

Subsequently, a second letter, this time from his brother Reginald, suggested help in getting out of prison if Malcolm would give up pork and stop smoking cigarettes. As it turned out, a number of members of the Little family in Detroit and Chicago now identified with the Nation. Unbeknownst to Malcolm, Reginald's advice served as a kind of introduction to some of the basic disciplines associated with Muslim practice. This became clear when Reginald came to the prison and began to talk about Elijah

17. *The Autobiography of Malcolm X*, 179.

Muhammad. Through him and other family members, Malcolm became acquainted with the combination of black nationalist and Muslim rhetoric characteristic of the Nation. He then began a correspondence with the leader, who encouraged Malcolm to "have courage."

Through family members, followed by exchanges with Elijah Muhammad, Malcolm X began to hear God's call. Such small steps as changing his diet and giving up smoking suggest the beginnings of a response. As with the Prophet and his companions, or again with al-Ghazali, the practice of prayer constituted a decisive step for Malcolm X. God calls human beings; they respond by calling on God, and then by calling others to follow suit. So we read:

> Regularly my family wrote to me, "Turn to Allah . . . pray to the East."
> The hardest test I ever faced in my life was praying. You understand. My comprehending, my believing the teachings of Mr. Muhammad had only required my mind's saying to me, "That's right!" or "I never thought of that." But bending my knees to pray—that *act*—well, that took me a week. You know what my life had been. Picking a lock to rob someone's house was the only way my knees had ever been bent before. I had to force myself to bend my knees. And waves of shame and embarrassment would force me back up. For evil to bend its knees, admitting its guilt, to implore the forgiveness of God, is the hardest thing in the world. It's easy for me to see and to say that now. But then, when I was the personification of evil, I was going through it. Again, again, I would force myself back down into the praying-to-Allah posture. When finally I was able to make myself stay down—I didn't know what to say to Allah.[18]

Eventually, Malcolm thought of something to say, and came to understand the performance of *salat*.[19] He also began to call others to faith. Writing letters to associates from his former life convinced him that one of the chief obstacles to success in this regard would be his lack of education, however. Study—in the sense of a systematic program of self-education—followed prayer and other disciplines. In an effort to build vocabulary, he undertook a project of copying the dictionary line-by-line, page-by-page; at the end of each day's endeavor, he reviewed the results in order to be able to recall the words when they appeared in books.

18. *The Autobiography of Malcolm X*, 195–96.
19. See the account in *The Autobiography of Malcolm X*, 222.

"Seek knowledge, even though it be in China." "The acquisition of knowledge is compulsory for every Muslim, whether male or female." Having already encountered the Prophet's sayings, we can put Malcolm's calling and effort in a Muslim context. At this point in his story, one might even say that the quest for knowledge was Malcolm's jihad, his effort in the service of God.

Following release from prison in 1952, he became one of the best-known spokespersons for the Nation of Islam, combining calls for African Americans to return to the "natural religion for the black man" with denunciations of American racism. Malcolm attracted national and even international attention, so that some in the Nation began to see Malcolm as a rival to Elijah Muhammad. After a period in which the leader ordered the disciple to cease speaking in public, the two men parted ways. A new period of searching began for Malcolm X, as he reconsidered what he had learned from Mr. Muhammad. Part of this involved a realization that solving problems of racial injustice would require cooperation between people of different faiths. But Malcolm also gained an increasing awareness of the historical, global realities of Islam, which led to his decision to make the pilgrimage to Mecca.

In the report of Gabriel's questions to the Prophet, making *hajj* or the pilgrimage to Mecca is one of the five pillars of Islam. Provided one is able to do so, each Muslim should make this journey at least once in the course of one's life. For Malcolm X, the experience proved startling. From the beginning of the journey, his account makes mention of the interaction between Muslims of all races and colors. He realized the practice of denouncing the "white devil" was not about skin color, but rather about an attitude associated with hateful acts. Islam provides a cure for the disease of race prejudice. Writing to associates back in the US, Malcolm mentioned what he saw in Mecca:

> There were tens of thousands of pilgrims, from all over the world. They were of all colors, from blue-eyed blonds to black-skinned Africans. But we were all participating in the same ritual, displaying a spirit of unity and brotherhood that my experiences in America had led me to believe never could exist between the white and the non-white. America needs to understand Islam, because this is the one religion that erases from its society the race problem. Throughout my travels in the Muslim world, I have met, talked to, and even eaten with people who in America would have been considered "white"—but the "white" attitude was removed

from their minds by the religion of Islam. I have never before seen *sincere* and *true* brotherhood practiced by all colors together, irrespective of their color.[20]

Upon his return to America, Malcolm X began to forge alliances with people of all races and religions in an effort to serve the cause of justice. In February of 1965, when he fell to an assassin's bullet, Malcolm had barely begun this new dimension of his vocation.

With respect to the idea of calling in Islam, however, perhaps his most important legacy had to do with the subsequent career of Warith Din Muhammad, one of Elijah's sons. W.D., as he was known, was a confidant of Malcolm X, and encouraged Malcolm's attempts to connect with historic Islam. Acclaimed as the leader of the Nation following his father's death in 1975, W. D. Muhammad quickly moved away from some of the Nation's most characteristic themes, and eventually announced that he and his followers would join standard Sunni mosques, no longer maintaining a separate "black Muslim" identity. To respond to God's call—to say "Here I am, O Allah, ready to serve"—required working with people of all races and creeds in the service of justice.

Conclusion

In considering the three stories outlined in this chapter, I want to highlight six main points with respect to the idea of calling in Islam.

First, God calls human beings to submit—that is, to become Muslims. God's call is extended to each and to all. In some sense, God's call relates to our very nature as creatures. As we saw in the discussion of Qur'an 7:171–72, there is a primordial covenant between God and humanity, and thus human beings know that God is their Lord. One can even say that this truth about human beings applies more generally, so that all creatures are called to praise God. All things come from God, and to God all things return.

Second, God's call is "written on" the hearts of human beings. All people have the capacity to reflect on the signs presented in the natural world, family life, and history, which are meant to lead us to God and for which we learn to give thanks. More often than not, however, human beings do not see the signs and express gratitude. Thus God sends prophets to remind

---

20. *The Autobiography of Malcolm X*, 390–91.

people of the reality in which they live. By preaching and example, these messengers mediate God's call. The greatest of them bring scriptures and found communities so that the mission may continue. Through the centuries, all people have a chance to hear the news.

Third, God's call can come in extraordinary forms. Muhammad's encounter with Gabriel provides the most important example of this. More typically, the call comes by means of other people, as it did in Malcolm X's story. His brothers and sisters, and the patient counsel of Elijah Muhammad, helped him to begin the journey. Interaction with the great variety of believers present at the Hajj moved him further along. Al-Ghazali's story also points in this direction: interaction with the Sufis helped him discover the light by which God penetrated his heart.

Fourth, prayer—calling upon God—is a critical step in the response to God. At the beginning of his ministry, Muhammad taught his companions the ritual of *salat*. If you would respond to God in faith, he seems to say, the first step is to acknowledge dependence on Him. For al-Ghazali, prayer was critical, in abandoning self-glory and as a vehicle by which God opens one's heart to receive that gift by which a human being develops trust in and reliance upon God. And for Malcolm X, bending the knees and bowing in prostration before God struck a blow against pride—the kind of attitude by which a person resists the notion that we belong to God, and only through acknowledgment of this does a human being experience true freedom.

Fifth, even as one responds to the divine summons by calling upon God, Muslim tradition stresses the importance of extending the call to other people. Once again, the story of the Prophet provides a paradigmatic example. Recitation of the Qur'an and the practice of prayer constituted an invitation to all. In Mecca, then in Medina, believers heard and said, "Here I am, Lord." Subsequent generations continued the practice; al-Ghazali's Sufis took the message of Islam from the heartland of the Middle East and North Africa to Southeast Asia and into Central, West, and East Africa. Malcolm X proclaimed the faith in North America, first to African Americans, then to all people.

One can combine such practices of piety with all sorts of worldly work. Throughout the centuries, we find Muslims as merchants, soldiers, politicians, physicians, scientists—so long as the work is honest, and one observes the "limits set by God," worldly activity is a kind of service. Thus, following a lecture I gave at the Islamic Center of Jacksonville, Florida, a few years back, I was not surprised to find that the congregation included doctors, students, school teachers, housewives, providers of daycare, and

business people, in addition to the Imam or prayer leader. In a contemporary context, Muslims are of course affected by developments in technology and changing patterns of social interaction. The basic notion of calling
remains consistent with that of earlier generations, however. God calls, and
human beings respond "Here I am, ready to serve."[21]

Sixth, historical and social-political contexts shape the way one carries
out his or her calling. In the first decade after his encounter with Gabriel,
Muhammad focused on preaching, and told his companions to overcome
their opponents through patient endurance and exemplary behavior. Eventually, the activities of the anti-Muslim forces reached a level that called for
something different. Muhammad moved his community to Medina, and
began to lead in the manner of diplomats and military commanders. Subsequent generations continued in this vein, building an imperial state that
placed Muslims in control of vast territories. At the same time, many kept
alive the practice of calling individuals to faith—emphasizing the importance of the religious and spiritual aspects of Islam, and reminding others
that political power is not an end in itself. At the pinnacle of al-Ghazali's
career, in a position to advise officials at the Abbasid court and to influence
the practice of Islam throughout the empire, the great scholar left in order
to devote himself to spiritual disciplines. Holding power can provide opportunities to serve, but it also acts as a temptation, distracting one from
that which is truly important. In another context, when Malcolm X heard
God's call, he understood it as a summons to social and political activism,
as well as to the life of the spirit. Breaking the chains of racial oppression
actually involved both of these things—that is, a life of prayer and other
disciplines and of work to combat injustice.

With these points in mind, I turn to consider two aspects of Islamic
thought and practice that are related to calling that challenge how contemporary Muslims appropriate their tradition today. Both are controversial
in Muslim communities, and an adequate explanation of each would take
me beyond the scope of this chapter.

First, the three stories focus on men. How does the idea of calling in
Islam relate to women? All Muslims agree that, as a matter of principle,
God's call goes forth to both men and women. All human beings are sum-
moned by their Creator. All are called to respond by calling upon God, and

---

21. A nice illustration of the variety of ways contemporary Muslims think about these
matters may be found at the website of the "My Jihad" project, accessed June 15, 2015, http://
myjihad.org/about/.

by extending God's call to others. Men and women are equal with respect to God's mercy and compassion. Male and female alike will answer for the good and bad they have done on the Day of Judgment.

That said, there is much in Muslim tradition to suggest that men and women are to play different social roles. Historically, many authorities hold to a notion of complementarity. The Qur'an declares that men "are the protectors of women" (4:34), and this verse is often cited in connection with judgments indicating that men are the proper leaders in the family and in society. Women's roles involve support for the men. In particular with respect to the family, the proper form of activity for women involves establishing and maintaining a household and caring for children. Such judgments do not envision a significant public role for women; indeed, they can be understood as actively restricting women's access to public life.

Following Malcolm X's release from prison, he moved in with one of his brothers. His account of the order of the household is consistent with the notion of complementary roles: upon rising, Malcolm and his brother performed their ablutions in preparation for prayer, followed by the brother's wife, then the children. As they prayed, they formed in ranks, so that Malcolm's brother led the ritual, with Malcolm immediately behind, and the wife and children in the rear. The order is as it should be, according to Malcolm X. Islam makes men the protectors of women, not the other way around. When Malcolm married, he envisioned a similar order for his household.

That is hardly a complete picture, however. Malcolm's wife was a nurse working in a public setting. And, in the period of reflection following his separation from the Nation of Islam, Malcolm pondered the example of his sister Ella, whose independence and entrepreneurial activity allowed her to fund his pilgrimage to Mecca. Shouldn't the faith have a place for women like these?

Amina Wudud, a Muslim scholar and author of *Inside the Gender Jihad*, takes up the role of women in Islam.[22] For Wudud, the relatively conservative approach of much Muslim tradition on these matters should be in question. The Qur'an's basic judgment is that men and women are equal before God. While there are verses that support male headship, reading these in the context of seventh-century Arabia makes it clear that the direc-

---

22. Amina Wudud, *Inside the Gender Jihad: Women's Reform in Islam* (New York: Oneworld Publications, 2006).

tion of Islam was progressive. For Wudud and others like her, this means that the call to serve involves working toward greater opportunities for women as well as men.[23]

Second, with respect to jihad, the activities of groups like ISIS, Boko Haram, al-Shabab, and al-Qa'ida raise important questions about calling. All claim the mantle of jihad and present their programs as a response to God's call. Yet there are many Muslim scholars who argue that these "jihad-ists" misconstrue Muslim tradition, and that their actions belie the claim to serve the cause of justice. Authorities at al-Azhar in Egypt, in Saudi Arabia, and elsewhere call on the tradition of *ahkam al-jihad* or "judgments pertaining to armed struggle." According to this tradition, for fighting to qualify as just, it must be authorized by a legitimate government, for a just cause, and conducted in a manner consistent with the orders of the Prophet. The orders include "do not kill children"—or in other texts, do not directly and intentionally target children, women, the old, and others who do not ordinarily participate in military activities.[24]

Many Muslims object to the way the jihadists seem to suggest that the term only refers to armed struggle. The literal translation of jihad is "effort." In the Qur'an, the term is usually joined with the phrase "in the path of God." Throughout the history of Islam, people have connected the notion of jihad with a variety of activities—in one sense, the idea is that any and all forms of effort aimed at serving God may be construed as jihad. Prayer, fasting, giving to charity, making the pilgrimage to Mecca are connected with jihad, as are calling others to faith or working in ways that build up one's community.

At the very least, a broader interpretation of jihad indicates that we need not—and I think should not—take the jihadist groups' claims at face value. Understanding the political and religious situations in the Middle East and other zones of conflict is not an easy matter. For some, at least, trying to obtain such understanding through studies of history, politics, economics, and religion may itself be a kind of jihad—an exertion of effort in the service of justice, and thus a response to the call of God.

---

23. Alongside the discussion by Wuhud, Ziba Mir-Hosseini's description of the debate over women's roles in contemporary Iran illustrates the variety of opinion. See *Islam and Gender: The Religious Debate in Contemporary Iran* (Princeton: Princeton University Press, 1999).

24. For a discussion of these matters, see John Kelsay, *Arguing the Just War in Islam* (Cambridge, MA: Harvard University Press, 2007).

Resources

Cook, Michael. *The Koran: A Very Short Introduction.* Oxford: Oxford University Press, 2000.

———. *Muhammad.* Oxford: Oxford University Press, 1983.

Enayat, Hamid. *Modern Islamic Political Thought.* Austin: University of Texas Press, 1982.

Fernea, Elizabeth Warnock. *Guests of the Sheik: An Ethnography of an Iraqi Village.* New York: Anchor Books, 1989.

Hashmi, Sohail H., ed. *Islamic Political Ethics: Civil Society, Pluralism, and Conflict.* Princeton: Princeton University Press, 2002.

Hourani, Albert. *Arabic Thought in the Liberal Age, 1798–1939.* Cambridge: Cambridge University Press, 1983.

Manning, Marable, and Hishaam D. Aidi, eds. *Black Routes to Islam.* New York: Palgrave Macmillan, 2009.

Mir-Hosseini, Ziba. *Islam and Gender: The Religious Debate in Contemporary Iran.* Princeton: Princeton University Press, 1999.

Rahman, Fazlur. *Major Themes of the Qur'an.* 2nd ed. Chicago: University of Chicago Press, 2009.

Schimmel, Annemarie. *Mystical Dimensions of Islam.* Chapel Hill: University of North Carolina Press, 1975.

5

Worship, the Public Good, and Self-Fulfillment

Hindu Perspectives on Calling

ANANTANAND RAMBACHAN

In 2013, Hawaii's Congressional Representative, Tulsi Gabbard, the first Hindu to be elected to either chamber, created history by using the Bhagavadgītā for her swearing-in ceremony. In various interviews since her election, Gabbard, a combat veteran of the Iraq war, spoke of the significance of the Bhagavadgītā's teachings in her life. The teachings inspired her to a life of service based on a model of servant leadership. She uses the terminology of the text to describe herself as a *karma yogi* (a practitioner of the spirituality of action—*karma yoga*), a teaching she hopes to share with her colleagues in Washington.[1]

The Bhagavadgītā, however, in addition to its commendation of a spirituality of action in the world, had an even more specific meaning and value for Representative Gabbard as a military veteran. The dialogue between the teacher, Krishna, and his friend and student, Arjuna, occurs on a battlefield just before the commencement of a great war. In Iraq, surrounded by death and destruction, Gabbard found strength in Krishna's teachings on the immortality of the *ātman,* the indestructible human self. The *ātman,* instructed Krishna, cannot be severed by weapons, burnt by fire, drowned in water, or dried by wind. It is eternal and all pervading.[2]

First thing in the morning and the last thing at night, I meditated upon the fact that my essence was spirit, not matter, that I was not my physical

1. "The Indian American Contenders," *New America Media,* accessed April 27, 2015, http://newamericamedia.org/2012/10/the-indian-american-contenders.php.
2. See Richard Davis, *The Bhagavad Gita: A Biography* (Princeton: Princeton University Press, 2014), 209–10.

body, and that I didn't need to worry about death because I knew that I would continue to exist and I knew that I would be going to God.[3]

The Bhagavadgītā, as we shall see, continues to be a significant Hindu text informing and inspiring the choices that Hindus make about the meaning and character of their lives in the world. Although particularly significant, as we see in the case of Gabbard, the Bhagavadgītā is one of several sacred texts in the Hindu tradition, reflecting its rich diversity.

What is spoken of today as "Hinduism" is an astonishingly diverse phenomenon, suggested by the word "Hindu" itself. This term has been used at different times, and even at the same time, to signify geographical, religious, cultural and, in more recent times, national realities. "Hindu" is the Iranian variation for the name of a river that the Indo-Europeans referred to as the "Sindhu," Greeks as the "Indos," and the British as the "Indus." Hindu traditions have always been varied, reflecting India's rich diversity of geography, culture, and language. These traditions, on the whole, do not problematize religious diversity or see it as something to be overcome.

It is helpful to think of Hinduism as a family name, recognizable through shared features, but preserving also the uniqueness of its individual members. The traditions comprising this ancient extended family continue to intermingle, influencing and being influenced by each other. If we keep this fact of diversity in mind, generalizations made in this essay will not mislead.

For these reasons, it is helpful to take note, at the inception, of the problems presented to the Hindu tradition by the word "religion." Although some of the phenomena encompassed by the term existed and continue to exist in India, "religion" carries its own assumptions. Among these are membership in specified organizations or congregations, uniform beliefs and rituals, ordained clergy, centralized and hierarchical authority, a single scripture, and heresy and sanctions, of one kind or another, for apostasy. If some constellation of these factors is central to the meaning of religion, Hindu traditions will be excluded. Hindus do not require membership in a congregation or denomination, do not offer a creedal statement to which one must subscribe in order to be admitted, do not

---

3. "America Elects Its First Hindu to Congress: A 31-year-old Female Iraq War Vet," *Daily Mail*, accessed April 27, 2015, http://www.dailymail.co.uk/news/article-2229712/America-elects-Hindu-Congress-31-year-old-female-Iraq-War-vet-Tulsi-Gabbard.html.

have a single ritual, do not excommunicate, and do not have institutions or spokespersons who speak authoritatively for all Hindus.

The languages of India do not have an easy equivalent for the term "religion." Religion dualistically implies a sphere of life that is nonreligious. The Sanskrit word, *dharma,* is often mistakenly equated with "religion," but the former is far more comprehensive than "religion." While including those dimensions of life, such as sacred spaces and rituals, that are considered religious, *dharma* also encompasses food and eating practices, dress, fine arts, occupation, and law. *Dharma* and its opposite, *adharma,* are not equivalent to the religious and secular. The root of *dharma* is *dhr,* meaning to support or sustain. *Dharma* refers, therefore, to all beliefs, values, and practices that are viewed as promoting the well-being of the universe. Beliefs and actions that cause fragmentation and chaos constitute *adharma.* Instead of "Hinduism," many Hindus speak of their tradition as *Sanātana Dharma* (Eternal Way).[4] The comprehensiveness of *dharma* is a valuable Hindu resource for thinking about the theme of this book, callings.

Reflecting the diversity of Hinduism, Hindus look to a vast array of sacred texts, some in Sanskrit, and others in the vernacular languages of India, for guidance.[5] Most Hindus, however, recognize the four Vedas, Ṛg, Sāma, Yajur, Atharva (ca. 1200 BCE or earlier) that include the Upaniṣads (ca. 500 BCE or earlier) as an authoritative and foundational revelation. Other important texts include the Mahābhārata (ca. 400 BCE–400 CE), the Rāmāyaṇa (ca. 400 BCE–300 CE), and the previously mentioned Bhagavadgītā (150 BCE–150 CE). Although I will draw from a variety of Hindu texts, the discussion that follows relies, in a special way, on the Bhagavadgītā.

The Bhagavadgītā, widely abbreviated as the Gītā, is a dialogue of seven hundred verses, arranged in eighteen chapters, between Krishna and his friend Arjuna. It constitutes chapters 23–40 of book 6 of the Mahābhārata. The conversation between Krishna and Arjuna occurs on the eve of an epic battle. Krishna, who has volunteered to serve as Arjuna's charioteer, is instructed by Arjuna to drive his chariot between the two armies so that he can survey the opposing forces. Although justice is on the side of Arjuna, the prospect of having to fight against his relatives and teachers saps all

---

4. Describing *dharma* and *adharma* is a matter of continuing debate within the Hindu tradition.

5. The earliest Hindu texts, the Vedas, are written in Sanskrit, as well as other important religious works such as the Bhagavadgītā, the Mahābhārata, and the Rāmāyaṇa. Although there are few speakers of Sanskrit, it continues to be an important language for Hindu prayer and ritual.

enthusiasm from Arjuna and plunges him into a moral and spiritual crisis. A discussion ensues, in which Krishna instructs Arjuna about the nature of work and duty and the importance of fulfilling social obligations.[6] The authority and significance of the Bhagavadgītā is connected undoubtedly with the fact that Arjuna discovers (chapter 11) that his advisor is none other than God, in one of his human incarnations (*avatāra*).[7]

Fredrick Buechner, a Christian preacher and novelist, has written that God calls human beings to the work "(a) that you need most to do and (b) that the world most needs to do have done. . . . The place God calls you to is the place where your own deep gladness and the world's deep hunger meet."[8] Buechner, it seems to me, is suggesting that good work occurs at the intersection where individual inward fulfillment and world need meet. Buechner's description of good work as expressing one's inward character and as meeting societal needs appears to me to coincide with two key and often-employed terms in the Bhagavadgītā: *svabhāva* and *svadharma*.

Concepts of Calling: *Svabhāva* (Individual Nature and Calling)

Svabhāva (*sva*, meaning "one's own" and *bhava*, "nature") refers to the intrinsic nature of the human being. The Bhagavadgītā (18:41; 18:42; 18:47) speaks of and commends work that flows out of one's nature (*svabhāvaprahbavair*), that is born of one's nature (*svabhāvajam*), and that is even ordained by one's nature (*svabhāvaniyatam*).[9] The author clearly suggests (18:48) that one should not relinquish work that is in harmony with one's innate character (*sahajaṁ karma na tyajet*). Such work, teaches Krishna, should not be given up, even though lacking perfection. All work, after all, notes Krishna, is imperfect (*sarvārambhā hi doṣeṇa*).

Underlying the Bhagavadgītā's insistence on the performance of work that expresses one's nature is the idea that such work affords a deeper

---

6. *Dharma* also has the meaning of duty and obligation.

7. The Hindu Vaiṣṇava tradition (centered on the nature of God as Vishnu) emphasizes the teaching on the *avatāra*, or the advent of God in our world. Krishna and Rama are two of the significant *avatāras*. The Bhagavadgītā (chapter 4) includes a special discussion on the *avatāra*.

8. Cited in William C. Placher, ed., *Callings: Twenty Centuries of Christian Wisdom on Vocation* (Grand Rapids: Eerdmans, 2005), 3.

9. Numbers refer to chapter and verse of the Bhagavadgītā. See *Shrī Bhagavadgītā*, trans. Winthrop Sargeant (Albany: State University of New York Press, 1993).

fulfillment. When an individual's nature does not flow into appropriate work, there is frustration and unhappiness. In Buechner's words, there is no "deep gladness." The Catholic poet-priest Gerard Manley Hopkins (1844–1889) spoke of each self as endowed with a distinctive nature, a unique constellation of characteristics that find expression and fulfillment in activity. Such activity reveals something of God.[10]

As the imperishable seed, origin, and foundation of the universe (9:18), God must be regarded as the source of the distinctive natures of human beings. One achieves life's highest purpose by worshipfully offering one's work to God who is the source of all life and who exists in all (18:46). Since the Hindu tradition, however, teaches a doctrine of rebirth (*punarjanma/saṃsāra*) until liberation (*mokṣa*), it is possible to posit that individual nature is not unalterably fixed, but open to change. The Hindu tradition, therefore, offers to us the possibility of callings that may differ with each new birth or even in the course of a single life. In the Bhagavadgītā, the student, Arjuna, clearly has the nature (*svabhāva*) of a warrior and political leader. Yet Krishna assures him, at the end of the sixth chapter, that the practice of religious discipline (*yoga*) results in rebirth in a family of *yogis* with an orientation to a life of spirituality. One assumes that his inward orientation will also be different. The underlying argument in the Bhagavadgītā, however, about the need for harmony between inner disposition and outward activity is not altered by this possibility of multiple callings across the rebirth cycles. Whatever one's calling, there is deeper fulfillment when the outward and inward exist in some harmony. Perhaps flexibility in understanding callings is a useful resource in an age in which we see more of such choices in a single lifespan. *Svabhava* does not have to be treated as inflexible and may be expressed in a variety of activities.

Douglas J. Schuurman describes the multitude of different gifts reflected in human beings and notes the difficulties of "discovering and developing our aptitudes."[11] The challenges of discerning one's *svabhāva* are no less for Hindus and reflect many of the difficulties shared across religious traditions. In India and many ancient societies, occupations were transmitted within families. Many traditional occupations in India, such as serving as temple or family priests, the making of icons (*mūrtis*) for

---

10. See Kristin Johnston Largen, *Finding God among Our Neighbors* (Minneapolis: Fortress, 2013), 177–80.

11. See Douglas J. Schuurman, *Vocation: Discerning Our Callings in Life* (Grand Rapids: Eerdmans, 2004), 143.

Hindu temples, and construction or agriculture, are still practiced today. The choice of family occupations is understandable in a historical context where educational opportunities were limited and not institutionalized and where skills were transmitted in families. Even so, Hindu society exemplified a certain flexibility and mobility and recognized that the family profession may not always be in harmony with an individual's *svabhāva*.

Chāndogya Upaniṣad (4.4.1–4.9.2) narrates the story of Satyakama, a young boy who wanted to study the Vedas. Studying was a privilege accorded only to those born in a family of priests (*brahmins*).[12] Satyakama was well aware of the caste requirements for such study and went to his mother. "Mother," said Satyakama, "I want to become a Vedic student, so tell me what my lineage is." "Son," she replied, "I don't know what your lineage is. I was young when I had you. I was a maid then and served and had a lot of relationships. As such, it is impossible for me to say what your lineage is. But my name is Jabala and your name is Satyakama. So you should simply say that you are Satyakama Jabala." Encouraged by his mother's response, Satyakama went to a teacher of the scriptures, Haridrumata Gautama, and asked to study the Vedas. As expected, the teacher immediately inquired about his lineage. Satyakama repeated exactly what his mother told him. Impressed by his truthfulness, and seeing this quality, rather than his birth, as the requisite qualification for study, Gautama accepted Satyakama as his student. A well-known story about Valmiki, the author of the Sanskrit version of the Ramāyaṇa, represents him as a hunter before he became a renowned poet. There is much evidence in the Mahābhārata of debates about whether *svabhāva* is determined by birth in a particular family or by individual disposition and personal cultivation of skills and appropriate values.

In spite of many prominent examples of such flexibility in the choice of work, it is also true that Hindu society exemplified a certain rigidity in the caste system. Caste is a hierarchical ordering of human society into four groups. The *brāhmaṇas* (priests) occupied the top, followed by the *rājanyas/kṣatriyas* (soldiers), *vaiśayas* (merchants and farmers), and *śūdras* (laborers). The first three groups were regarded as the *dvijas* or twice-born and entitled to perform and participate in Vedic ritual. Generally, male

12. I narrated and reflected on the story of Satyakama in "Satyakama: The Boy Who Did Not Know His Father," in *Faces of the Other,* ed. Hans Ucko (Geneva: World Council of Churches, 2005), 34–37. See *The Upanishads,* trans. Patrick Olivelle (Oxford: Oxford University Press, 1996).

members of these three groups alone underwent the initiatory ritual (*upa-nayana*) that enabled them to study the Vedas. Those who were not, for one reason or another, included in the fourfold classification were deemed outcastes or untouchables.[13] The rigidity of caste and the insistence on hereditary work were reinforced by interpretations of the doctrine of *karma* to explain birth in a particular caste as the just consequence of actions performed in previous lives. The teaching on *karma*, essentially a moral law that stipulates a causal relationship between actions and effects, was utilized to legitimize a hierarchical social structure. Such interpretations insisted on the necessity to perform caste work.[14]

The nature of work was one of the major questions of debate and division between the famous untouchable leader, B. R. Ambedkar (1891–1956), and Mahatma Gandhi (1869–1948). Gandhi believed that the phenomenon of untouchability was a corruption of the authentic teachings of the Hindu tradition and must be eliminated by reform. Ambedkar, on the other hand, contended that caste and untouchability were a fundamental part of the tradition. His conversion to Buddhism, months before his death in December 1956, reflected his deep disillusionment with the Hindu tradition.[15]

Although Gandhi advocated for the abolition of untouchability, he was in favor of the retention of the fourfold *varṇa* system and hereditary occupations. He believed that hereditary occupations were consistent with the equal value of all work. The untouchables would become part of the group of manual workers. He believed that, through a change of heart, all groups could be considered equal. Ambedkar, on the other hand, argued for the right to choose one's work and saw inequality and caste as inseparable.[16] He had greater faith in a new legal system and in a political struggle for minority rights. Frustrated over his failure to secure temple entry and other religious rights for untouchables, and the slowness of the Hindu tradition to change, Ambedkar converted to Buddhism, and almost 200,000 untouchables followed him.

---

13. Many so-called untouchables speak of themselves as Dalits (oppressed/crushed).

14. In Sanskrit, the word *varṇa* is used often for the four major groups and *jāti* for the many subgroups that continue to develop. For a discussion of these two categories and their interrelatedness see David R. Kinsley, *Hinduism: A Cultural Perspective* (Englewood Cliffs, NJ: Prentice Hall, 1993), chapter 8.

15. For an account of Ambedkar's views see B. R. Ambedkar, *Annihilation of Caste* (The Annotated Critical Edition), ed. S. Anand (London: Verso, 2014).

16. See Christophe Jaffrelot, *Dr. Ambedkar and Untouchability: Fighting the Caste System* (New York: Columbia University Press, 2005).

Today, around 14–15 percent of the population of India, consisting of approximately 160–180 million people, is labeled "untouchable" or members of the "Scheduled Castes" in the terminology of the Indian constitution.[17] Although the constitution of independent India stipulates that "the State shall not discriminate against any citizen on grounds of religion, race, caste, sex, place of birth," the phenomenon of untouchability persists, especially in rural India, and work choices still are limited by circumstances of birth. We must acknowledge, however, that changes are under way. The impact of legislation, urban life, democracy, freedom, equality, and feminism are transforming age-old attitudes and customs. In addition, the modern era is also witness to increasing self-awareness among the Dalits and their readiness to organize themselves to agitate for justice.

Schuurman discusses the way in which Christian reformers, such as Calvin and Luther, interpreted the understanding of vocation within the limits of a conservative social hierarchy thought to be divinely ordained.[18] Religious legitimacy was conferred upon persons occupying traditional positions of power. Schuurman calls for a focus on "aspects of the doctrine of vocation that criticize hierarchies—whether based on gender, race, or class—and which point to mutuality between men and women, and among all people."[19] Although there is nothing inherently wrong if an individual chooses to follow a traditional family occupation, provided that he or she has the right disposition (*svabhāva*) for such work, a better society is certainly one in which work choices are not determined and limited by circumstances of birth. Choice is the ideal of many contemporary societies that aspire toward universal education and opportunities that are not limited by family work. One of the aims of such education is to offer learning experiences in which students have the opportunity for self-discovery and occupational choices that express interest and inward disposition.

It is important, to me, that the Hindu tradition retain the insight of work that expresses inner disposition and interest (*svabhāvajam karma*) but sever the connection with any insistence on hereditary occupation, a central feature of caste hierarchy. Ideally, the work that one does should be the work that one wants to do. Choosing one's work will certainly contribute to a higher level of meaning and fulfillment in work. In fact, theo-

17. On the statistics, Internet Fact Archives, "Scheduled Castes of India," accessed April 27, 2015, http://www.faqs.org/minorities/South-Asia/Scheduled-Castes-of-India.html.

18. Schuurman, *Vocation*, 103–4. See also Schuurman's chapter, "Calling in a Protestant Key," in this volume.

19. Schuurman, *Vocation*, 111.

logically, at the heart of the Hindu tradition, there is a vision of life that invalidates the assumptions of inequality and limited choices evident in caste. The Bhagavadgītā (13:28; 18:61) speaks repeatedly of God as present equally and identically in every being. God's immanence is the source of human dignity and equal worth, which supports freedom of work choice and equality of opportunity based on abilities and interests, and gives foundation to the argument against oppressive hierarchies. Rather than assuming that birth determines *svabhāva,* we would be entrusted as individuals, families, and communities with the task of helping each other discern the work for which we are best suited. Hindu society continues to move away from choosing occupations based on a person's birth. There is a need now for guidance and support to help a new generation of Hindus choose meaningful work.

Concepts of Calling: *Svadharma* (the Social and Cosmic Significance of Callings)

Self-understanding and choosing work that expresses one's own nature are necessary, in the Hindu tradition, for meaning and fulfillment. *Svabhāvajam karma* or work that flows out of inner disposition helps us to avoid alienation from self and consequently from work. The focus on *svabhāva* alone, however, gives the impression of a highly individualistic understanding of the meaning of work and the process of choosing such work. In the Bhagavadgītā, however, one's individual nature cannot be considered separately from the fact that one belongs to an interrelated family, social, and cosmic order. Life is not possible outside of this interdependent order. Krishna (3:16) likens the interrelated whole to a revolving wheel (*pravartitaṁ cakraṁ*) that functions well through the cooperation of all its parts. If the meaning of human life cannot be conceived apart from this wider reality, then the meaning of work must be seen also in this context. Work, in the Hindu tradition, gains meaning when it expresses one's nature, but its meaning is enhanced by considering its social and cosmic significance.

Throughout this discussion, we have employed the English word "work" to describe the field of action in which one expresses one's self. As with "religion," however, there is no simple Sanskrit equivalent. The Sanskrit term for individual nature is, as already noted, *svabhāva.* The activity in which one expresses one's *svabhāva* is referred to in the Bhagavadgītā as *svadharma*.[20] This term is very suggestive and broader in scope than "work." It embraces all human activity.

The key to understanding the meaning of *svadharma* is, of course, *dharma*. It is derived from the root *dhr*, meaning "to support." *Dharma* embraces the corpus of values and actions that, in the widest sense, sustains existence. It makes possible unity and the flourishing of individuals, families, and communities. The opposite of *dharma* is *adharma*, the source of disunity, fragmentation, and chaos. The fundamental principles of *dharma* are derived from an understanding of the interdependent character of life. Each one exists in a complex web of relationships that includes other human beings, other species, and the natural world. We are inseparable from and continuously nourished by this web. We thrive and prosper because we are the continuous beneficiaries of the activities of the whole.

The interdependent and interrelated nature of existence is an argument that few will contest. It is a truth affirmed by the expanding horizons of our understanding of existence. Much less attention, however, is given to our moral obligations in an interdependent world. In the Hindu view, each one has a moral obligation to contribute to the sustenance of the whole of which he is a part and which makes existence possible. The Bhagavadgītā (3:12) speaks of a thief as one who enjoys what is received from creation without giving back anything. The text commends (3:11) mutual giving and nourishing (*parasparaṁ bhāvayantaḥ*) as the way to human flourishing. One of the many meanings of *dharma* is "duty" or "obligation" and Hindus speak often of "work" as duty.

In Hindu society, the *dharma* of a human being includes all of the ways in which she fulfills obligations to others. The complexity and diversity of the ways in which our lives are connected with others are reflected in the multiple classifications of *dharma*. There are general obligations (*sāmānya dharma*) required of all human beings. Although lists vary in texts, these usually include noninjury, truthfulness, compassion, and self-control. In addition to these general obligations, there are obligations connected with the particular stage of one's life (*āśrama dharma*). An unmarried student has obligations that are different from a married person.[21]

20. The term and its variations are used five times in the text (3:35 twice; 18:47; 2:31; 2:33).

21. Karl Barth recognizes the opportunities and limits of each stage of life. Barth identifies three stages with distinct opportunities: youth, middle age, and old age. The Hindu tradition speaks of the stages of the student, the householder, the forest-dweller, and the renunciant. See Schuurman, *Vocation*, 145–46.

What we have already spoken about as *svadharma* is another example of a specific obligation. This is the obligation connected with what is regarded as one's work or profession, even though the meaning of the term should not be limited to work for which one receives remuneration. Situating such obligations within the matrix of *dharma* considerably enhances their significance. It emphasizes the universal community to which we belong and helps us to see our work as necessary to the well-being of this community. Through a vision of the whole, the significance of our particular role is illumined and its meaning deepened.

Let us consider, for example, a worker who is employed in a plant where heart-lung machines that support the body during cardiac surgery are manufactured. The worker works in the section of the factory making the tubes that connect the patient to the machine. This worker, however, does not understand the purpose of the tubes since he has no comprehension of the total product. Work of this kind helps the worker to satisfy his daily needs, but has very limited meaning beyond this purpose. He cannot identify with the daily tasks involved. Suppose this worker understands the purpose of the tubes and the necessity of the heart-lung machine in saving lives. Such an understanding will transform the worker's perception of his work and himself, adding significance and meaning to daily tasks. In a similar way, understanding work as *svadharma* adds meaning and value to work by situating its significance in relation to the universal community.

Svadharma also adds a moral consciousness to work and to all human activity. Work is not only the expression of our special individual nature. It is also the special contribution that we make to the universe. Although there are some who choose not to engage in work that is beneficial to others and who are content to receive without giving, such conduct is morally deplorable. It is also shortsighted since our failure to nourish the community that sustains us results in our own deprivation. *Svadharma* excludes work that intentionally harms others. Although granting value to work that expresses one's nature, the Bhagavadgītā does not give a license for action that inflicts suffering on the community. The teaching on *svabhāva* is not meant to legitimize every desire and inclination. The Bhagavadgītā (7:11) gives its approval only to those desires that are consistent with *dharma*.[22] Without *svadharma*, *svabhāva* may lack moral purpose and direction. *Svadharma* is one way of fulfilling our debt to the universe community.

---

22. See Calvin's criticism of those who abuse the idea of vocation for selfish purposes. Schuurman, *Vocation*, 96–97.

The unity of *svabhava-svadharma* reminds us of the need to be attentive to both self and the other. Neglect of one's self impedes one's ability to give generously to others.

Twice in the Bhagavadgītā (3:20; 3:25), Krishna uses the important expression *lokasaṁgraham*. *Loka* is an inclusive word referring to the universe in its entirety. *Saṁgraham* means well-being. We may equate *lokasaṁgraham* with the universal common good, provided that our focus is not anthropocentric and includes a concern for all beings and the natural world. In both verses, Krishna instructs Arjuna to consider the public good in all that he does. Activity that does not contribute to the public good cannot be described as *svadharma*. Good work in the vision of the Bhagavadgītā contributes to the flourishing of the world.[23] Clarity about this is important in making work choices.

Human obligations (*dharma*), as noted earlier, are complex and depend, among other things, on one's stage of life and one's work. As a husband (*pati*), a father (*pitṛ*), and a son (*putra*), I have obligations (*dharma*) to my wife, children, and parents. As a professor (*ācārya*), I have obligations to my students (*ācārya dharma*). In the fulfillment of all of my obligations, and all are important, I must not harm the common good. It is possible to imagine ways in which one's family loyalty, for example, may be expressed in ways that hurt the public good. In the same way, one's work in the public or private sector, one's loyalty to one's nation, political party, or religious community, must be expressed in ways consistent with the public good. In the Hindu tradition, the public good is an important norm for measuring the value and the meaning of all that we do.

Living Out a Calling: The Unity of Life and Callings as Worship

With its emphasis on the interdependent character of existence and the fulfillment of obligations, it is no surprise that the Hindu tradition likens the universe to a cosmic person. The Puruṣasūkta hymn of the Ṛg Veda (10:90) describes the universe as emerging from the body of the cosmic person and equates various elements in nature (sun, moon, air, earth) with specific parts of the cosmic body.[24] The underlying purpose of the

---

23. Determining the public good is not always easy and requires the exercise of discernment. It is helpful to remember Krishna's observation that all work is imperfect.

24. The hymn is also controversial for its description of the four *varṇas* as emerg-

metaphor is to highlight the unity and interdependent functioning of the world. A healthy human body is one in which each organ serves the whole in accordance with its unique character. The proper functioning of the whole, in turn, nourishes each organ.[25] If an organ does not contribute to the functioning of the body, like a thief in the example of the Bhagavadgītā (3:12), the body is hurt, but also the organ. The human body is a model of the harmony of *svabhāva* and *svadharma,* since each organ serves the body (*svadharma*) through the expression of its uniqueness (*svabhāva*). The realization of our individual potential is important not only for our personal fulfillment but also for the common good. The community is diminished when, for whatever reason, a human being fails to realize her worth and potential. It is imperative, therefore, that communities promote values and opportunities that enable human self-fulfillment in terms of both *svabhāva* and *svadharma.*

Although a concern for the common good does not have to be connected with a religious worldview, the Bhagavadgītā and most Hindu traditions certainly assume this connection. *Svabhāva* and *svadharma* have religious meaning, and this meaning informs how these are lived out in various contexts and roles.

At the heart of this religious meaning is a theology of all work as worship, enunciated throughout the Bhagavadgītā. According to the Bhagavadgītā (18:46), "A human being attains life's highest purpose by worshipping with his own work (*svakarmaṇā*), the One from whom all beings originate and who exists in all."[26] The text (9:27) commends the offering of all actions to God in worship. "Whatever you do, whatever you eat, whatever you offer in worship, whatever you give, do it as an offering to me."[27] In each phrase the word *yat* (whatever) is repeated. The intent of the text here is to unify human life by including all actions and activities and commending the performance of these as worship. Worshipful actions, it is important to remember, are not only the heroic actions of Arjuna in the Bhagavadgītā or Mahatma Gandhi leading a freedom movement. Worshipful actions are also not limited to what is usually described as work.

---

ing from different parts of the cosmic body: mouth (*brahmins*), arms (*kṣatriyas*), thighs (*vaiśayas*), and feet (*śūdras*). This may be read as legitimizing the fourfold system.

25. We have noted and reiterate the ways in which this metaphor may be used to justify an oppressive system through the undermining of freedom to choose one's work. This fact, however, must not also blind us to its constructive insights.

26. My translation.

27. My translation.

All actions are included and the value of every action is enhanced and sanctified when it is performed as an offering to God.

In the Bhagavadgītā, the essence of worship is an offering or an undertaking motivated by the love (*bhakti*) of God. In the verse (9:26) preceding the one cited above, Krishna identifies love of God as the affection that makes an action one of worship. "One who offers to me, with love, a leaf, a flower, a fruit, or water, that offering of love I accept, from one who is earnest." The Bhagavadgītā does not ignore the moral choices that we must make when we act. We have already noted Krishna's teaching that all actions must be performed with concern for the common good. The point is that such actions become acts of worship when the underlying motivation is the love of God. The love of God (*bhakti*) and the performance of action (*karma*) unite when all actions are performed worshipfully. The theology of action as worship is referred to in the Hindu tradition as *karma yoga*. Offering one's actions (*karma*) to God spiritualizes and transforms them into a religious way (*yoga*) of being. It relates work to what has ultimate meaning.

One of the primary characteristics of *karma yoga* or the spirituality of action is what the Bhagavadgītā, in several verses, speaks of as the renunciation of the fruit of action or nonattachment to the results of action (*karma phala tyāga*). Actions (*svadharma*) in the teaching of the Bhagavadgītā (3:4–5) cannot and should not be given up. One does not gain spiritual liberation by turning away from one's obligations to family, community, or world. This is one of the important teachings given by Krishna to Arjuna, when Arjuna expressed a desire to seek liberation through the path of renunciation. Although one exercises choice in the selection of action, one must recognize that one cannot control or guarantee the outcome of one's actions. Choice is limited to one's motivation and the means employed. One of the most often-quoted verses (2:47) in the text states, "Your choice is in action alone; never in the results. Do not be attached to the fruits of action, but do not be attached also to inaction." In *karma yoga,* one attends to those matters over which one has some choice: one's motivation, the nature of one's work, and the means employed. The meaning of the action, however, is not exhausted by its outcome. In the vision of the Bhagavadgītā, uncertainty about the outcome ought not to deter from engagement in action. Fear of failure must not hamper good work. Offering an action to God grants meaning to the action even when the specific goal is not attained. The significance of human action is not to be measured only in relation to outcomes. *Karma yoga* reminds us also that the consequences of our actions are not always immediately discernible. What appears to be a failure in the short term may not be so when judged from a longer perspective.

The Bhagavadgītā makes a unique contribution to the Hindu understanding of the significance of life and action in the world and, consequently, to our thinking about callings. In Hindu society, at the time of the Bhagavadgītā, the roles and responsibilities of individuals were clearly stipulated. As a soldier, Arjuna had an obligation to defend his community against violence and injustice. Faced with the unpleasant duty of having to stand against teacher, relatives, and friends, he expressed a desire to withdraw from society and to pursue a religious life in solitude and with freedom from social obligations. The manner in which Arjuna described his choice suggests that he understood the committed pursuit of the religious life to require renunciation and the entry into monasticism (*saṃnyāsa*). Becoming a monk would free him from traditional family and social obligations. The Hindu tradition holds liberation (*mokṣa*) to be the highest goal of human life. He expected his teacher, Krishna, to approve of his wish to live the religious life by turning away from conventional roles in society. Underlying his request is the view that the life of the monk is superior religiously to the life of the person active in family and community.

Though affirming liberation at life's highest end, Krishna does not argue for the superiority of monasticism. He challenges the view (chapter 3) that the life of renunciation is superior and virtuous. There is no natural connection between renunciation and liberation. Monks do not cease to be active since the maintenance of bodily life is impossible without action (3:4-8). After establishing that monks, like other human beings, are active, Krishna specifies the kinds of actions that are compatible with the religious life. In doing so, he offers a new understanding of the meaning of renunciation. Renunciation is not the literal relinquishing of obligations in the world, but the overcoming of the selfish motive in action. It is the performance of action for the public good (*lokasaṃgraham*); it is nonattachment to the results of action (18:11); it is the worshipful offering of all actions to God (9:27-28). Such actions contribute to the well-being of the world, are compatible with the religious life and conducive to liberation. These are the insights that guide committed Hindus in living out the meaning of their callings in the world.

It is important to clarify, however, that Krishna does not denounce the life of the renunciant. In fact, he also commends it, but only as a choice among other choices. It is not the only way to live out a religious commitment.

The Bhagavadgītā's teachings on renunciation enabled a Hindu activist like Mahatma Gandhi to spiritualize an intensely political life. The Bhagavadgītā's reinterpretation of renunciation made it possible for him to follow his political calling while preserving his deep religious commitments. His political and his religious life were inseparable and had the one aim of knowing God. Gandhi wrote:

> I count no sacrifice too great for the sake of seeing God face to face. The whole of my activity whether it may be called social, political, humanitarian or ethical is directed to that end. And as I know that God is found more often in the lowliest of His creatures than in the high and mighty, I am struggling to reach the status of these. I cannot do so without their service. Hence my passion for the service of the suppressed class. And as I cannot render this service without entering politics, I find myself in them.[28]

Sustaining Callings: The Significance of Divine Immanence

Concern for the common good (*lokasaṁgraham*) and the theology of work as worship unite in a special way in one of the core and often-repeated insights of the Bhagavadgītā. This is the teaching that God exists equally in all beings. "God exists in the heart of all beings" (18:61). "The Supreme Lord exists equally in all beings; the Imperishable in the perishing. One who sees this, sees truly" (13:27). "One who sees Me everywhere and sees everything in Me never loses Me and is never lost from Me" (6:30). "I am the self, existing in the heart of all beings" (10:20). Service offered to the needy is the service of God. As a contemporary Hindu monk, Swami Tyagananda, puts it, "If God dwells in me and in everyone and everything in the world, then no matter who I am dealing with and who I am working for, I am really dealing only with God and working only for God."[29]

Some of the most often-quoted teachings on this insight came from the famous Hindu teacher Ramakrishna (1836–1886), the *guru* of the

---

28. Mahatma Gandhi, *All Men Are Brothers: Autobiographical Reflections* (New York: Continuum, 2001), 68.

29. Swami Tyagananda, *Walking the Walk* (Calcutta: Advaita Ashrama, 2014), 52.

Swami Vivekananda (1863–1902).[30] Speaking to his disciples on one occasion about the meaning of compassion, Ramakrishna explained that they should see the service of others as the service of God. "No, no; it is not compassion to *jivas* (living beings) but service to them as Shiva (God)." Ramakrishna obviously wanted his students to understand service as a privilege and honor that must be exercised in humility as a worshipful act. His words had a powerful impact on his young disciple, Vivekananda, who vowed "to proclaim everywhere in the world this wonderful truth I have heard today. I will preach this truth to the learned and to the ignorant, to the rich and the poor, to the Brahmana and the Chandala."[31] The Ramakrishna Mission, founded by Swami Vivekananda in 1897, uses the word "service" (*seva*), instead of "compassion" (*dayā*).

The implications of divine immanence for a theology of service in the Hindu tradition seem to coincide with a Christian understanding of divine incarnation. Schuurman reflects on the significance of this Christian teaching. "Theologically, the doctrines of providence and incarnation come into play here. Fulfilling a station's lawful duties is a participation in God's provident ways and recipients of services are Christ incarnate within human need. Thus Luther says God milks the cows through milkmaids, and he encourages fathers to imagine they are holding the baby Jesus in their hands when they change their infant's dirty diapers."[32] Schuurman cites Jesus's parable (Matt. 25:31–36) about the separation of the sheep and the goats that speaks of Jesus as incarnate in the needy. "Truly I tell you, whatever you did for one of the least of these brothers and sisters of mine, you did for me."

One of the important resources and modes of thought in the Hindu tradition for the spiritualization of human activity in all spheres of life is the fact that, traditionally, there is no sharp distinction between the secular and sacred.[33] I commented earlier on the absence of an easy Sanskrit equiv-

---

30. For a summary of Ramakrishna's life see Christopher Isherwood, *Ramakrishna and His Disciples* (Calcutta: Advaita Ashrama, 1974). For Swami Vivekananda, see Swami Nikhilananda, *Vivekananda: A Biography* (Calcutta: Advaita Ashrama, 1975).

31. Cited in Gwilym Beckerlegge, *Swami Vivekananda's Legacy of Service: A Study of the Ramakrishna Math and Mission* (New Delhi: Oxford University Press, 2006), 94–95. The translations in parenthesis are my own. Brahmana and Chandala refer to members of the highest caste and the lowest.

32. Schuurman, *Vocation*, 6–7.

33. The separation, however, is becoming a feature in the lives of many Hindus and may result in a greater compartmentalization of human life.

alent for "religion." As Troy Wilson Organ noted, "Hinduism as a religion and Hinduism as a culture are so intertwined that we can never be sure whether a certain mode of behavior is Hindu or Indian."[34] In principle, the Hindu tradition does not privilege religious vocations such as the work of the temple-priest (*pūjari*). In practice, however, certain occupations, such as those involving sanitation work and leather products, were considered "impure," and those who performed such work were relegated to the lower rungs of the caste ladder or even considered as outcastes. One of Gandhi's main concerns, despite his conservative views on caste, was to advocate for the dignity of all labor and to set an example by performing the work of all castes.[35] He justified his political activism in an understanding of the unity of human life and its religious foundations. It was a frequent topic of his reflections. "The whole gamut of man's activities today," wrote Gandhi, "constitutes an indivisible whole. You cannot divide social, economic, political and purely religious work into watertight compartments. I do not know any religion apart from human activity."[36]

The absence of any sharp secular-sacred divide is reinforced by the fact that the spirituality of the Hindu tradition is not anti-materialistic or life-negating. The goals that make for a full human life have been classified as fourfold. These are *artha* (wealth), *kāma* (pleasure), *dharma* (virtue/ethics), and *mokṣa* (liberation). While historically approving the voluntary renunciation of greed and materialism, Hinduism has never given its blessings to involuntary poverty and material deprivation. Wealth (*artha*) is a legitimate goal of life. *Kāma* includes sensual as well as aesthetic enjoyment. Sculpture, music, and dance flourished with the blessings of the Hindu tradition and Hindus love to celebrate life through these forms. The work of artists can be understood as religious offering, and classical dance performances begin with prayerful invocations.

Kāma legitimizes the human need and capacity for pleasure; the necessities of life are to be enjoyed as a way of fulfilling human nature. Hindus are not so spiritually minded that they despise the gain and enjoyment of the world. The spiritualization of human life is not its reduction to an ascetic minimum. Wealth and pleasure, however, must be sought and en-

34. Troy Wilson Organ, *Hinduism: Its Historical Development* (New York: Barron's Educational Series, 1974), 10. Organ also comments on the difficulty of separating religion and philosophy in Hinduism.

35. Gandhi opposed untouchability and inequality, but argued for the system of hereditary occupations.

36. Gandhi, *All Men Are Brothers*, 63.

joyed in ways that are consistent with moral values (*dharma*), the third of the four goals. *Dharma* asks that we broaden our perspective to incorporate the good and well-being of the community. It reminds us that our rights are only possible and meaningful in a context where equal, if not greater, recognition is given to our duties and obligations. The personal attainment of wealth and pleasure by inflicting pain and suffering on others, or by denying them the opportunity to freely seek these two ends, is opposed to *dharma*. In Hindu mythology the symbol of *dharma* is the bull, whose four feet are truth, purity, compassion, and generosity. A life of moderation, in which wealth and pleasure are in harmony with virtue, is conducive to life's highest goal, liberation (*mokṣa*). All callings are to be fulfilled with attentiveness to *dharma*.

Even as the four goals of life give a religious legitimization to the fulfillment of our basic human needs and are conducive to life's ultimate good, the Hindu ideal of life's four stages sanctifies our lives in each of life's important phases. Each stage is referred to, in Sanskrit, as *āśrama,* and each one has its own objectives as well as duties and responsibilities. A religious ritual (*saṃskāra*) is performed before the entry into each stage of life. The first or student stage is the period of formal education. Knowledge is sacred and its pursuit is a privileged commitment. Students are expected to build moral character through the practice of self-control, noninjury, truth, and generosity. The second stage begins with marriage, which is regarded as a sacrament in Hinduism and not just a legal contract between two adults. Marriage is understood as a religious order in which husband and wife look upon each other as partners in the attainment of wealth, pleasure, virtue, and liberation. There are daily religious obligations that include prayer, the service of elders, study, and sharing.

After raising and educating one's children and preparing them for adult life, elderly couples gradually withdraw from family responsibilities and devote more time to religious study and practice. They are referred to as forest-dwellers because, in the past, some persons sought the peace and simplicity of forest dwellings to study and contemplate. Since persons in this stage are rich in experience and wisdom, they are seen as capable of serving their communities as counselors, peacemakers, and teachers. They focus outwardly in the service of others and inwardly on their spiritual growth. Life does not lose meaning as one grows older physically, but offers new opportunities for religious growth and discovery. While quite rare today, some Hindus do enter a fourth stage where they intensify their religious lives and their focus on liberation. They are referred to as renunciants since they live lives of poverty and chastity in pursuit of liberation, the highest and ultimate goal of life. These are the monks and nuns of Hinduism who generally reside in monasteries and devote themselves to study, meditation, and teaching. The point of specifying goals and stages is to help us integrate all pursuits and periods of life and to infuse these with religious meaning.

Modern Challenges and Opportunities to Exercising Choices in Calling

Insistence on hereditary work, and lack of opportunities, are important ways in which human choices are frustrated. Impediments, however, take many forms. Although contemporary society idealizes individual choice, it also presents difficulties in the exercise of such choice.

To know oneself requires self-attentiveness; it requires solitude and the joy of being with oneself. Contemporary culture, on the other hand, tends to be extrovert, distracts from deep engagement with self, and is often not conducive to solitude and contemplation. In so many ways, it offers opportunities for diversion from self and self-understanding.

In addition to its extroverted orientation, contemporary culture encourages consumerism and measures success, and even human worth, by material assets. As such, it exerts strong pressures to select work primarily on the basis of income possibilities and not on the basis of aptitude (*svabhāva*) and concern for the common good (*svadharma*). We see examples of this in many professions. Many physicians lack compassion and concern for public health that are necessary for good medical practice. There are teachers, unfortunately, who do immeasurable and sometimes irreparable damage to the minds of children because they have no love for learning or nurturing this love in others. The significance of aptitude (*svabhāva*) is not meant to encourage indifference to economic needs in choosing work. The Hindu tradition upholds wealth (*artha*) as a necessary and legitimate goal of human life. It does not, however, have to be the single factor determining choice.

The challenges of choosing work that offers opportunities for self-expression are not limited to contending with wider social values. A young Hindu may have to struggle also with family expectations and pressures. As a Hindu parent, I am aware of the preference of many Hindu parents for professions that are lucrative and socially prestigious (such as medicine, law, and engineering) and the pressures exerted on children to choose such work.[37] There is less family support for the study of the humanities and the fine arts, and for careers in these fields. Although parental hopes and aspirations for children are appropriate and understandable, these become problematic when the child is regarded only as instrumental for the achievement of parental ambitions with little regard for the child's *svabhāva* and fulfillment. Freedom is a necessary condition for human flourishing in work, and where such freedom is curtailed by parental desire, growth is thwarted and self-expression stifled. Children do not thrive without loving parents, but love must be offered with the detachment that enables a child to cultivate and fulfill her own potential and nature.

Although the Bhagavadgītā suggests that there is special fulfillment in performing work that expresses one's *svabhāva,* it does not imply that such work is always easy to choose or to perform. One may have to make choices that are painful and that one prefers to avoid. Arjuna in the Bhagavadgītā is a good example of this predicament. Although he is a soldier by training and disposition, faced with the challenge of having to fight a just war against teachers, friends, and family, he expresses a desire to walk away from the field of battle into monasticism and a quest for liberation (*mokṣa*). Krishna persuades him that his desire for world-renunciation is both flawed and unnecessary. Liberation does not require walking away from obligations in the world.

In the course of their conversation (3:35) we have these intriguing words of advice from Krishna: "It is better to do one's own work, though deficient, than the work of another done efficiently. Death in the performance of one's work is better; the work of another is full of fear." This verse may be read very conservatively as supportive of hereditary occupations and the hierarchical ordering of caste. It could be interpreted as enjoining persons to continue performing inherited work. On the other hand, we may read Krishna's words as offering an insightful caution about the temptation of being seduced by the prospect of easy success as a way of avoiding more difficult choices in action. One may try to evade one's commitments because of fear of failure, dangers involved, feelings of inadequacy, or the temptation of quick success. Although such a choice is possible, Krishna suggests there will always be an inner conflict and a deep and nagging pain. It is possible to choose and succeed in work that does not flow from

---

37. A recent Bollywood movie, *3 Idiots,* comically highlights the family pressures in making career choices.

svabhāva, but there is a price to be paid. There are social costs, as well as inner disharmony. In the case of Arjuna, for example, the social cost is not standing against a tyrannical and unjust rule.

We may understand Krishna's words better through the lives of outstanding proponents for justice like Martin Luther King Jr. (1929–1968) and Mahatma Gandhi. They were both gifted and talented individuals who may have achieved success outside the arena of a risky social and political struggle. It is difficult, however, to imagine that they would be at peace with themselves if they had avoided the field of struggle for justice. Society would be poorer without their struggles. They are luminous examples of human beings who risked and offered their lives to do work of the most demanding kind. Gandhi was born into a caste of merchants and trained as a lawyer. He discovered in South Africa that his work was in the struggle against injustice. In this struggle, he found ways to incorporate his legal training and knowledge.

The choices of Gandhi's sons, however, were limited by his own preferences for them. The freedom in choosing a calling that he exercised was not extended to his sons. As one of Gandhi's biographers put it, "Gandhi wanted a helper; Manilal wanted freedom. He thought of becoming a lawyer or doctor; his father was training him to be a minor saint."[38] Another son, Harilal, openly rebelled against his father, converted to Islam, and became an alcoholic.[39]

Retrieving and Reforming Traditions

Hindu society, like many traditional societies, exemplified the custom of following family occupations. This is understandable in a context of limited choices and the preservation of skills and expertise within families. With the growth and expansion of economic and educational opportunities in India, the tradition of adhering to family occupation is rapidly changing. This is also true in the growing Hindu diaspora in places such as North America, Europe, Africa, and the Caribbean. In this changing context, what resources, ideas, and practices are available to Hindus in choosing callings? Who will Hindus turn to for guidance in making such significant decisions? When one follows the work of the family into which one is born,

38. Louis Fischer, *The Life of Mahatma Gandhi* (New York: Harper & Row, 1983), 94.
39. See Fischer, *Life of Mahatma Gandhi,* 205–14.

there is no struggle with choice. This, however, is no longer the case for most Hindus, who are increasingly making individual choices.

For these Hindus, the tradition offers valuable resources, some of which will have to be interpreted anew in the light of contemporary realities. I have cited several of these in my discussion above, but wish now to make a few concepts more explicit. Prominent among these are the teachings on *svabhāva* and *svadharma*. *Svabhāva* suggests that a meaningful calling must bear some relation to a person's inner disposition and interest. What a person chooses to do should be an expression, ideally, of who she is. This is a valuable idea that should be retrieved by relinquishing the argument that individual disposition is fixed by birth. Freely choosing a calling that is in harmony with one's inner nature is conducive to deeper fulfillment.

In a similar way, the Hindu teaching on *svadharma* must be disconnected from the obligation to perform caste-ordained work. The emphasis must be on choosing and performing callings that are consistent with the public good. *Svadharma* can be linked fruitfully with the Bhagavadgītā's idea of *lokasaṁgraham,* that is, keeping a concern for the universal common good in all that one does. Work that causes suffering to others is not consistent with *svadharma* or *lokasaṁgraham. Svadharma* and *lokasaṁgraham* are not anthropocentrically limited. I believe that a new generation of socially and ecologically conscious Hindus will find this interpretation of *svadharma* appealing and attractive.

Although the concepts of *svabhāva* and *svadharma* are discussed in a sacred text, the Bhagavadgītā, they can serve as guiding values even for those with minimal or no Hindu religious commitment. Identifying deeply with one's calling and having a concern for the universal common good are not limited to persons with religious faith. Both are examples of religious teachings that may inform secular choices and even have value for persons who are not Hindus.

For Hindus seeking to express their religious commitments in choosing and performing work, *svabhāva* may be understood as divine gift (*prasādam*), and the fulfillment of *svadharma* as worship. The Hindu theological understanding of work as worship (*karma yoga*) offers the possibility of spiritualizing work and unifying the meaning of being religious. All that is done for the love of God, in all of life's multiple roles and relationships, become acts of worship. The religious way of being offered by Krishna in the Bhagavadgītā does not call us away from the world or from life in family and community. It invites a transformation of work through an attitude of worshipfully offering all that we do to God (*īśvara arpaṇa buddhi*) and a concern for the common good (*lokasaṁgraham*). The Hindu tradition does not compartmentalize life or distinguish the secular and religious spheres. It offers a spirituality that is neither anti-materialistic nor life denying. This life- and world-affirming understanding of the religious life is a valuable resource for Hindus when interpreting the meaning of religious commitment in contemporary societies.

The Sanskrit term *bhakti,* used to refer to the love of God, is derived from the root *bhaj,* meaning "to attend upon," "to adore," or "to share." In the Hindu tradition, the worshiper of God (*bhakta*) commonly regards herself as the servant (*sevaka*) of God. The Hindu emphasis on divine immanence offers a special way of understanding the meaning of loving and serving God. Care and attentiveness to the needs of others are ways of serving God who is present equally in all beings. This teaching continues to be a deep source of inspiration for Hindus seeking to relate religious teachings to lives of service in the world. It was the inspiration for Swami Vivekananda to found the Ramakrishna Mission with a focus on monks serving the community. In a famous and often-quoted speech at the Rameswaram temple in southern India (1897), Swami Vivekananda spoke of the immanence of God (Shiva) and its significance for our relationships with the needy. "He who sees Shiva in the poor, in the weak and in the diseased, really worships Shiva; and if he sees Shiva only in the image, his worship is but preliminary. He who has served and helped one poor man seeing Shiva in him, without thinking of his caste, or creed, or race, or anything, with him Shiva is more pleased than with the man who sees Him only in temples."[40] Hindu worship, in temple and home, involves hospitality offerings to God consisting of necessities such as water, food, and clothing. Extending such hospitality to needy human beings is certainly a way of serving God that is theologically validated in Hindu teachings.

One of the urgent needs of contemporary Hindu communities is making available to a new generation of Hindus those teachings of the tradition that are central and relevant for decisions about callings. Hindu priests have great expertise in the performance of domestic and temple ritual. Generally, however, they receive little or no theological training and are not expected to function as religious teachers or disseminators of wisdom. The religious teacher (*guru*) is expected to have theological training and is in a better position to guide Hindus in making decisions about choices

40. See Swami Vivekananda, *The Complete Works,* 8 vols. (Calcutta: Advaita Ashrama, 1964–1971), 3:140.

in work. Even so, there is a need for better training of Hindu priests and teachers to offer guidance on such a consequential decision. While many institutions of higher learning offer guidance to students on career and life choices, Hindus cannot leave this matter to such agencies. It is important that Hindus who want to live faithfully in the world from the deepest teachings of their tradition have access to the relevant resources. Hindu temples and leaders need to do more in this regard.

Conclusion

In this discussion, we relied significantly on the teachings of Krishna in the Bhagavadgītā for resources on Hindu teaching about calling. I emphasized his call for infusing all human actions with new meaning by transforming these into worship. Although the Hindu tradition commends particular acts of worship, the aim is to overcome the identification of worship with distinct actions performed only at certain times and places. The intention is to overcome the compartmentalization of human life by discovering the joy and beauty of understanding all roles in life as callings and offering all actions to God.

There are other ways, however, in which Krishna teaches us about callings and especially through his life as narrated in the Bhāgavata Purāṇa.[41] As a child, he is playful, mischievous, and energetic. He is the delight of everyone in his village, reveling in joyful play (*līla*) as an end in itself. The text offers significant descriptive detail about Krishna's relationship with his mother, Yashoda. The special bond between mother and child is highlighted, especially in the intimacy of nursing. "Hari (Krishna) approached his mother as she was churning, desiring to drink her breast milk. He climbed on her lap. Looking at his smiling face, she allowed him to drink from her breast, which was leaking milk from affection."[42]

God is always with Yashoda and she experiences the mystery of God in the most unexpected and ordinary acts between mother and child. The following account is quite typical in the Bhāgavata Purāṇa:

> On one occasion, picking up the child and raising him on to her lap, the beautiful Yasoda suckled him at her lactating breast, full of affection.

41. See *Krishna: The Beautiful Legend of God,* trans. Edwin F. Bryant (London: Penguin, 2003).
42. *Krishna: The Beautiful Legend of God,* 45.

When her son had almost finished drinking, the mother began caressing his sweetly smiling mouth. As he yawned, she saw in there the sky, the sun, the moon, fire, air, the oceans, the continents, the mountains and their daughters (the rivers), the forests, and moving and non-moving living things.[43]

The message is clear. God is always present, and the ordinary and intimate moments of life are occasions when the divine is discovered. Even as Arjuna did not have to leave the field of battle and take monastic vows to find God, Yashoda finds God everywhere in the fulfillment of her calling as a mother and in caring for and playing with her child. If, as the Hindu tradition teaches, we understand God to be present everywhere and we see everything existing in God, God never ceases to be with us. Every act, role, obligation, and relationship occurs within God, becomes possible because of God, and gains ultimate significance through God.

Resources

Ambedkar, B. R. *The Annihilation of Caste*. The Annotated Critical Edition. Edited by S. Anand. London: Verso, 2014.

Davis, Adam, ed. *Hearing the Call across Traditions: Readings on Faith and Service*. Woodstock, VT: Skylights Paths, 2011.

Gandhi, M. K. *The Bhagavad Gita According to Gandhi*. Radford, VA: Wilder Publications, 2012.

Minor, Robert N. *Modern Indian Interpreters of the Bhagavadgita*. Albany: State University of New York Press, 1986.

Organ, T. W. *Hindu Quest for the Perfection of Man*. Columbia, SC: South Asia Books, 1994.

Rambachan, Anantanand. *A Hindu Theology of Liberation*. Albany: State University of New York Press, 2015.

———. *The Hindu Vision*. Delhi: Motilal Banarsidass, 1999.

Sundararajan, K. R., and Bithika Mukherji, eds. *Hindu Spirituality: Post Classical and Modern*. New York: Crossroad, 1997.

Tagore, Rabindranath. *Gitanjali*. Delhi: General Press, 2012.

Vivekananda, Swami. *Karma Yoga: The Yoga of Action*. Mayavati: Advaita Ashrama, 1999.

43. *Krishna: The Beautiful Legend of God*, 39.

6

The Calling of No-Calling

Vocation in Nikaya and Mahayana Buddhism

MARK UNNO

The concept of "calling" may be applicable to Buddhism, but generally not in as straightforward a manner as in other religions due to the nature of Buddhism as a religion, basic assumptions about "calling," and the logic implicit in these assumptions. For instance, calling in the Abrahamic traditions illuminates the relationship between God, a transcendent being, and the followers. Whether understood literally or metaphorically, God is often depicted in personalized terms, making "calling" an ideal term to describe the relationship to the Divine: God "calls" to his believers. The divine-human relationship generally reflects a "two-worlds" worldview, a qualitative difference between God and a Divine realm, on the one hand, and human beings and an earthly, mundane realm, on the other. Calling bridges these two qualitatively different worlds that diverge in the very nature of their existence. In contrast, Buddhism tends to emphasize *awareness* and *awakening,* such as karmic awareness and awakening to no-self, emptiness, and oneness in compassion.

Buddhism, in its roughly 2,500-year history, has had many twists and turns—so many, in fact, that it can be difficult to make generalizations about how Buddhists would generally interpret the idea of "calling." Buddhism's diversity can be compared with the Abrahamic religions in one example. In each of the three Abrahamic traditions, there is significant agreement about central, canonical religious texts: the Hebrew Bible in Judaism, the Old and New Testament in Christianity, and the Qur'an in Islam. Imagine a religion in which there are hundreds of sacred scriptures, all attributed to the same founding figure, and scores of sectarian developments, and equally multitudinous ways about speaking about the nature of reality, with little overall agreement. Such is the case with Buddhism.

Nevertheless, I will draw some broad historical strokes. The historical development of Buddhism can be divided into two large movements: Nikaya Buddhism and Mahayana Buddhism. Nikaya Buddhism is represented in the Nikaya literature, the earliest layer of Buddhist scripture, recorded a few centuries after the passing of the historical Buddha Śākyamuni (ca. sixth–fifth century BCE), focusing on his exploits and the lives of his followers: monks, nuns, and laity. One form of this school remains today: the Theravada, which is found throughout much of South and Southeast Asia, including Sri Lanka, Thailand, and Burma. Mahayana Buddhism, the Buddhism of the "Great Vehicle," is based on scriptures compiled from the beginning of the Common Era onwards and is found in North (Tibet, Nepal, and Mongolia)[1] and East Asia (China, Japan, and Korea).[2] Mahayana Buddhists have referred to followers of the earlier Buddhism as "Hinayana," the "Lesser Vehicle," but as this is a derogatory term, some scholars use the more neutral descriptor, "Nikaya Buddhism."[3]

In the early Buddhism of the Nikaya literature, the center of the stage is largely occupied by Śākyamuni Buddha as a human figure teaching his human followers, both renunciants and laity. He emerges as a figure that has rejected and left behind the Hindu religious order, which includes the structure of society in a hierarchical caste system, overseen by the all-encompassing deity Brahman. The Buddha does not emerge as a divine figure himself, and does not exhort others to follow him based on his personal authority, but rather tells them to serve as "lamps unto themselves," illuminating their realization of the Dharma, or teachings. The path of the Buddha in this early account in some ways represents a rejection of religion, understood theistically. The Buddha responds neither to a god who

1. Buddhism in North Asia—Tibet, Nepal, Mongolia—recognizes a third major development, the Vajrayana, the Diamond Vehicle, above the Mahayana, but in general considers Mahayana the umbrella term.

2. Vietnam, although geographically in Southeast Asia, has been shaped more by Mahayana Buddhism coming from China and elsewhere, rather than Nikaya Buddhism.

3. "Nikaya Buddhism" is a coinage of Professor Masatoshi Nagatomi of Harvard University who suggested it to me as a usage for the eighteen schools of Indian Buddhism, to avoid the term "Hinayana Buddhism," which is found offensive by some members of the Theravada tradition. Robert Thurman, "The Emptiness That Is Compassion: An Essay on Buddhist Ethics," *Religious Traditions* 4, no. 2 (Oct.–Nov. 1981): footnote 10.

calls nor to a singular higher principle, nor does he wield the authority of the divine, as he sought peace and repose in an otherwise tumultuous world filled with suffering.

Mahayana Buddhism, initiated with the compilation of a new set of scriptures that were attributed to the historical Buddha centuries after his passing, consists of hundreds of deities, and numerous world-systems, somewhat like the many galaxies that have been found to populate our physical universe, but each with its own cosmic buddha. Ultimately, cosmic buddhas do not inhabit a different level of being from humans. The nature of everything is said to be "emptiness," devoid of any intrinsic, conceptually identifiable essence. Mahayana Buddhism, adopting forms of logic from Hinduism, operates on the basis of a nondiscursive logic: "both/and," "neither/nor," such that the cosmic buddhas are ultimately empty: they are both personal and impersonal, both exist and do not exist, ultimately neither exist nor do not exist. In a word, reality as such is "beyond words."

One of the largest developments of East Asian Buddhism, Pure Land Buddhism, refers to the "call of Amida Buddha," the cosmic buddha of infinite light. The practitioner of Pure Land Buddhism responds to the "primal vow of Amida," the vow to bring all sentient beings to awakening or enlightenment. Yet, as will become evident, Amida is not a transcendent deity, and shares the nature of emptiness with everything and everyone else: Amida is both personal and impersonal, exists and does not exist, just like the sentient beings that are to be saved by Amida's primal vow. This is, as it were, the call of no-calling, of the voiceless voice.

In Nikaya Buddhism and Mahayana Buddhism, including Pure Land Buddhism, there is no God as a singular, ultimate reality. Buddhism has generally not subscribed to a two-worlds worldview as the theistic religions have. Instead, everything is interrelated, more like a web or net, where a change in any one aspect affects all others. Interrelatedness does not mean that a sense of calling cannot be distilled from the history of Buddhism. Yet, because of the diverse range of practices, conceptions, and deities within Buddhist history, and its vast web of interrelations, the account given here is necessarily selective and episodic. Within the development of both Nikaya and Mahayana Buddhism, specific moments have been chosen to illustrate what in Buddhism might resonate with a sense of calling.

In Nikaya Buddhism, the primary goal or calling is to awaken to the tranquil repose of *nirvana,* and thereby attain liberation, *mokṣa,* from the bonds of suffering in human existence. Secondarily, those who have attained *nirvana* are called to teach others the path to *nirvana*. Three episodes have been selected to illustrate early Buddhist notions of calling: the Buddha's leave-taking on his spiritual quest for awakening, the moment of his awakening and the beginning of his teaching career, and the entry of the Buddha's son Rāhula into the sangha, the monastic community.

In Mahayana Buddhism, the order is reversed: the primary calling is to manifest compassion for all beings in order to bring them to awakening first, and only then attain awakening for oneself. I have selected three episodes to illustrate Mahayana senses of calling: one from the *Vimalakīrti—nirdeśa-sūtra* (The Holy Teaching of Vimalakīrti), involving a lay spiritual teacher; one from the *Liuzu Tanjing* (the Platform Sutra of the Sixth Patriarch) of Chan/Zen Buddhism, describing the transmission of the Dharmaseal of awakening from one Zen master to another; and one from the life of Shinran, the founder of Shin Buddhism, the largest sect of Pure Land Buddhism in Japan, in which he declares himself to be "neither monk nor layman." Before recounting these episodes, however, I will introduce key Buddhist concepts relevant to calling.

Key Teachings

Nikaya Buddhism

Four sets of categories can be helpful to understand the Nikaya literature: the Three Treasures, the Three Baskets of sacred literature, the Four Noble Truths, and the Three Marks of existence.[4]

The Three Treasures are: Buddha, the awakened one; Dharma, the teaching; and Sangha, the community of monks and nuns. The Three Baskets of sacred literature are Sutra, the sayings/teachings of the Buddha; Śāstra, the commentary that explains the teachings of the Buddha; and Vinaya, the rules and regulations governing the Sangha, the monastic community.

The Four Noble Truths are: suffering, cause, end, and path. First, life

---

4. For a more detailed explanation of early Buddhist teachings and categories, see Peter Harvey, *An Introduction to Buddhism: Teachings, History, and Practices* (New York: Cambridge University Press, 1990). Harvey also provides the original vocabulary for various terms in Pali, which is the language of the Nikaya literature.

is filled with suffering, which is, second, caused by human attachment to preconceptions of how things are, or how they should be. Third, there is an end to this suffering that can be attained by following the Eightfold Noble Path, broadly applicable to both renunciants and laity, which includes right thought, right intention, right speech, right action, right livelihood, right effort, right mindfulness, and right concentration.[5] Cultivating this path leads to the purification of karma and the attainment of *nirvana* and awakening. After awakening, this path continues as the expression of the life of enlightenment.

Although there is not room here to explain all eight aspects of the noble path, it is worth highlighting "right livelihood," as it has a direct bearing on calling. It generally means undertaking wholesome and virtuous livelihoods, ones that demonstrate cardinal precepts such as honesty and care for the life of sentient beings, and that are conducive to realizing *nirvana*. It also means avoiding unwholesome livelihoods, in particular those that involve harm to sentient beings and the taking of lives: weapons makers, slave traders and purveyors of prostitution, those who raise and slaughter food-source animals, producers of intoxicants and poisons. The underlying rationale is karmic: livelihoods entailing destructive actions lead to impure karma, taking one further away from enlightenment.

The early Buddhist view of right livelihood brings complications, however. Most people in India ate meat, so that butchers were essential to society, yet they were regarded as karmically impure and inferior. The same is true for weapons makers, who were needed for warriors, who were considered noble. The Buddha himself came from the warrior class. Thus, right livelihood potentially reintroduced a class-based system of karma that the Buddha is said to have rejected.

The Three Marks of Existence are: suffering, impermanence, and no-self. Suffering recapitulates the first of the Four Noble Truths, accentuating its significance. Attachment causes suffering because everything, without exception, is impermanent. According to this view, even the Buddhist teachings will someday disappear, only to reappear in a new form. The heart of the problem for human beings is that the very self is impermanent,

---

5. It is problematic to attribute the Eightfold Noble Path to all Buddhists. Mahayana Buddhists, for example, reject any pan-Buddhist doctrine or dogma as absolute. East Asian Buddhists since the medieval period widely rejected this path also as too "gradual," and instead advocated the path of "sudden awakening." Pure Land Buddhists, in particular Shin Buddhism, rejects the idea that human beings can follow this path, especially in the corrupt age, including ours.

which is to say, there is no eternal essence or soul of any kind, nothing that one can cling to within oneself. Even "life" and "death" are illusory labels that fall away in the attainment of *nirvana*. If one were to place this in the context of "calling," then, the Buddhist is called to seek liberation from the illusory opposition of life and death and to realize that there is no permanent or eternal self, a calling of no-calling from the self of no-self.[6]

Mahayana Buddhism

Mahayana Buddhists continued to use the categories of Nikaya Buddhists but in a more flexible manner. The keys to understanding Mahayana Buddhism can be found in the following three notions: the twofold truth, the bodhisattva ideal, and *upāya-kauśalya* or skillful means.

The twofold truth was articulated by the first philosopher-master of Mahayana Buddhism, Nāgārjuna.[7] It consists of conventional truth and highest truth, which are like two sides of the same coin rather than two separate truths. Often rendered as form and emptiness, respectively, form refers to the world understood through the filter of words and concepts; it is the world understood through the human conventions of language. Emptiness, *śūnyatā*, characterizes the highest truth beyond words. It is reality freed from the divisions and separations imposed by categorical thinking. There is nothing wrong with the categories of language *per se*,

6. Early Buddhists, including Mahayana, are not called to sustain life *per se*. Buddhism is generally not life-affirming (nor life-denying). The goal is awakening and liberation from having to live or having to die (cycle of life and death). Ultimately life and death turn out to be illusory. Human life is specifically cherished, not for its own intrinsic value, but because human beings are well disposed to attaining awakening and liberation. This shows a significant difference between Buddhism and some other religions regarding basic existential assumptions. The precept on not-harming life (*ahimsa*) has more to do with self-contradiction (taking life to sustain one's own) than it does affirmation of life. The real problem is attachment to life, as well as attachment to death. Relative to some other religions, Buddhists may appear to be aloof for these reasons. Buddhists are not detached, but seek to live in nonattachment, since life and death are illusory, not intrinsically real. Ultimately, reality, nirvana, is said to be "unborn" (*asaṃskṛta*) in the sense that "coming into existence" is regarded as illusory.

7. Nāgārjuna, born in present-day Sri Lanka, was a monk of the second or third century. Several treatises are attributed to him, but the main work is the *Fundamental Verses on the Middle Way* (Skt. *Mūla-madhyamika-kārikā*). Nāgārjuna is recognized as the first Mahayana master by all Mahayana schools and sects.

but true awareness of reality beyond words can only be attained by the mind emptied of dogmatic attachments and preconceptions. Once free of dogmatic preconceptions, reality as such (Skt. *tathatā*)[8] discloses itself as a dynamic web of interdependence in which all beings and things coalesce in each moment as a self-expression of the empty cosmos. Phenomena arising in interdependent co-origination (Skt. *pratītya-samudpada*) are the positive expression of emptiness, disclosing the oneness of reality in its vivid unfolding.

Emptiness is similar to no-self, *anatman,* in Nikaya Buddhism, in which the self has no conceptual essence but is nevertheless unfolding dynamically as an impermanent self. However, there is a difference between *anatman* and *śūnyatā.* Nāgārjuna formulated emptiness in part as a criticism of what he perceived to be the dogmatism of the Nikaya Buddhists. While they may have understood that the self is without any conceptual essence, they seemed to him to set up dogmatic orthodoxies concerning the Buddhist teachings, the Dharma. Thus, Nāgārjuna developed the emptiness critique in part to target attachment to religion as much as attachment to self. He warned that one should not even become attached to the concept of "emptiness," and thus taught the "emptiness of emptiness," *śūnyatā-śūnyatā.* In one form or another, virtually all schools of Mahayana Buddhism subscribe to the twofold truth: conventional and highest truth, form and emptiness.

The bodhisattva ideal, in one of its classical formulations, states that the bodhisattva, as a seeker of enlightenment, refuses to attain enlightenment by him or herself unless all other beings first attain enlightenment. The philosophical basis for this lies in emptiness. If the true nature of reality including the self is emptiness, then the true nature of the self is empty of any categorical oppositions: male/female, self/other, human/nonhuman, and so forth. In emptiness, all conceptual distinctions lose their holding power, and the separation created through the use of words and concepts dissolves, thus giving way to the flow of a oneness beyond words. The true nature of the self turns out to be emptiness/oneness in which all beings are inseparable from oneself. In such a view, it makes no sense for one person to attain awakening before everyone else. For the true self to attain awakening, all beings must attain awakening. Putting other

---

8. "Skt." is an abbreviation for "Sanskrit," the language of classical India and of Mahayana Buddhism. The Buddha is said to have spoken in Pali, related to Sanskrit, and the language of the Nikaya scriptures.

beings before oneself, as the bodhisattva is said to do, assures that the seeker of enlightenment does not render an egalitarian view in which one sees oneself as slightly "more equal" than others. The call to bodhisattva-hood, if it can be described as such, is to realize the self of emptiness, which is also the self of oneness with all beings, in which they are all led to liberation from attachment.

Skillful means, or *upāya-kauśalya,* refers to the skillful adaptation of the Dharma beyond words to the specific circumstances of the moment: the varying capacities of practitioners; the changing circumstances of time, place, and culture; and the various factors of diversity for which the Dharma must be adapted. For Mahayana Buddhists, it is more important to be faithful to what they perceived to be the wordless spirit of the Buddha's awakening rather than the literal categories of the Nikaya Buddhists, which may have been appropriate for the time of the historical Buddha but were not suitable for later centuries and other cultures. Yet, even within the Nikaya literature, the Buddha is touted for his ability to adapt his teachings according to the differing capacities of his followers. If the call of bodhisatt-vahood is to become one with all beings in liberation, then skillful means is the wide array of approaches available to this realization.

Narratives of Calling

Nikaya Buddhism

The origin story of the Buddha is well known and widely considered to have a substantial basis in history.[9] Born Siddhartha Gautama (ca. 500–400 BCE) of the Śākya clan in Northern India, he was a member of the *kṣatriya* or warrior class or caste, princely heir to the throne. At the age of twenty-nine he abandoned what would have been his calling within the existing Hindu caste system in favor of an individual quest for awakening. Overly protected within the royal palace where he had spent his entire life, he was overcome with a sense of dis-ease in the face of the illness, old age, and death that awaited him. For six years he wandered among philosophers, ascetics, and various religious teachers in the coalescing *śramaṇa* culture of holy seekers lying outside the boundaries of the traditional caste structure, until at the age of thirty-five, he attained *bodhi,* awakening, and

---

9. See Harvey, *An Introduction to Buddhism,* 9–27.

the realization of an unconditioned truth, *nirvāṇa,* that released him from the continual cycle of rebirth and existence. Thenceforth, he came to be known as Śākyamuni Buddha, the Awakened One, the Sage of the Śākya Clan, and commenced a teaching career that spanned forty-five years until he entered into ultimate *nirvana,* or *parinirvāṇa* (Pali: *parinibbāna*), at the age of eighty.

Although there is no God who calls, one could say that Siddhartha set out on his spiritual journey due to an inner calling rooted in his deep dissatisfaction with life, not from the exhortation of an external authority. His story shares some features of what Kathleen Cahalan describes concerning calling in the Catholic tradition in the sense that there is a special life of sacrifice for which Siddhartha is called. On the one hand, he could be accused of being selfish for abandoning not just his princely status but also his familial obligations: to his father, his wife, and his newborn son. On the other hand, his departure can also be seen as a great sacrifice in the service of a higher religious life. One could imagine that the youthful prince agonized over his decision, that he loved his family and suffered all the more knowing the pain his departure would cause them. He had no assurance that his quest for spiritual peace and repose would ever be fulfilled. He could easily die of injury, illness, or starvation. Yet, he risked everything because he could not suppress his spiritual yearning.

Soon after attaining awakening, the Buddha realized that the illusory bonds of the self had been forever broken and liberation attained:

> Through many a birth in saṃsāra have I wandered in vain, seeking the builder of this house (of self). Repeated birth is indeed suffering! O house-builder, you are seen! You will not build this house again. For your rafters are broken and your ridgepole shattered. My mind has reached the Unconditioned; I have attained the destruction of craving.[10]

He did not then proceed immediately to show others the path to liberation. Rather, his initial thought was to spend the rest of his days in repose and peace, and then attain final *nirvana,* never having to be reborn again. The truth he had awakened to was unconditioned, beyond literal description, and could not easily be taught; in fact, he would likely have to contend with the confusion and misunderstanding of others:

---

10. Acharya Buddharakkhita, trans., *Dhammapada,* verses 153–54, accessed January 7, 2012, http://www.accesstoinsight.org/tipitaka/kn/dhp/dhp.11.budd.html.

When the Blessed One was newly Self-awakened . . . this line of thinking arose in his awareness: "This Dhamma that I have attained is deep, hard to see, hard to realize, peaceful, refined, beyond the scope of conjecture, subtle, to-be-experienced by the wise. . . . For a generation delighting in attachment, . . . this/that conditionality and dependent co-arising are hard to see. This state, too, is hard to see: the resolution of all fabrications, the relinquishment of all acquisitions, the ending of craving; dispassion; cessation; Unbinding. And if I were to teach the Dhamma and if others would not understand me, that would be tiresome for me, troublesome for me."[11]

This doubting about his ability to convey the path of liberation to others is in turn presented as a moment of decision as to the question of the Buddha's calling:

Then Brahmā Sahampati, having known with his own awareness the line of thinking in the Blessed One's awareness, thought: "The world is lost! The world is destroyed! The mind of the Tathagata, the Arahant, the Rightly Self-awakened One inclines to dwelling at ease, not to teaching the Dhamma!" Then, just as a strong man might extend his flexed arm or flex his extended arm, Brahmā Sahampati disappeared from the Brahmā-world and reappeared in front of the Blessed One. Arranging his upper robe over one shoulder, he knelt down with his right knee on the ground, saluted the Blessed One with his hands before his heart, and said to him: "Lord, let the Blessed One teach the Dhamma! Let the One-Well-Gone teach the Dhamma! There are beings with little dust in their eyes who are falling away because they do not hear the Dhamma. There will be those who will understand the Dhamma."

Brahmā Sahampati is a deity that descends to appeal to the Buddha's sense of compassion.[12] An invention of Buddhist writers, this deity in modern terms could be said to represent the Buddha's conscience. In the early Buddhist scriptures, however, it represents the second moment of his calling: the first,

11. Thanissaro Bhikkhu, trans., "Ayacana Sutta," *Samyutta Nikāya* 6.1, accessed January 7, 2012, http://www.accesstoinsight.org/tipitaka/sn/sn06/sn06.001.than.html.

12. This is not *the* Brahman, the all-encompassing deity of Hinduism, but rather one of many possible deities presented as the voice of compassion and conscience. In fact, Sahampati is unknown outside this particular reference, a momentary narrative creation that brings the Buddha's mindset into relief.

to rise up and seek the spiritual path, and the second, to go forth and teach out of compassion for other suffering beings. Spreading his teaching marks the beginning of the sangha, the Buddhist community of monks and nuns.

The third moment of calling involves his son Rāhula. As mentioned earlier, when Siddhartha Gautama renounced his status as prince and set out as a wandering seeker, he had already been married and had a child, a baby boy named Rāhula.[13] Thus, he abandoned not only his princely calling but also his calling as husband and father. Years after he attained awakening and became the Buddha, he returned to the Śākya Kingdom when his son was a full-grown adult. Inspired by the spiritual presence of his father, Rāhula declared that he, too, wished to renounce his status as princely heir to the throne to join his father's sangha. The Buddha's father King Śuddhodana (Pali: Suddhodana), by now elderly, strongly objected; he had already lost his son, and to lose his only grandson was too much to bear. The Buddha insisted, however, that his son's wishes be respected and that he be allowed to join the sangha. Yet, recognizing his father's anguish, he told the king that he would grant any wish that he could fulfill, other than returning the grandson Rāhula. King Śuddhodana then made one request, which the Buddha granted, became codified in the *vinaya,* and still holds true in many Buddhist cultures today: If a son wishes to become a Buddhist monk, then he must receive the permission of his parents.[14] In today's world, this often extends to parents of other faiths or normative commitments. For example, if a man wishes to renounce his social ties and become a Buddhist monk, and his Christian parents object, then there are Buddhist orders that will not ordain him because it goes against the *vinaya.* Thus, the suffering of the king, as father and grandfather, was transformed into compassion for the suffering of other parents (and grandparents).

In these stories of early Buddhism, we thus find at least three kinds of calling: the calling to seek enlightenment in the renunciant path of a monk or a nun, the calling to teach other renunciants the path to awakening, and the calling to extend compassion and the teachings to laypeople. All three kinds of calling can also be found in Mahayana Buddhism, but the Mahayana brings into view a whole other set of concerns including types and dimensions of calling, the status of lay versus ordained, and the dissolution of core categories for defining Buddhism as a "religion."

13. See, for example, Bhikkhu Bodhi, "The Buddha and His Dhamma," accessed March 6, 2015, http://www.accesstoinsight.org/lib/authors/bodhi/wheel433.html.

14. Richard F. Gombrich, *What the Buddha Thought* (London: Equinox, 2009), 177.

Mahayana Buddhism

Whereas early Buddhism emphasized *anātman*, no-self, as the lack of any fixed, essential conception of selfhood, Mahayana emptiness extended this to all phenomena, negating the reification of all concepts, including religious dogma, even emptiness itself. Philosophically, this was intended to dissolve barriers and oppositions, including those involving religious hierarchies of ecclesiastical status and gender. While historically the male monkhood continued to dominate Buddhist institutions into modern times, ideologically the Mahayana reflects a movement away from the monastery-centered perspective toward a more lay-oriented ideal.

The following three narratives provide a sampling of what might be considered calling in the Mahayana scriptures: one from the *Vimalakīrti— nirdeśa-sūtra* (The Holy Teaching of Vimalakīrti),[15] that of the illness of Vimalakīrti the merchant; an episode of the illiterate woodcutter from the *Liuzu Tanjing* (Platform Sutra of the Sixth Patriarch)[16] of Chan (Jpn. Zen) Buddhism; and an autobiographical moment from the life of Shinran, the founder of Shin Buddhism, the largest sect of Japanese Pure Land.

The Holy Teaching of Vimalakīrti, an early Mahayana sutra that was likely composed in the first couple of centuries of the common era, became widely read and influential, especially in East Asia, and is cited by various schools of Buddhism including Faxiang (Skt. Yogācāra) and Chan/Zen. It begins with Śākyamuni Buddha instructing his disciples go pay their respects to a lay bodhisattva named Vimalakīrti, a merchant, a householder, and a family man. He has fallen ill, and the Buddha is sending his disciples to wish him well. They refuse, however, complaining that Vimalakīrti always exposes their deficient understanding. Finally, Mañjuśrī, the wisest of the bodhisattvas, agrees to go, and the others follow him to Vimalakīrti's residence. There, after conveying his sympathies, Mañjuśrī asks Vimalakīrti a series of questions that Vimalakīrti answers from the standpoint of emptiness. Finally, Mañjuśrī asks him about his illness.[17]

MAÑJUŚRĪ: Householder, of what sort is your sickness?
VIMALAKĪRTI: It is immaterial and invisible.

15. Robert A. F. Thurman, trans., *The Holy Teaching of Vimalakirti* (University Park: Pennsylvania State University Press, 1987).
16. Philip Yampolsky, trans., *The Platform Sutra of Hui-neng* (New York: Columbia University Press, 1967), 125–53.
17. Thurman, *Vimalakirti*, 44.

MAÑJUŚRĪ: Is it physical or mental?

VIMALAKĪRTI: It is not physical, since the body is insubstantial in itself. It is not mental, since the nature of the mind is like illusion.

MAÑJUŚRĪ: Householder, which of the four main elements is disturbed—earth, water, fire, or air?

VIMALAKĪRTI: Mañjuśrī, I am sick only because the elements of living beings are disturbed by sicknesses.

MAÑJUŚRĪ: Householder, how should a bodhisattva console another bodhisattva who is sick?

VIMALAKĪRTI: He should tell him that the body is impermanent, but should not exhort him to renunciation or disgust. He should tell him that the body is miserable, but should not encourage him to find solace in liberation; that the body is selfless, but that living beings should be developed; that the body is peaceful, but not to seek any ultimate calm. He should urge him to confess his evil deeds, but not for the sake of absolution. He should encourage his empathy for all living beings on account of his own sickness, his remembrance of suffering experienced from beginningless time, and his consciousness of working for the welfare of living beings. . . . Thus should a bodhisattva console a sick bodhisattva, in such a way as to make him happy.

In their exchange, Vimalakīrti tells Mañjuśrī that the suffering of all beings is the source of his own suffering, such that his illness is his expression of emptiness, oneness, and great compassion.

While Vimalakīrti is a fictional, idealized character, it is not as if he is merely depicted as a seamless, superhuman figure. Particularly in the last statement cited above, Vimalakīrti describes what it means to abide both in the highest reality of emptiness/oneness and this world of vicissitudes: that to live the truth of emptiness is in fact to live in the very depths of this suffering world itself.

For example, one should be aware of the inherent instability of embodied existence and its attendant ills; yet, one should not retreat into a solipsistic meditative state: "He should tell him that the body is miserable, but should not encourage him to find solace in liberation." Implied in this is a criticism of early Buddhist monasticism and its retreat into renunciation and solitary meditation. Rather, one should balance living in this world of suffering with having one's center in the depths of meditative tranquility.

One should be aware that "body" is merely a social construction, a human convention, and does not actually exist in any reifiable sense; nevertheless, one should honor and respect the empirical body as the conduit to awakening: "The body is selfless, but . . . living beings should be developed." That is, the process of religious awakening involves the transformation of consciousness, from a view of the body as "real," something that is the possession and "property" of the ego self, to a view of the body as an open conduit of compassion to the human and larger sentient community.

The realization of emptiness gives rise to the awareness of others' suffering as inseparable from one's own, and the unfolding of great compassion in bodhisattva service: "He should encourage his empathy for all living beings on account of his own sickness, his remembrance of suffering experienced from beginningless time, and his consciousness of working for the welfare of living beings."

In this Mahayana vision, the bodhisattva ideal is based on the loosening of conceptual boundaries and the realization of oneness through compassion. As such, religious calling comes not at the behest of a transcendent absolute but arises from profound suffering immanent to life itself; this is the impetus behind the bodhisattva vow. Vimalakīrti also represents an inversion of the prior monasto-centric hierarchy. He is a layman, a family man, a lowly merchant; he enters into places of commerce, drinking establishments, homes of friends and family, but he is not perturbed, does not lose his equanimity or composure. Ordinary daily life becomes the realization of the inseparability of *samsara* and *nirvana,* the life of vicissitudes and the truth that liberates. Yet, this does not mean he is unfeeling or detached. His *modus operandi* is *nonattachment,* neither attachment nor detachment, in which the karmic awareness of the suffering of others becomes Vimalakīrti's own, only to be transformed into great compassion.

Above all, the fact of Vimalakīrti's illness illustrates the bodhisattva ideal of Mahayana Buddhism: He refuses to be liberated from suffering until all beings attain liberation. Vimalakīrti the layman represents a philosophical overturning of the earlier Buddhist monastic hierarchy, displacing it with a demonstration of bodhisattva compassion. Vimalakīrti, along with other characters of early Mahayana literature, began to emerge around the first or second centuries.

In turning to the episode of the illiterate woodcutter from the Platform Sutra of Huineng, a Chan/Zen Buddhist scripture likely compiled during the eighth century, we find another such overturning. The protagonist of the Platform Sutra is an illiterate woodcutter who is a "southern barbarian," a trope for the uneducated and uncultured.[18] One day, on one of his work errands, he hears a monk reciting verses from the Diamond Sutra and, immediately inspired, seeks out the monk's master Hongren, the Fifth Patriarch, or fifth-generation Chan master as counted from the founder Bodhidharma. Hongren tells the young woodcutter that he cannot become a monk as he is uncultured and illiterate, but entreated by the aspirant, allows that he can be a servant of the temple, preparing firewood and engaging in other manual tasks; already at this point, Hongren glimpses the woodcutter's superior realization. As Hongren is also preparing to retire, he must name a successor. To make a long story short, it is the illiterate woodcutter who demonstrates his keen intuition and superior wisdom. Deciding that the woodcutter is the one capable of becoming his true successor, Hongren bestows him with the Dharma name Huineng (wise and capable), and presents him with the transmission of the seal of awakening in the form of his robe and begging bowl.

However, Hongren knows that this will cause problems. His monks will be incited to jealousy and raise objections. He instructs Huineng to escape at night and stay out of sight, and only much later reemerge to take the Dharma throne as the Sixth Patriarch after things have calmed down. Although he follows his master's instructions, Hongren's monks eventually find out and go in pursuit of Huineng. Finally, one of the monks by the name of Huiming catches up to him and demands the return of the bowl. Huineng points out that Huiming is not really after the bowl, that his true desire is for genuine awakening, and guides Huiming to realization. Huiming departs gratefully, leaving Huineng unharmed. Huineng lives for some years in the woods, suffering from isolation, deprivation, and difficult circumstances. Along the way he instructs hunters and others he encounters, and finally emerges to take his rightful place as the Sixth Patriarch.

Here again, there is an implicit criticism of the monastic intellectual elite. An illiterate woodcutter turns out to be more enlightened than all of the monks who have been engaged in Buddhist practice for many years. Yet, when they pursue him out of their jealousy, Huineng does not criticize them or put them in their place; instead, he compassionately brings Huiming to his own awakening. Unlike Vimalakīrti, however, Huineng does become a monk and is in fact anointed as the Sixth Patriarch. This brings us closer to the historical reality of Mahayana Buddhism, which

---

18. Yampolsky, *The Platform Sutra*, 126–35.

for all its scriptural valorization of laity and women continued for most of its history to place great importance on male Buddhist masters and their institutional authority.

The third episode of calling in Mahayana Buddhism is taken from the life of Gutoku Shinran (1173–1262). He was the founder of Jōdo Shinshū, known as Shin Buddhism in the West, which became the largest sect of Japanese Pure Land Buddhism. Whereas in Zen Buddhism, the central practice is seated meditation, in Shin Buddhism, the central practice is the invoking or chanting of the Name of Amida Buddha. The Name consists of the six-syllable phrase, Namu Amida Butsu, which is a transliteration of the Sanskrit, Namō Amitābha Buddha, meaning, "I bow and entrust myself to the Buddha of Infinite Light." The "Namu" or "I" in this case refers to the practitioner who is filled with the blind passion of attachments. "Amida Butsu" refers to the manifestation of emptiness as infinite light or illumination. Since the illumination of emptiness is a dynamic unfolding from moment to moment, the Name might be better rendered, "I entrust myself to the awakening of infinite light." The repetitive invoking of this name is a kind of contemplative practice, but because it arises from emptiness, the chanting of the Name is said to arise not from the ego's own self power but from "other power," meaning the power that is other than ego, or the true nature of the self as emptiness. A respected lay Shin Buddhist teacher from the modern period, Wariko Kai, composed a poem that expresses this well. She states,

> Mihotoke no na wo yobu waga koe wa
> Mihotoke no ware wo yobimasu mikoe nari keri

> The voice with which I call Amida Buddha
> Is the voice which Amida calls to me.

This is the voiceless voice of the boundless compassion of emptiness arising to embrace and dissolve the foolish attachments of the practitioner. Thus, we have here a genuine sense of calling, yet because of being based in emptiness, it is a calling of no-calling.

As Shinran states, Amida Buddha turns out to be *upāya,* a skillful means of leading the practitioner to compassionate liberation from the bonds of attachment, just like Vimalakīrti's illness, and the illiterate wood-cutter showing the learned monks the path to awakening. According to Shinran,

What is called the unsurpassed Buddha has no form. Due to having no form, it is called the spontaneous dharma-nature [*jinen hōni*]. . . . We learn to listen deeply [to the voiceless voice of] Amida in order to be led to the awareness of formlessness. Amida Buddha is the skillful means for us to realize [this formless] spontaneity. . . . One should not be constantly thinking about this matter of spontaneity. If one thinks about this spontaneity too much, one will take the meaning of what has no meaning [i.e., emptiness], and turn it into something that appears to have [some specific] meaning. This is the inconceivable buddha-wisdom.[19]

Shin Buddhism arose in medieval Japan as a lay-centered movement, outside the control of the established sects. As it gained popularity, it posed a threat to the established ecclesiastical authorities, and they were successful in petitioning the Japanese emperor to defrock and banish its leaders, including Shinran who was exiled into the countryside. He had broken protocol by openly marrying, having children, and working along with his wife Eshinni, who took a nun's name, wore robes, and worked as Shinran's partner in ministering to peasants in outlying regions.

At the very end of his main philosophical work, Shinran states, "Thus, I was neither monk nor layman."[20] This was a historical statement describing his situation as an outlaw monk living like a layman. In addition, it was a statement of Mahayana philosophy, going beyond the false distinction between clerics and laity. Furthermore, it can be taken as Shinran's own confession as a foolish being filled with attachment, unworthy to be regarded as a good monk or a good layman, and *thereby* embraced, illuminated, and dissolved into the flow of boundless compassion and infinite light. This final statement is reflective of Shinran's entire life, called by Amida Buddha from the depths of his own being, and like so many episodes in Mahayana Buddhism, upsetting the apple cart of conventional religious expectations.

Practices Sustaining Calling of No-Calling

In the West, in particular in Europe and North America, the image of Buddhism has been closely associated with seated meditation including

---

19. Shinran, *Mattōshō*, in *Shinran chosaku zenshū* (*SCZ*), ed. Daiei Kaneko (Kyoto: Hōzōkan, 1964), 587.

20. Shinran, *Kyōgyōshinshō*, in *SCZ*, 340.

participation in workshops and retreats held at Buddhist centers. Historically and into the present, the vast majority of Asian Buddhists have not engaged in seated meditation and associated yogic practices. For laity, contemplative practice is much more likely to take the form of chanting the Name of Amida Buddha, other cosmic buddhas, or prayers that invoke a range of Buddhist deities. While monastics continue to wield a great deal of institutional authority, lay teachers and practitioners, men and women, have also played prominent roles in contexts other than yogic practice.

In the US, Buddhists constitute about 1 percent of the population, and among them, there are more lay-based movements—such as Shin Buddhism and Soka Gakkai International, with their central practices invoking cosmic buddhas, bodhisattvas, and scriptures through chanting their names—than those movements that rely on some form of seated meditation practice and related practices derived from monastic traditions, such as Zen, Tibetan Vajarayana, and Vipassana-based mindfulness. However, in the US, even in the case of teachers coming from monastic traditions, most of the American teachers have not been celibate, with the majority married or in committed partnerships. In some Asian cultures, such as Japan, the majority of priests are married even in monastic traditions such as Zen, but in monastically derived traditions, they will have trained for some time in single-sex monasteries or convents, anywhere from six months to several decades.

While in Asia, there are Buddhist temples, in the US, there are both temples and "centers," the latter a Western innovation, in which there are usually just a handful of full-time religious teachers in residence, and laypeople participate in weekly, monthly, and other periodic services, workshops, and retreats. These centers tend to be based on models of individual practice with some degree of community, and centers are often run entrepreneurially to attract and cultivate followers. A particular feature of these centers is that they are mixed-gender, unlike Buddhist monasteries in Asia that are segregated similarly to Catholic monasteries and convents. Sexual scandals involving Buddhist teachers and their students, especially involving the abuse of religious authority, have been of particular concern in the mixed-gender setting of American Buddhist "centers" (although such scandals have not been limited to heterosexual relations).

The part-time center participation model stands in contrast with ethnic Asian "temples." These ethnic temples are generally community-based, with weekly services but many other group activities throughout the week such as study classes, Buddhist choir practice, and sports clubs. As an example, in Japanese American Shin Buddhist temples in the early-to mid-twentieth century, members donated to their temples upwards of 50 percent of their often extremely modest household incomes, and the ministers themselves were sustained purely by *dāna,* or religious donations. In turn, the temples functioned almost like extended families that provided all manner of spiritual and material support to families in need. In effect, the temple members, although lay, necessarily lived lives of renunciation with the religious life as the core. This is no longer the case as temple ministers have become modestly salaried, and youth leave for college and/or work, often never returning to the temples.

There is a relatively small yet growing percentage of Shin temples that have become ethnically and racially more diverse, sometimes incorporating aspects of both "temple" and "center" cultures. In terms of "calling," early ethnic temples were more communal, with members called in service to temple life, and centers more individualistic in the way each practitioner is called to practice, following the beat of his or her own drum, with consequently higher turnover rates in terms of center participation.

Calling versus Career

Buddhism in the contemporary US faces particular challenges, especially in relation to the center model, of which teacher-student sexual concerns is only one example. More generally, the combination of intensive meditation practice, including retreats of a week or more, on the one hand, and the demands of lay life, on the other, can be especially stressful. The traditional system of monastic training was not designed to facilitate the transition back-and-forth between the hustle and bustle of lay life and the deep quietude of the intensive retreat setting. As Willoughby Britton has documented, the result is often difficulty both in transition and in the practice itself, with a number of students falling into disturbing mental states as a result.[21]

The renunciant path of monastics looks very different from the life of laity, despite exemplars depicted in sacred writings such as Vimalakīrti the

---

21. Willoughby Britton, "Meditation Nation," *Tricycle,* accessed June 28, 2015, http://www.tricycle.org/trikedaily/meditation-nation.

layman; the path of yogic practice that involves far more than seated med-itation is not for the faint of heart. One way of understanding the complex-ity faced by those who feel called to the life of intensive Buddhist practice in the West is to place it in the larger context of the work of religious calling versus the work carried out in one's career.

The life of religious calling for a monk or a nun in principle entails renunciation of mundane desires—for family, material success, social sta-tus, and the like. Alms-begging, a practice common to monks and nuns in much of Asia, is emblematic of this renunciation. In Japan, for exam-ple, Zen monks are not even allowed to touch alms with their hands but extend their *kesa,* a cloth mantle symbolic of their entire robes, heads bowed, to receive *ofuse* (Skt. *dāna*) in humility. Moreover, these alms are not their own to keep individually but used to sustain the entire monastic community.[22]

In contemporary American culture, such a way of life would amount to the renunciation of a career that entails self-promotion, the search for social recognition, and the accrual of wealth. Yet, the life of alms-begging is not really possible for even monks in the US, since we do not live in a culture that recognizes alms-begging as a culturally acceptable practice.

If the ideal of the life of a monk or a nun is based on renunciation, the career of a contemporary layperson is based on acquisition: the proactive accumulation of all forms of symbolic capital—social and material—that constitutes a significant marker of success. Unlike monks and nuns in the vision of traditional Asian Buddhist cultures, Buddhists in the US live and work in a culture defined by individual entrepreneurship. It is difficult to sustain a Buddhist center or career as a Buddhist teacher without self-promotion through social media, charging fees for workshops and retreats, and active recruitment of students and followers. Contemporary Asian Buddhist monks, nuns, and priests have also had to develop similar strat-egies, and it is not as if they did not actively pursue the accumulation of symbolic capital within their traditional, premodern contexts. However, there are significant differences between traditional Asian ideals of reli-gious calling and the way that Buddhist practice has come to be promoted in the contemporary US and in the West generally.

---

22. In actual practice, monks in Japan have other sources of income, such as "dona-tions" (Jpn. *ofuse*) received for performing funeral and memorial services. The example of alms-begging is simply given to illustrate the principle of renunciation, not the historical reality.

Three examples help to illustrate the complex intersection of calling and career for contemporary American Buddhists. One comes from an interview with Grace McLeod (1907–2006), a pioneering lay Buddhist who helped to nurture Shin Buddhist temples through many efforts, including creation of English-language teaching materials in the early- to mid-twentieth century. Another comes from a question posed to His Holiness the Fourteenth Dalai Lama, Tenzin Gyatso (b. 1935), on the occasion of his special lecture at the University of Oregon in 2013, regarding the balance between work and religious life. The third is taken from the life of author, feminist, and social activist Natalie Goldberg (b. 1948), and her attempt to negotiate her life as a writer and her devotion to Zen Buddhist practice.

Born in Anacortes, in Washington State, and raised Catholic, Grace McLeod encountered Japanese Buddhists in her twenties in the Seattle area and converted to Buddhism in 1948 along with her husband Hugh McLeod.[23] Although little known outside of her own circle of associations, she made major contributions to Buddhism internationally. Streams of prominent Buddhist teachers from high-ranking Tibetan lamas to Zen masters visited her in Seattle as she produced volumes of teaching materials for American Buddhists before it became popularized in the 1960s and 1970s. For nearly four decades, several of her publications were circulated to all of the Shin Buddhist temples in the US.

McLeod was in her seventies when the Sixteenth Karmapa, one of the highest-ranking Tibetan lamas, came to visit her from his renowned Rumtek monastery in Sikkim in North India. He asked her to visit him there, saying, "I have work for you." When she eventually arrived, he introduced her to the nuns there, calling her their "mother." In time, she helped to establish an international Buddhist convent in Sikkim, helping to raise the funds almost single-handedly. Gail Kaminishi, herself a long-time contributor to Seattle Betsuin temple and American Shin Buddhism, said of Grace, "She is truly like a bodhisattva, very committed to being in this world, helping others when and how she can."[24]

One wonders about the lack of wider recognition for McLeod's work,

23. The following account of Grace McLeod's life is taken from: Keith Ervin, "Grace McLeod, World Traveller, Potent Advocate for Buddhism," *The Seattle Times,* August 27, 2006, accessed July 2, 2015, http://community.seattletimes.nwsource.com/archive/?date =20060827&slug=mcleodobit27m; and Sienna Craig, "Under the Magnolia Tree: Days with Grace McLeod," unpublished essay, 2006.

24. Craig, "Under the Magnolia Tree," 3.

but she herself seemed to prefer it that way: "The problem," she said, "is that Western Buddhists have such a hard time not being proud of the teachings they receive, even though this is counter-intuitive."[25]

For McLeod, her calling to be a Buddhist was to be without ego, which comes very close to the meaning of Buddhist "no-self" and "emptiness." Since the passing of her husband Hugh in 1978, Grace had lived mostly alone, had very few needs or possessions other than her modest early twentieth-century home in Seattle, and, in many ways, had become like one of the nuns she had helped so much. Her Buddhist way of life was especially remarkable considering that she became a Buddhist when it was not fashionable, indeed when it made her the friend and ally of an oppressed ethnic, racial, and religious minority. Her life was one of calling, albeit a calling of no-calling, as it arose from no-self, non-ego, and returned quietly to no-self and to vast emptiness.

Grace's comment about Western Buddhists having "such a hard time not being proud" was directed, not so subtly, at the individualistic, self-promoting, entrepreneurial character of the many Western Buddhists she had encountered, especially in recent decades. While this criticism certainly seems valid, one could argue that it can be difficult to maintain and develop Buddhist centers in the US without this entrepreneurialism, without fee-based retreat centers, advertisements in *Tricycle: The Buddhist Review,* Buddhist center–related businesses such as organic eateries, paraphernalia stores, and the like. At what point does the life of a Buddhist teacher cease to be a life of religious calling and become a career? Can the two coexist, or are they mutually incompatible? These questions also arise for lay Buddhists, as the next episode shows.

After nine years of cooperative planning between Maitripa Tibetan Buddhist College in Portland, Oregon; the Eugene Sakya Center; and the University of Oregon (UO), His Holiness the Fourteenth Dalai Lama arrived for one afternoon lecture presented to a packed audience of 12,000 at Matthew Knight Arena at the UO, along with events at our partner institutions. After concluding his presentation on "The Path to Peace and Happiness in the Global Society," for which the Dalai Lama received a long, standing ovation, he responded to three pre-taped video questions from those who were in attendance. One was from Jennifer Burton, staff member at the UO Center for Multicultural Academic Excellence:

25. Craig, "Under the Magnolia Tree," 9.

Sometimes in professional life aggressiveness and self-centeredness are rewarded more than compassion and care for others. Since it is not possible because of financial and family obligations for the average person to withdraw from the professional world, how can people be altruistic and maintain *bodhicitta,* the aspiration for enlightenment, and still thrive in their jobs?[26]

The response from the Dalai Lama was brief yet to the point,

> In order to help others more effectively, . . . to help other . . . people, first you yourself [must] be healthy. If you, yourself [are] sick, then how [can you] care for other sick people? . . . So, in order to help other people, you yourself must be fit, . . . including economic condition [finances]. . . . Balanced with sense of concern [for] others' well-being.

This exchange is telling, both in terms of the question and the answer. The question went to the heart of the problematic intersection of calling and career. The answer addressed the need to develop spiritual resources and a balanced approach. Jennifer Burton, identifying herself with the Buddhist teachings, was asking how one could be giving and selfless when career and job often seemed to require self-promotion and selfishness. The Dalai Lama's response did not directly answer her question. Instead, he seemed to suggest that one must be spiritually and financially robust enough (healthy enough) to be able to give to others, and that one must balance concern for others with concern for self.

Religions including Buddhism often tout virtues such as generosity, unselfishness, love and compassion for others, that is, a life of renunciation that entails abandoning selfish concerns in order to cultivate a life of religious virtue. Yet, as Burton indicates, success in lay society often entails competition and self-promotion, a point that is especially poignant for her, as she advocates for minority students whose needs go unrecognized, and voices unheard.

For laypeople who spend a large proportion of their time at work, and attempt to derive meaning from it, a meaningful career is difficult to disentangle from success in a competitive marketplace. Unselfishness can

26. The Fourteenth Dalai Lama, Tenzin Gyatso, "The Path to Peace and Happiness in the Global Society," University of Oregon, May 10, 2013, accessed July 2, 2015, https://www .youtube.com/watch?v=LW42SqUqbjM, 1.12.33.

be an important virtue in the workplace, but being a good team player or listing volunteer work on one's resumé is of a completely different order of unselfishness from Buddhist no-self or the realization of emptiness. The former is often based in self-interest, the latter in non-self.

In the context of calling and career, the Dalai Lama's response may be understood in at least two ways. (1) One must have enough in reserve—spiritually, emotionally, materially—to be able to give without suffering compassion fatigue. (2) For laypeople, it is unreasonable to renounce personal desires for self, family, and friends. Instead, one needs to strike a balance between one's calling as a Buddhist and one's work and career that entail some degree of selfishness, including the job of simply feeding one's family. The balance between life in society that is necessarily competitive, on the one hand, and a life of Buddhist calling that entails renunciation of personal desires and socially defined success, on the other, continues as a prominent theme in the following episodes, taken from a memoir by Natalie Goldberg, writer and Zen Buddhist practitioner.

Best-selling author Natalie Goldberg recounts her path to becoming a writer as well as Zen Buddhist practitioner in her memoir, *A Long Quiet Highway*. Both are presented as paths that take one deep into the truth of the self. Even her Zen master Dainin Katagiri seems to think the writing life can be a practice like Zen Buddhism:

> "Make writing your practice," Roshi [my master] told me.
> "Oh, no, I can't. My brain," I pointed to my head, "I can't shut it up."
> "If you commit to it, writing will take you as deep as Zen," he told me.[27]

Eventually, Katagiri tells her she will have to make a decision: Choose writing or Zen.

> Once I went to Roshi when I lived in Minnesota and told him, "When I'm at Zen center, I feel like a writer. When I'm with writers, I feel like a Zen student."
> "Someday you will have to choose. You're not ready yet, but someday you will be. Writing and Zen are parallel paths, but not the same."
> We never spoke about it again. I continued to write; I continued to sit [in meditation practice at Zen center].

27. Natalie Goldberg, *A Long Quiet Highway: Waking Up in America* (New York: Bantam Books, 1993), 183.

Three months after I finished [composing *Writing Down the*] *Bones,* I went camping alone one weekend in August by the Chama River. . . .

I made breakfast of brown rice and roasted nuts over a fire and then packed up. . . . Pink cliffs shot up from the dry desert to my left and the Chama River and its valley spread out to my right.

I'd gone about three miles when suddenly I burst out crying. . . . I repeated over and over: "I chose being a writer. I chose being a writer. I chose being a writer," and sobbed and sobbed. Before that moment I had no idea that that question had been working in me so deeply. . . .

Why did I have to choose? I don't know if we do really choose. Eventually, I think something chooses us and we shut up, surrender, and go with it. And the difference between Zen and writing? In writing you bring everything you know into writing. In Zen you bring everything you know into nothing, into the present moment where you can't hold onto anything.[28]

As a woman and a Jew growing up in places and at a time when she felt displaced in the dominant culture, writing was a way for Goldberg to find her voice, to establish her identity in society, in the world of form. Zen practice was her way of going deep within, connecting with her deepest, truest self, which for her was the self of emptiness and oneness with everyone and everything. Writing and Zen were close but not the same. Writing was a way to bring her depth out into the world; Zen was a way of freeing herself from the oppressive world and finding her true self, beyond words. Writing became a meaningful career for Goldberg, but she would likely object to the characterization of her writing life as a "career." It carries a much deeper meaning for her than what is usually thought of as a successful career, one that brings financial success and social status.

Neither Goldberg nor Katagiri ever make clear why she had to choose Zen or writing. Goldberg continued her Zen practice even as she chose the path of writing, so the choice was not to eliminate one in favor of the other. Rather, the decision seemed to be a matter of commitment. One cannot truly deepen one's practice unless one commits to a vehicle that will take one to greater realization. It can be likened to the fact that it is very difficult to become a virtuoso violinist and pianist at the same time; you can play both, but you have to commit to one.

Still, writing as a path and Zen as a path are not the same in the way

28. Goldberg, *A Long Quiet Highway,* 190–92.

that becoming a violinist or a pianist might be regarded. Writing is an inherently social activity, an act of human communication that entails some degree of competitive success. It just wouldn't have been the same if no one bought Goldberg's books, attended her writing workshops, or followed her on Facebook, validating her voice, "I'm here, and people recognize my existence." Of course, one can be recognized as an accomplished Buddhist practitioner, but many great Buddhists go nameless, their virtue inconspicuous. Nevertheless, Katagiri tells Goldberg that writing can take her as deep as Zen practice, that it can be a kind of Buddhist practice without carrying that label: "If you commit to it, writing will take you as deep as Zen." The art, discipline, or vehicle itself is not as significant as one's commitment.

Whether going from form to emptiness deep in Zen practice, or from emptiness to form bringing the depths out into the light of day in writing practice, as human beings both Katagiri and Goldberg have to live in society (form) but aspire not to be defined by it (emptiness). In fact, both Katagiri and Goldberg end up being Zen practitioners and writers, each publishing books, each getting married, each continuing Zen practice throughout their lives, each needing students to be teachers of their art. The life of a writer and that of a Zen teacher are vastly different, but also not so different, according to Goldberg and Katagiri, if one goes deep enough into either one. Both carry dimensions of calling and of career, each path with its need for social recognition, and equal aspiration to be free of this need. It could be that both "writer" and "Zen master" as defined by the voices in *A Long Quiet Highway* contain profound self-contradictions that are embedded in their respective paths, and possibly in human life itself.

The Dalai Lama takes a view similar to Katagiri, that the choice of the path itself is less significant than the commitment to cultivate it, whether Buddhist or non-Buddhist, or even religious or nonreligious. Of his consistent emphasis on compassion as the basis for genuine human existence, he states, "I am convinced that everyone can develop a good heart and a sense of universal responsibility with or without religion."[29] In this sense, a specifically religious sense of calling is less significant for these Buddhist teachers than a clear view of human life and death, and a truth that is free from ideological attachments.

---

29. The Fourteenth Dalai Lama, Tenzin Gyatso, "Nobel Peace Prize Acceptance Speech," accessed July 3, 2015, http://www.dalailama.com/messages/acceptance-speeches/nobel-peace-prize.

Conclusion

As can be seen from the discussion above, there are a number of ways in which dimensions of Abrahamic conceptions of calling resonate with Buddhist notions. At the same time, there are significant differences. In a view of selfhood that emphasizes no-self, emptiness, and great compassion, it may be more significant to think about what is most helpful for a given person within the context of the moment, than about any one specific aspect of their life, including religious calling or even religious identity. Or, one might say, religious calling can be an important component of considering what can be said and done for a person given the karmic limitations and possibilities of the moment.

Making one's faith explicit seems foundational to a life of religious calling in the Abrahamic traditions. As an example, for a Christian, being called to faith in Christ can be the most defining moment of the formation of their religious identity. In contrast, to be a real Buddhist, it may be necessary to forget that one is a "Buddhist." The path to being Buddhist, to realizing no-self, can be understood as forgetting the self, loosening the boundaries between self and other, Buddhist and non-Buddhist, religious and nonreligious. According to the Zen Master Dōgen (1200–1253), "To study the Buddha Way is to study the self. To study the self is to forget the self."[30] Or, as the Vietnamese monk, socially and environmentally engaged activist Thich Nhat Hanh states, "The way of nonattachment from views is the basic teaching of Buddhism. . . . We are determined not to be idolatrous about or bound to any doctrine, theory, or ideology, even Buddhist ones. Buddhist teachings are guiding means [*upāya*] to help us learn to look deeply and to develop our understanding and compassion."[31]

"Calling" can be a helpful category for thinking about the life of a Buddhist, but it is not a primary concept in the way it might be for Abrahamic religions. Especially in Mahayana Buddhism, it can be seen as one component within a larger, fluid, contextual view of empty Buddhist teachings as *upāya* or skillful means. This consideration of calling in a Buddhist framework has been necessarily selective, episodic, a constructed account.

---

30. Dōgen, "Genjōkōan," *Shōbōgenzō,* vol. 1, ao 319-0, annotated by Yaeko Mizuno (Tokyo: Iwanami Shoten, 1993), 54. Norman Waddell and Masao Abe, trans., "Shobogenzo Genjokoan," by Dogen Kigen, *The Eastern Buddhist* 5, no. 2 (October 1972): 134.

31. Thich Nhat Hanh, *Being Peace* (Berkeley, CA: Parallax Press, 1987), 90–91.

It will have more than served its purpose, however, if it provides a basis for further exploration.

Resources

Chadwick, David. *The Life and Zen Teaching of Shunryu Suzuki.* New York: Harmony Books, 2000.

Dalai Lama. *Ethics for the New Millennium.* New York: Riverhead Books, 2001.

Dresser, Marianne. *Buddhist Women on the Edge: Contemporary Perspectives from the Western Frontier.* Berkeley, CA: North Atlantic Books, 1996.

Goldberg, Natalie. *A Long Quiet Highway: Waking Up in America.* New York: Bantam, 1993.

Guenther, Herbert, trans. *The Life and Teaching of Naropa.* Boston: Shambhala, 1995.

Hanh, Thich Nhat. *Being Peace.* Berkeley, CA: Parallax Press, 1987.

Haas, Michaela. *Dakini Power: Twelve Extraordinary Women Shaping the Transmission of Tibetan Buddhism in the West.* Boston: Snow Lion, 2013.

Kaye, Les. *Zen at Work.* New York: Three Rivers Press, 1997.

Kornfield, Jack. *After the Ecstasy, the Laundry.* New York: Bantam, 2001.

Kottler, Arnold. *Engaged Buddhist Reader.* Berkeley, CA: Parallax Press, 1999.

O'Halloran, Maura Soshin. *Pure Heart, Enlightened Mind: The Life and Letters of an Irish Zen Saint.* Boston: Wisdom Publications, 2007.

Unno, Taitetsu. *River of Fire, River of Water.* New York: Image, 1998.

7

The Cultivation, Calling, and Loss of the Self

Confucian and Daoist Perspectives on Vocation

MARK BERKSON

Deep reflection on the notion of calling brings one far beyond the question of "making a living," and ultimately into the question of making a *life*. While we might begin the inquiry into calling with a focus on jobs and careers, we will inevitably arrive at fundamental existential questions such as "What is a good human life?" and "What is a self?" The study of what has traditionally been called "vocation" might initially seem like a practical exploration of work, but it ultimately makes philosophers and theologians of us all.

It is important to move beyond a focus on words such as "work," "job," and "career," and bring in the literally evocative concept of "vocation." The etymology of the word draws us into philosophical reflection about the meaning of being "called." What are we being called to do? Who/What is doing the calling? Who is the being who is called?

In this chapter, I examine the two most important indigenous Chinese religious and philosophical traditions—Confucianism and Daoism—during their origins and early development in the "Golden Age" of Chinese thought, the classical period of the sixth through the third centuries BCE. The classical Confucian tradition will be represented by its three most important figures: Confucius (Kongzi, 551-479 BCE), Mengzi (372-289 BCE), and Xunzi (312-230 BCE). The Daoist perspective will be represented by Zhuangzi (ca. 369-286 BCE).[1] Despite vast geographic and

---

1. There is much debate about the meaning and scope of the term "Daoism." This term encompasses texts of the classical period that are considered foundational to what is sometimes called "philosophical Daoism" (primarily the *Daode Jing* and *Zhuangzi*), sectarian

temporal distance between them and us, these thinkers have important contributions to make to a discussion of calling. The significant differences between these schools and the Abrahamic, monotheistic traditions with which many Americans are familiar, as well as the differences among the Chinese thinkers themselves, make them valuable participants in this conversation. The word "calling" has no exact equivalent in Confucian or Daoist thought, but I will show that there are many related and analogous concepts.

The concept of calling includes three aspects: first, the activities and practices in which one engages regularly (i.e., the projects to which one devotes one's *time*); second, the *self* that is cultivated through these activities; and third, the *others* with whom and on whose behalf one does these activities. When exploring the Confucian and Daoist traditions, I will focus on the concepts of time, self, and relationship. Any work that one does, whether paid or not, involves these components, which give rise to these questions. In terms of time: How will I be spending my time? How will I experience time when engaged in this activity? How does my work, in artist Eugène Delacroix's words, "give value to time"?[2] In terms of self: Am I well suited for this activity? Does it make good use of my particular talents and gifts? Will it bring me joy and fulfillment? What kind of person will this activity make me? In terms of relationships: With whom and for whom will I be working? How will this activity impact others (e.g., people, animals, the environment)?[3]

Therefore, we can say that a reflection on calling involves thinking about how being unfolds through time and in relation to others. Confucianism and Daoism give us two radically different ways of thinking about

---

traditions (sometimes referred to as "religious/liturgical Daoism"), practices of physical and spiritual transformation (including the pursuit of longevity and immortality), and what is often labeled "folk" or "popular" Daoism. I am selecting Zhuangzi for inclusion in this chapter, both because of the powerful challenge that his voice can present to our conventional ideas of calling, and also because of the profound influence he has had on East Asian religion (particularly forms of Buddhism, such as Chan/Zen). As his perspective is distinctive, I will often use the term "Zhuangzian" to describe his thought, rather than "Daoist." The Romanization system that I will use throughout this chapter is Pinyin (so "Dao" will be used instead of "Tao").

2. Michele Hannoosh, *Painting and the Journal of Eugène Delacroix* (Princeton: Princeton University Press, 1995), 13.

3. See my discussion of the relationship between self and temporality, in "Conceptions of Self/No-Self and Modes of Connection: Comparative Soteriological Structures in Classical Chinese Thought," *Journal of Religious Ethics* 33, no. 2 (June 2005): 293-331.

self, time, and relationships. In addition, Confucians and Daoists use a word that will be central to a discussion of calling—Dao, or Way.[4] They ask: "Is what I am doing in accordance with the Dao?" The word has both descriptive and normative dimensions. The Dao is both the way things are, the Way of the Cosmos/Nature, and also the way that one should live if he or she wants to accord harmoniously with the way things are. However, these two schools conceive of the Dao differently—Confucians emphasize the *social* aspects of the Dao (the way that people should live together in society) and the Daoists focus on the Dao as the movement and activities of the *natural* world, the rhythms and cycles of Nature as a whole, and the diverse multiplicity of created beings.[5]

Classical Confucian and Zhuangzian voices are distinct in this volume because they do not devote significant attention to metaphysics, theology, and the question of post-death existence. The Confucian thinker Xunzi, for instance, rejects supernaturalism and articulates a largely humanistic (and deeply spiritual) vision. For this reason, most insights of the classical Confucian and Daoist traditions are available to everyone without requiring them to accept supernatural or metaphysical claims, making them valuable resources for secular humanists and the growing number of Americans who identify as "spiritual, but not religious."

The Confucian Tradition

The historical period in which both the Confucian and Daoist traditions arose was one of great conflict and violence, as a number of warring states vied for supremacy. The states' rulers sought advice from philosophers representing different schools, at times arranging debates among them. Sages from these different schools, including Confucius and his followers, sought to influence policy and gain positions in their courts. Philosophy was not an armchair exercise; it was linked with statecraft and could be a

4. While the concept of Dao would seem to be associated primarily with the Daoists, whose school contains the word in its name, all of the various schools of this period used the term. Dao in its ordinary usage means "way" or "path." Each of these schools was proposing a way, a dao.

5. While the Confucians emphasize the social dimension, they also reflect on the relationship between human beings and the larger natural world. On this ecological dimension of the Confucian vision, see P. J. Ivanhoe, "A Happy Symmetry: Xunzi's Ethical Thought," *Journal of the American Academy of Religion* 59, no. 2 (1991): 309-22.

risky activity. The philosophers' ultimate goal was to find a way to restore order and greatness to China amidst chaos and fragmentation. The Legalists advocated policies of strict reward and punishment, the Mohists articulated a form of state consequentialism, and the Confucians focused on returning to the greatness of a past Golden Age by preserving and transmitting the texts and rituals of the sages of the past. The Confucian goal was social harmony achieved through the cultivation of moral individuals and strong families, and their methods emphasized education and ritual rather than coercion.

Classical Confucianism does not aim for an end such as salvation. It aims for perfected moral character, meaningful human relationships, and an ordered, harmonious society. It beautifully articulates the ways in which the meaning and purpose of our lives can be seen primarily in three realms: human relationships characterized by love, mutual respect, and benevolence; work and participation in public life that contribute to the greater good; and self-cultivation through education, ritual, the arts, and physical practices. The Confucian texts do not merely aim to give readers guidance on how to be a "good Confucian." They are telling us how to become excellent human beings.

Self, Time, and Relationship

The *Analects* provides a concise autobiographical statement of Confucius that can serve as a "calling story" in miniature:

> At fifteen I set my mind upon learning; at thirty I took my place in society; at forty I became free of doubts; at fifty I understood Heaven's Mandate; at sixty my ear was attuned; and at seventy I could follow my heart's desire without overstepping the bounds of propriety. (2.4)[6]

In essence, his story is a cultivation narrative that begins with a commitment to education in youth, continues with a deepening understanding of Heaven (including an "attuned ear," better to hear a call with), and

6. When a book and verse number are given for the *Analects,* the reference is to the translation by Edward Slingerland in P. J. Ivanhoe and Bryan Van Norden, *Readings in Classical Chinese Philosophy* (Indianapolis: Hackett, 2005).

culminates in a person whose spontaneous actions and desires accord with the moral Way (Dao) by which society is ordered and harmonized. Confucius was seventy when he achieved this ability, and it is a characteristic of Confucians that they emphasize the need for perseverance to sustain the lifelong project of self-cultivation. A passage from the *Analects* reads, "A shi (scholar-official) must be strong and resolute, for his burden is heavy and his way is long. . . . His way ends only with death—is it not long?" (8.7).

The Confucian notion of temporality sees the human life in terms of narratives. A life unfolds in stages, which are marked by rites of passage (e.g., the "capping ceremony," marriage, the sixtieth birthday). There are tasks, roles, and virtues appropriate to different stages of life because our body and mind develop in stages.[7] Contemporary Confucian scholar Tu Weiming describes the ideal Confucian narrative as described in the *Book of Rites*:

> The "capping ceremony" (*guan li*) is performed on a man's twentieth birthday and declares that he has come of age.[8] But only after he has married and become a father in his thirties is he considered a full participating member of society. His career as a scholar-official normally begins at forty. . . . If all goes well, he reaches the apex of his public service at fifty, and he does not retire from it until he is well over seventy. The "capping ceremony" is also preceded by an equally elaborate process of maturation: education at home begins at six . . . etiquette at eight . . . formal schooling at ten, and by thirteen the student will have studied music, poetry, dance, ritual, archery and horsemanship. Thus from childhood to old age the learning to be human never ceases.[9]

The story of Confucian progress is a more or less orderly series of discrete stages based on our physical and psychological changes over time.

---

7. Much of this is explained in terms of changes in our *qi* over time, and for Confucians and Daoists alike, working with the *qi* is an essential part of cultivation. There are no English words that correspond directly to *qi*. Common translations include "psychophysical energy" and "vital breath."

8. The capping ceremony was a ritual in which a young man would receive a cap to wear, indicating that he would now be considered an adult and had reached marriageable age. Young women would participate in an analogous hair-pinning ceremony.

9. Tu Weiming, *Humanity and Self-Cultivation: Essays in Confucian Thought* (Berkeley, CA: Lancaster-Miller Publishers, 1978), 35.

The three essential elements of the narrative are education, family life, and public service. All ideal calling narratives would have these three elements.[10]

From a Confucian perspective, the cultivation of the self through ritual and learning is the essential humanizing activity and thus what we are all called to do. The individual life is framed by the tradition's ideal narrative of development and self-cultivation, which provides the path by which one measures one's progress. For Confucians, selfhood depends on narrative temporality.[11]

In the narrative, birth and death are the primary "bookends." These endpoints, however, must be understood as ellipses rather than final periods, as one's life narrative is inextricably connected with one's ancestors and descendants. Confucians owe it to their ancestors to continue the family line and thus are "called" by the tradition to have children.[12]

One of the philosophical divides that occurs in the Chinese tradition is the role that human nature plays in the cultivation of self. Human nature is "worked on" in some way, although this way differs among thinkers. Mengzi believes that our nature is naturally oriented toward the good (e.g., toward concern for others), and cultivation of the self is seen as tending to human nature while it grows. Agricultural metaphors are employed to describe the process. For example, Mengzi describes our natural moral inclinations as "sprouts" that must be nurtured, but not pulled, in order to grow properly (2A2, 2A6). For Mengzi, self is understood as the full *realization* of nature.

Xunzi, in contrast, believes that our nature is composed primarily of

---

10. Traditionally, these narratives applied only to men. However, many philosophers have critiqued the patriarchal elements of Confucianism and shown that the Confucian vision can be freed from these elements with no diminishment—and in many ways with enhancement—of its power. See Chenyang Li, ed., *The Sage and the Second Sex: Confucianism, Ethics, and Gender* (Chicago: Open Court, 2000), and Li-Hsiang Lisa Rosenlee, *Confucianism and Women: A Philosophical Interpretation* (Albany: State University of New York Press, 2006).

11. For two contemporary philosophical discussions of the role of narrative in the understanding of the self, see Alasdair MacIntyre, *After Virtue: A Study in Moral Theory* (Notre Dame: University of Notre Dame Press, 1984), and Charles Taylor, *Sources of the Self: The Making of Modern Identity* (Cambridge, MA: Harvard University Press, 1989).

12. In popular Chinese religion, this view is expressed by the practice of keeping the ancestors "alive," well, and connected with the family by ritually feeding them. Living descendants are always needed to continue these ritual offerings. Without these, the ancestors, who could be very helpful to a family, might become hungry ghosts that cause trouble.

selfish appetites, so the work of coming into selfhood is one of reforming and reshaping human nature. Xunzi uses metaphors of craftsmanship to describe the process, comparing moral cultivation to the "steaming and bending" that one uses to "make wood straight as a plumb line into a wheel" (256). For Xunzi, human nature is not a moral force, but is rather the disordered raw material that must be shaped and molded into something harmonious and beautiful, a task accomplished through learning and ritual. For Xunzi, then, the cultivation of the self is understood as the *reforming* of nature.

The Confucian project is called "self-cultivation" not only because there is a strong element of individual effort involved—along with the effort of our parents, teachers, and others—but also because the self is the ultimate achievement. It is essential to keep in mind that the Confucian understanding of the self is not that of the autonomous, separate agent, as is often understood in the West. Rather, the self is, to a very large extent, relationally constituted; we are fundamentally the nexus of relationships that shape us and give our lives meaning. We cultivate ourselves with the guidance of, alongside, and for the sake of others. We are who we are because of those we have loved, lived with, and learned from.

In order to engage in self-cultivation, each person must begin with the question, "Who am I?" For some Westerners, this question might involve seeking some inner essence that defines them outside of any particular "role" they might play.[13] For the Confucian, the answer to "Who am I?" is more straightforward. A Confucian would instruct us to think of the relationships that make us who we are and that make our lives meaningful. In my case the answer would be that I am a father, husband, son, brother, friend, teacher, student, citizen, and colleague. Some of these relationships will have to do with areas traditionally understood as "work," such as my role as a professor, which itself has various components (teaching, scholarship, and service). Others have to do with being a member of a particular community, such as my family, my circle of friends, or my country.

What, then, is my calling considered from a Confucian perspective? I am called to be the best of each of these roles that I can, to fulfill my responsibilities to, and to contribute to the well-being of, the others in each

---

13. Some of my students say that when they reflect on the question of who they truly are, they try to bracket all of the roles they play and think about who they are when they're alone.

of those relationships (I cannot be a husband without my wife or a teacher without my students). The Confucian's task, then, is to reflect on what it *means* to be a good parent, child, spouse, student, and so on.[14]

Receiving a Calling

Confucius In monotheistic traditions, a person or community is called by God, although the conception of how God calls varies in each. Confucianism has what might be called a this-worldly and humanistic focus, exemplified in Confucius's response to being asked about serving ghosts and spirits, "You are not yet able to serve people—how could you serve ghosts and spirits?" (11.12).

At the same time, the concept of *Tian* plays a significant role in Confucian thought. The term is often translated as "Heaven," which is problematic given how different the Confucian term is from its meaning in the Abrahamic traditions. However, there is some justification for translating *Tian* as "Heaven" in the thought of Confucius and Mengzi (but not Xunzi).[15] For Confucius and Mengzi, there is a sense that *Tian* is a moral force and that the structure of the cosmos is a deeply moral one. *Tian* endows us with morality and moves us in the direction of goodness and harmony if we pay attention to it and accord with it.

In some ways, *Tian* resembles the God of the Deists and might be understood like "Providence," a moral force providing guidance and supporting those who act in accord with the destiny it decrees; it gives an overarching moral structure to the universe. Confucius is confident in his mission (even when threatened by soldiers in Kuang) because he believes he is, in a sense, called by *Tian*. "Is not culture now invested here in me? If Heaven intended this culture to perish, it would not have given it to those of us who live after King Wen's death. Since Heaven did not intend that this culture should perish, what can the people of Kuang do to me?" (9.5). Elsewhere he declares, "It is Heaven itself that has endowed me with virtue" (7.23). One of his disciples explicitly describes Confucius as being

14. See Douglas Schuurman's discussion of Luther's notion of "fulfilling a station's lawful duties" in Douglas Schuurman, *Vocation: Discerning Our Callings in Life* (Grand Rapids: Eerdmans, 2004), 6-7.

15. While *Tian* is not a moral force for Xunzi, he sometimes uses it to mean "sky," in which case it could be rendered "Heaven" (e.g., *Tiandi,* "Heaven and earth," *Tianxia,* "all under Heaven"). I am indebted to Eric Hutton for this point.

on a Heavenly mission: "Heaven . . . intends him for sagehood" (9.6). One admirer proclaims to Confucius's disciple, "Heaven intends to use your Master like the wooden clapper for a bell" (3.24).

While Heaven does not speak in revealed words to Confucians, *Tian* expresses its "will" through *Tian Ming,* the "Heavenly Mandate or Decree." Confucius states, "The gentleman stands in awe of . . . the Mandate of Heaven" (16.8), a decree that Confucius came to understand at age fifty in his cultivation narrative.[16] The concept of *Tian Ming* predates Confucius, and is often used to explain the defeat of one ruler or dynasty and the ascendance of another. Throughout history and to the present day, many Chinese have believed that Heaven's displeasure with a ruler is expressed through powerful displays of calamitous weather or natural disasters. When the bad ruler is defeated, the new ruler will proclaim that his success is a sign that the Mandate of Heaven has passed to him. In this sense, Heaven can be said to "speak" to human beings by indicating its approval or disapproval.[17]

Is *Tian* "transcendent"? One way to understand how there might be something transcendent in Confucianism is to look at the *Great Learning* (*Daxue*). The text describes the ancient sages: "Their hearts being rectified, their persons were cultivated. Their persons being cultivated, their families were regulated. Their families being regulated, their States were rightly governed. Their States being rightly governed, the entire world was at peace."[18]

The human project of self-cultivation is set in widening concentric

16. Confucius uses "gentleman" in a moral sense (like "cultivated person"), not in the sense of social status. For Confucius, titles such as this are earned; they are not something one is born with.

17. Rodney Taylor argues that the religious dimension of Confucianism comes largely from the role of Heaven as an "absolute," and that the Confucian tradition "provides a way for the individual to move toward that which is identified as the absolute. This movement toward the absolute is a process of . . . ultimate transformation." Rodney Taylor, *The Religious Dimensions of Confucianism* (Albany: State University of New York Press, 1990), 3. Heaven, which exerts the "pull" that moves human beings on the spiritual path, is what provides Confucianism with its soteriology, a means of entering into a "transformed state of being." Robert Eno writes, "Prescriptively, Tian provides reasons to act in certain ways in the future: we should do X because Tian wants us to and/or will reward us." Robert Eno, *The Confucian Creation of Heaven: Philosophy and the Defense of Ritual Mastery* (Albany: State University of New York Press, 1990), 82.

18. James Legge, *The Four Books* (Boston: Elibron Classics, 2000), 359. I modified the translation slightly.

rings of relationship, and coming to understand this interconnected web helps one understand the relation of the self (the microcosm) with the larger, ultimately macrocosmic, level. In the *Great Learning,* the levels are: self, family, society/state, and world. Confucianism sees the world composed of levels of relationships, each of which both transcends and includes the smaller levels. The self is transcended by, but included in, the family; likewise with family and society, society and world. The whole is always "greater than the sum of the parts," but it is ultimately just made up of all the parts (there is no dualistically transcendent component). The Confucian cosmos is organismic, and a common metaphor, particularly in later Confucianism, describes all of humanity and the world as one body. One works on transforming the world by cultivating the self, leading Tu Weiming to call the worldview "anthropocosmic." He writes, "To fully express our humanity, we must engage in a dialogue with Heaven because human nature, as conferred by Heaven, realizes itself not by departing from its source but by returning to it. . . . Humanity is Heaven's form of self-disclosure, self-expression, self-realization."[19]

Mengzi Mengzi portrays human nature by providing a map of the human heart-mind.[20] Its four characteristics are the senses of compassion, respect/deference, shame, and right and wrong. When these incipient dispositions are cultivated through Confucian education and ritual, they will blossom into full-blown virtues (benevolence, propriety, righteousness, and wisdom, respectively) that are able to provide inner guidance as a person navigates the challenges of life. The heart is the inner moral compass that gives direction.

For Mengzi, Heaven "calls" each human being by endowing us with an inner moral sense, the good nature with which each of us is born. When we listen to the moral guidance within, we are attending to the call of Heaven. Mengzi explains, "To fully apply one's heart is to understand one's nature. If one understands one's nature, one understands Heaven. To preserve one's mind and to nourish one's nature is the means to serve Heaven" (7A1).[21]

19. Tu Weiming, *Centrality and Commonality: An Essay on Confucian Religiousness* (Albany: State University of New York Press, 1989), 102.

20. The word *xin* in classical Chinese thought is often translated "heart-mind" to show that the thinkers did not consider cognitive and affective capacities to exist separately.

21. When a book and verse number is given from Mengzi, the translation used is Bryan Van Norden's *Mengzi* in Ivanhoe and Van Norden, *Readings in Classical Chinese*

For Mengzi, our calling is to nurture our moral heart, listen to it, and follow its guidance, which is why the practice of introspective reflection (*si*) is important for Mengzi. Primarily through looking inward, a person discovers their path. Moral natures also show themselves in other ways, such as spontaneous actions that reveal inborn compassion, a sense of satisfaction in performing good actions (which is why ritual can help strengthen these dispositions), and thought experiments that reveal true feelings and values.

However, introspection alone is not sufficient. While all people possess a moral heart, not everyone attends to it, understands it, or hears its "voice" amidst the loud, demanding shouts of appetites and desires. For this reason, we must have teachers, wise friends, and mentors in order to point out aspects of ourselves that we do not see.[22] Mengzi tells the story of a king who failed to see his moral nature, assuming that he only had the capacity to be a powerful, greedy ruler rather than a benevolent leader. Mengzi reminded the king of an episode in which the king spared the life of an ox being led to sacrifice because he was "moved by pity for the animal." Upon reflection, the king realized that he did have compassion, telling Mengzi, "Though the deed was mine, when I looked into myself I failed to understand my own heart. You described it for me and your words struck a chord with me" (L1A7).[23] We can fail to see vitally important parts of ourselves, which is why we sometimes need others to reveal us to ourselves.

In Mengzi's thought, it is clear that the call is coming from one's heaven-endowed heart. The form that this call takes can be understood,

---

Philosophy. When the book and verse numbers are preceded by an "L," the translation refers to D. C. Lau, *Mencius* (New York: Penguin, 1970).

22. Mengzi sees the value of a teacher quite differently than Xunzi. Mengzi says that teaching involves "transforming influence, like that of timely rain . . . helping the student to realize his virtue . . . and develop his talent . . . answering his questions . . . and setting an example" (7A40). The teacher functions primarily to show a student her potential, to nurture it and guide its development, and to serve as an example of what a person who has done this work looks like. See *Mencius,* trans. D. C. Lau (New York: Penguin, 1970), 191. Xunzi, who does not believe that we have any inner moral guide, emphasizes the importance of teachers in imparting the actual *content* of the Way.

23. Mengzi points out that since we possess the inner resources we need to become fully moral people, we need only to "extend" these moral feelings to more and more people and situations, an act that can be understood as tending to and watering the sprouts of morality. Mengzi explains that "there is just one thing in which the ancients greatly surpassed others, and that is the way they extended what they did" (1A7).

in part, by one of the cardinal virtues for Mengzi—*Yi,* often translated as "righteousness" or "dutifulness." While there is much debate over the meaning of this character, the general sense involves notions of what is proper for one to do given who one is (i.e., roles in different contexts, relationships) and the situation. *Yi* can be defined as "what is appropriate."

Eric Hutton writes, "One's *yi* dictates what kind of person one ought to be, rather than specifying particular actions to do."[24] *Yi* is proper feeling and behavior given one's roles and relationships. The question Confucians must ask is, What is *yi* for each relationship I am in, each job that I do? For Confucians, the concrete content of *yi,* the proper behavior, is given by the *li,* or rituals. *Yi* is relevant for the notion of calling because it tells a person the obligations that are incumbent upon them given the relationships and activities they find themselves in, many of which are inherited rather than chosen. Confucians believe that we all come into this world with duties to ancestors and parents, for example. We also acquire duties and responsibilities over time depending on the commitments we make to certain people, communities, and organizations. The "call" that we will then experience comes not from a transcendent voice, but from the demands of righteous conduct in all of these contexts.

Xunzi For Xunzi, *Tian* does not respond to us or morally guide us, and it does not endow us with an inner moral guide. It does not care about us or intervene directly in human affairs. For these reasons, it is better understood in Xunzi's thought as "Nature" (rather than "Heaven"). Xunzi writes, "The activities of *Tian* are constant" (269), pointing out that they do not change just because a virtuous or vicious person is in power, and they are not influenced by our prayers or rituals.[25] We must fit harmoniously in with it, pay close attention to it (as a farmer follows the seasons and weather), and be grateful for all it gives us. The role of *Tian* for Xunzi is that it provides the patterns with which we must harmonize ourselves. *Tian* is majestic but indifferent; we can "marvel at it" and stand in awe of it, but there is no need for us to try to communicate with it.

For Xunzi, human nature is basically selfish and disordered. Xunzi

24. Eric Hutton, "On the Meaning of Yi for Xunzi" (unpublished MA thesis, Harvard University, 1996), 18.

25. When I cite translations of the *Xunzi,* a page number refers to the translation from Eric Hutton's *Xunzi* in Ivanhoe and Van Norden, *Readings in Classical Chinese Philosophy.* If the page number is preceded by a "W," it refers to the translation from Burton Watson, *Hsün Tzu: Basic Writings* (New York: Columbia University Press, 1963).

writes, "People's nature is bad. Their goodness is a matter of deliberate effort" (298). We need the humanizing, beautifying guidance of the tradition—especially rituals—to make us into good human beings. The path of self-cultivation, the way to which Xunzi believes we are called, is the never-ending effort to beautify our ugly nature, to control the forces within ourselves and harmonize with others. "Human nature is the original beginning and raw material, and deliberate effort is what makes it patterned, ordered, and exalted" (281).

But since Xunzi argues that we have no internal motivation to embark on that path (as Mengzi believes we do), what, in Xunzi's view, calls us to undertake the Confucian project of self-cultivation? For Xunzi, we are called by other human beings, living and dead, who have made our lives possible and whose love and support has sustained us—our ancestors and parents. We must live in such a way as to honor their commitment and sacrifices, which is why filial piety is one of the most important Confucian virtues.[26]

Xunzi believes that followers of the Confucian Way are also called by tradition, by the sages of the past who developed the Way, and by the teachers who have transmitted it ever since. Because, for Xunzi, there is no inner guide, one relies on teachers to show one the Way. The Confucian texts and rituals that make it possible to become good human beings are not products of heavenly guidance or a moral nature (as they are for Mengzi); they were developed through the efforts of the great sage kings, and without them human nature would lead to conflict and chaos. In explaining the origin of the Confucian rituals, Xunzi writes, "The ancient kings hated such disorder, and therefore they established ritual principles in order to curb it, to train men's desires and to provide for their satisfaction" (W89).

In addition, leaders call people to become public servants, to work for the good of society, and to serve their fellow citizens, creating a just and harmonious society. Furthermore, Confucians believe that people feel the pull of moral exemplars, those who model excellence. The *Analects* makes this point many times: "The virtue of a gentleman is like the wind, and the virtue of a petty person is like the grass—when the wind moves over the grass, the grass is sure to bend" (12.19). And when persons become

---

26. The expressions and obligations of filial piety remain even after one's parents have died. Confucius said, "One who makes no changes to the ways of his father for three years after his father has passed away may be called a filial son" (4.20).

more cultivated, they dedicate themselves to helping others—"Wanting to realize himself, (one who is benevolent) helps others to realize themselves" (6.30). As a person becomes more cultivated and comes to understand the beauty of the Dao, they begin to feel drawn toward it, and ultimately to love it.

To be called is to feel a pull toward some end. For Xunzi, the follower is pulled or called not by Heaven, but by the sages who developed and transmitted the humanizing Dao (and by the Dao itself), by parents and ancestors who have given life and love, by teachers and friends who guide and support, and by leaders who bring order to society. Ultimately, other human beings are the sources of a person's call. In the Confucian vision, *we are all calling each other.*

Living Out a Calling

What about the concept of "work," in the sense of occupation or profession? What do Confucian thinkers advise on the kinds of occupations to pursue? Confucius, his disciples, and much of his audience were focused largely on government service. They wanted to be scholar-officials who would serve in the state bureaucracy to help create a harmonious society through good governance. Confucius became a teacher because his political aspirations did not work out, but one could certainly say he found his true calling. He is considered China's foremost model of a teacher.[27]

Although Confucius's own political aspirations were not achieved, his disciples (and their disciples after them) came to dominate the Chinese imperial state. Knowledge of Confucian texts became essential to passing the examinations that would qualify one for a position as an official. Although the perfect society will never be achieved, a person has a responsibility to do their best to work toward making things better. Confucius's disciple Zilu says, "To avoid public service is to be without a sense of what is right. . . . The gentleman takes office in order to do what is right, even though he knows that the way will never fully be put into practice" (18.7).

While government service is one of the most important careers for a Confucian, Confucius points out that people do not have to directly serve in an official capacity in order to have an impact on the ordering of society.

27. His birthday is celebrated as Teacher's Day in Taiwan.

He explains, "In being a filial son and a good brother one is already taking part in government" (2.21).

The education that Confucius advocates can be seen as a version of the liberal arts, a curriculum that cultivates good human beings rather than creates narrow specialists. Confucius states, "The gentleman does not serve as a vessel (tool)" (2.12).[28] The purpose of a Confucian education is the formation of character, not job training, and Confucius advocates the study of those fields that will broadly develop the student's mind and body. He encourages his disciples to "[e]xplore widely in your cultivation of the arts" (7.6).

Confucius's own biography illustrates the role of "vocational luck" in our lives, as he was never able to get the job that would have enabled him to put his vision into practice. Sometimes, the job that would be most fulfilling, or that would enable a person to best serve others, does not become available. But vocation in its larger sense means that we still have a primary calling: developing our character. A Confucian perspective tells us that whatever our job is, we should take pride in it and do it to the best of our abilities, aiming not to be recognized but to be worthy of recognition. "Do not be concerned that no one has heard of you, but rather strive to become a person worthy of being known" (4.14). Confucius states, "One who is benevolent sees as his first priority the hardship of self-cultivation, and does not think about attaining any results or rewards" (6.22). Those who are truly called to an activity are not deterred by the lack of wealth or status. Confucius praises those who are committed to the path of self-cultivation despite difficult material circumstances. "What a worthy man was Yan Hui! Living in a narrow alley, subsisting upon meager bits of rice and water—other people could not have borne such hardship, and yet it never spoiled Hui's joy. What a worthy man was Hui!" (6.11).

Confucians do not reject material pleasures if they are gained ethically. Confucianism does not have an ascetic form and does not promote renunciation. One enjoys material goods and uses them wisely if they come, but remains cheerfully and doggedly on the right path if they do not. Confucius emphasizes the joy that can be found in study, music, and conversation. When asked to describe himself, he said, "Why not just say—He is the type of person who becomes so absorbed in his studies that he forgets to eat" (7.19).

Self-cultivation can be pursued outside of the workplace, through

28. See also verses 9.2 and 9.6.

an engagement with the arts, sports, literature, even good conversations over a nice meal and wine. A life of such things can be rich and meaningful regardless of how one earns a paycheck. People who are not fortunate enough to have fulfilling jobs can find joy in, and can develop themselves through, activities in life beyond the workplace. Any activity that challenges a person, brings them into a community of fellow practitioners, and enables the cultivation of virtues and the pursuit of excellence can be seen as a calling if pursued for the right reasons, regardless of whether it provides an income.

Daoism and Zhuangzi's Challenge: An Alternative View of Calling

Confucian thinkers focus on the importance of family, learning, the arts, and public service. Most people's lives include many, if not all, of these elements, and Confucians provide deep insights into their meaning and importance so that we do not take them for granted. Zhuangzi, on the other hand, powerfully challenges ordinary understandings of life and the nature of being human. He shows an alternative vision of how people might live and look at their lives. I will illustrate Zhuangzi's radical worldview with a "calling story" from his writings:

> Sir Motley of Nanbo made an excursion to the Hillock of Shang. There he saw an unusual tree so big that a thousand four-horse chariots could be shaded by its leaves. "Goodness! What tree is this?" asked Sir Motley. . . . Looking upward at the smaller branches, he saw that they were all twisted and unfit to be beams. Looking downward at the massive trunk, he saw that it was so gnarled as to be unfit for making coffins. If you lick one of its leaves, your mouth will develop ulcerous sores . . . "This tree is worthless," said Sir Motley, "and that is why it has grown so large. Ah! The spiritual man is also worthless like this." (M38-39)[29]

29. Page numbers given for a citation from Zhuangzi refer to the translation by Burton Watson, *Chuang Tzu: Basic Writings* (New York: Columbia University Press, 1964). When the page number is preceded by a "W" the translation used is Burton Watson, *The Complete Works of Chuang Tzu* (New York: Columbia University Press, 1968). When the page number is preceded by an "M" the translation used is Victor Mair, *Wandering on the Way: Early Taoist Tales and Parables of Chuang Tzu* (New York: Bantam, 1994). The *Zhuangzi* is a composite text, and many scholars believe that the historical Zhuangzi wrote only the seven "Inner Chapters."

One element that seems to be found in accounts of calling in virtually every tradition is that one's life be "useful" in some way, such as serving other people or God. Zhuangzi, on the other hand, extols the values of "uselessness." He tells a number of stories that illustrate the "usefulness of uselessness," including this one about a big tree: "Its trunk is too gnarled and bumpy to apply a measuring line to, its branches too bent and twisty to match up to a compass or square." Zhuangzi points out that because of the tree's shape, "Axes will never shorten its life, nothing can ever harm it. If there's no use for it, how can it come to grief or pain?" (30). Zhuangzi also describes the "useful trees" that so many admire: "These are trees that make their own lives miserable because of their abilities. Therefore, they cannot finish out the years allotted to them by Heaven but die midway. . . . I have finally learned what uselessness really means and that it is of great use to me" (M38).

In a story told about Zhuangzi's life, he is fishing by the river when he is approached by two officials who offer him a position running the affairs of a kingdom (an offer Confucians dream of). Zhuangzi, without even turning his head to face them, replies, "I have heard that there is a sacred tortoise in Chu that has been dead for around three thousand years. The king keeps it wrapped in cloth and boxed, and stores it in the ancestral temple. Now would this tortoise rather be dead and have its bones left behind and honored? Or would it rather be alive and dragging its tail in the mud? . . . Go away! I'll drag my tail in the mud!" (109).

While most people set goals and pursue them, Zhuangzi says the opposite: Don't strive. He suggests that people "relax and do nothing . . . or lie down for a free and easy sleep" (30). The notion of calling seen in Confucian thought (and theistic traditions as well) has the basic assumption that to live a meaningful life involves setting goals and having a purpose. But Zhuangzi does not look at life this way. Rather than think about life as having a direction, Zhuangzi describes the ideal way as "free and easy wandering."

For Zhuangzi, humans are simply manifestations of the Dao (the natural Way), and the human way of being is merely one among many, with no elevated status above the ways of eels, frogs, or birds (Zhuangzi's stories are filled with animal exemplars). Zhuangzi suggests that people live out their natural lifespans, simply and naturally, without becoming attached to things or taking life too seriously. He says, "The highest happiness, keeping alive— only nonaction (non-striving, effortless action) gets you close to this" (112).[30]

30. Burton Watson translates *wu wei* as "inaction," which is not an adequate translation

Striving and ambition lead to suffering and, too often in the chaotic and bloody Warring States period in China (475-221 BCE), an early death. Whereas Confucians would accept suffering and death for the sake of principle, courage, or loyalty, Zhuangzi wants none of it. Zhuangzi's rejection of so many values held dear by Confucians—ambition, courage, responsibility, the desire to make a difference—makes him a valuable interlocutor in a discussion of calling. Is there a notion of calling in Zhuangzi?

(No) Self, Time, and Relationship in Zhuangzi

It is helpful to look at the understandings of self, time, and relationship in Zhuangzi because his perspective is radical. It is not characterized by a sense of the narrative structure of life, which is essential to the Confucian vision. According to Zhuangzi, all narratives are based on constructions given by society (e.g., the appropriate time to do certain things, which roles should be occupied and when, and how they should be fulfilled). For Zhuangzi, such narratives are not natural, but are constructed overlays on top of, and often obstructing, what is actually underneath: a ceaseless flow of life that can be experienced in its immediacy at any time. Social conventions, abstract categories, and constructed narratives serve to cover up our connection with the Dao and must be stripped away.

Zhuangzi holds a "momentary" temporality that focuses on continuous, moment-by-moment transformation, a "ceaseless change" that emphasizes the endless transformation of things. Zhuangzi reminds us that nothing stays constant from one moment to the next. "The life of things is a gallop, a headlong dash—with every movement they alter, with every moment they shift. What should you do and what should you not do? Everything will change of itself, that is certain!" (103). As a result of this awareness, the sage lives entirely in the ever-changing present. In Lee Yearley's formulation, "Each new moment is grasped as it comes and surrendered as it goes. . . . Life is a series of new beginnings. Everything is unstable. . . . Change is the final reality. . . ."[31]

---

because "inaction" connotes quietude or physical stillness. As we will see, *wu wei* means effortless *action* that results from following the natural Dao rather than the conscious, striving mind.

31. Lee Yearley, "The Perfected Person in the Radical Chuang-Tzu," in *Experimental Studies on Chuang-Tzu,* ed. Victor Mair (Honolulu: University of Hawaii Press, 1983), 135.

Given that life consists of moment-by-moment transformation, the best way to live does not involve goal-oriented striving; instead, Zhuangzi counsels people to "ride along with things," and to freely "wander" rather than progress on a well-formulated path. Whereas the narrative-based understanding of life is often expressed by Confucians through the metaphor of a journey on the tradition's directed path, Zhuangzi's way is connected with a lack of direction, an aimless wandering.[32]

In terms of time, the Confucians emphasize the length of the human life and the need for perseverance along the way, but Zhuangzi repeatedly highlights life's remarkable brevity. "Man's life between Heaven and earth is like a white colt passing a crack in the wall—suddenly it's finished. Rapidly surging, all things come forth; smoothly subsiding, all things reenter" (M216-17). Life can be seen as an endless stream of continuously changing moments; at the same time, one's entire earthly life can be seen as but a moment itself.

As we have seen, the "self," for Confucians, indicates an achievement that requires cultivation over time, is grounded in narrative temporality, and involves categories by which a person understands who they are. I believe that if "self" is understood in this way, then Zhuangzi has a picture that can be described as "no self."[33]

When a person does not have a self or name to build up or defend, he cannot be injured by others' judgments or insults and cannot be moved by flattery or greed. Zhuangzi writes, "The whole world could praise Song Rongzi and it wouldn't make him exert himself; the whole world could condemn him and it wouldn't make him mope. . . . Therefore, I say, the Perfect Man has no self (*wu ji*) . . . the sage has no name (*wu ming*)" (W26).[34]

---

32. The narrative conception of self-cultivation leads many Confucians to employ the genre of travel accounts in telling their stories. Pei-yi Wu writes that for the Confucians, "Spiritual autobiography can and has been narrated as a travel account." Pei-yi Wu, *The Confucian's Progress: Autobiographical Writing in Traditional China* (Princeton: Princeton University Press, 1990), 95.

33. Zhuangzi's "no-self" differs in some ways from the Buddhist notion, as a thinker's conception of "no-self" will differ depending on the conception of "self" that he is rejecting. Zhuangzi is arguing against a Confucian notion of self while the Buddha argues against the conception of "Atman" (soul or self) found in the Upanishads. These two understandings of "no-self" share certain features, such as an understanding that everything is impermanent, leading to the belief that there are no eternal, immutable, autonomous elements of any being. See Berkson, "Conceptions of Self/No-Self," 312, 327.

34. Watson translates *ming* here as "fame," but I keep the literal translation "name." Another passage describes a sage as having "rejected self (*qu ji*)" (340).

For Zhuangzi, we are called to lose the very self that Confucians see as the highest achievement. In Zhuangzi's vision, the "self" is something that is constructed by the mind; when all of the concepts and categories used by the mind to label and identify ourselves are gone, the mind itself is clear, "like a mirror." In such a state, there is no place for the "self" to reside.

But how can a person rid themselves of ingrained habits of the mind, concepts and categories that develop and are internalized over a lifetime? Zhuangzi advocates contemplative techniques, such as "sitting in forgetfulness" and "the fasting of the mind," through which mental patterns (e.g., the tendency to identify with certain labels and judge according to certain norms) fall away. When a person engages in the "fasting of the mind," their "identity" dissolves.[35] In one passage, Yan Hui says, "Before I am able to exercise fasting of the mind, I truly have an identity. But after I am able to exercise it, I will no longer have an identity (there is no more Yan Hui)" (M32). What one is doing is "forgetting" all of those labels and categories with which one normally identifies and which can lock one into roles, ways of acting, and obligations. Labels have a false constancy that is at odds with the continuously changing nature of the world.

Another way to lose the self is through absorption in skillful activities. Zhuangzi's writing is filled with stories of masters immersed in skillful activity and physical labor such as a butcher, a wheelwright, a woodcarver, and a cicada catcher. Zhuangzi portrays them as exemplars because, in their humble work (without the benefit of formal, Confucian-style education), they demonstrate outstanding skill and craft, which itself reflects their mental, physical, and spiritual achievement. A famous example is that of Cook Ding, whose skill was described this way: "At every touch of his hand, every heave of his shoulder . . . zip! zoop! He slithered the knife along with a zing and all was in perfect rhythm. . . . '(S)pirit moves where it wants. I go along with the natural makeup, strike in the big hollows, guide the knife through the big openings, and follow things as they are'" (46-47). The skillful person is fully engaged in the activity and is thus able to move gracefully and in accordance with nature.

The skillful exemplars in Zhuangzi can be seen as being in the "flow state," a nondual awareness often experienced in the midst of skillful ac-

---

35. Zhuangzian forms of meditation seem akin to *zazen* (seated meditation) in Zen Buddhism. Zhuangzi had a profound influence on the development of East Asian Buddhism.

tivity, such as a musical or athletic performance.[36] For Zhuangzi, the word for such a state is *wu wei,* "effortless action."[37]

Through absorption in skillful activity, the narrative-producing, self-constructing mind moves out of the way and a worker *becomes* the work. Zhuangzi describes the masterful artisan Chui as one who "didn't let his mind get in the way" (128). A master diver explains the practice as "following along the way the water goes and never thinking about myself" (126). A woodcarver who is considered a genius (literally, as everyone who saw his work said that it "seemed to be the work of gods or spirits") said that he stills his mind until he no longer has "any thought of congratulations or rewards . . . praise or blame." He goes on, "The ruler and his court (who commissioned the woodcarver) no longer exist for me. My skill is concentrated and all outside distractions fade away" (127). The cicada catcher says, "I'm aware of nothing but cicada wings" (121). The contemplative practices and skillful activity described by Zhuangzi can best be understood through "momentary temporality," when one is aware only of the unfolding experience of the present moment. When one is able to experience the world as a continuous flow of moment-by-moment transformations, all notions of achievement (including "self," the ultimate Confucian achievement) disappear, leading to optimal experience, consummate skill, and a sense of joy.

Zhuangzian Cultivation Narratives

We have seen that Zhuangzi emphasizes the "momentary" dimension of life while the Confucians highlight the "narrative" dimension. At the same time, there are elements of cultivation narratives found in Zhuangzi, which

36. The idea of "flow" is explained in the work of psychologist Mihaly Csikszentmihalyi as the "merging of action and awareness," when "people become so involved in what they are doing that the activity becomes spontaneous . . . they stop being aware of themselves as separate from the actions they are performing." Mihaly Csikszentmihalyi, *Flow: The Psychology of Optimal Experience* (New York: HarperPerennial, 1990), 4. P. J. Ivanhoe looks at the role of skill stories in Zhuangzi in "Skepticism, Skill and the Ineffable Tao," *Journal of the American Academy of Religion* 61, no. 4 (1993): 639-54.

37. The term *wu wei* means "non action," but the Daoists often write the phrase "*wei wu wei,*" or "act non action." The phrase does not mean that no effort is required, but rather that action appears to flow without conscious effort, skillfully and spontaneously; the person is responsive and performs at the highest level without conscious striving. For an excellent treatment of this concept, see Ted Slingerland, *Effortless Action: Wu Wei as Conceptual Metaphor and Spiritual Ideal in Early China* (New York: Oxford University Press, 2007).

demonstrates the inescapability of the process of cultivation and narratives of development in a human life. The practices that lead to the forgetting of self (e.g., meditation, swimming, woodcarving, etc.) are difficult, require time to master, and have stages of development. Skill acquisition requires a narrative conception of cultivation. While Zhuangzi does not emphasize this aspect, he does allude to it, particularly in the context of the "skill stories." For example, Cook Ding, when asked about his skill, replies, "When I first began cutting up oxen, all I could see was the ox itself. After three years I no longer saw the whole ox. And now—now I go at it by *qi* and don't look with my eyes" (W46). The cicada catcher explains his skill this way:

> For the first five or six months I practice balancing two balls on top of each other on the end of the pole and, if they don't fall off, I know I will lose very few cicadas. Then I balance three balls and, if they don't fall off, I know I'll lose only one cicada in ten. Then I balance five balls. . . . No matter how huge Heaven and earth, or how numerous the ten thousand things, I'm aware of nothing but cicada wings . . . how can I help but succeed? (W120-21)

The highest state is one of complete absorption in and awareness of the activity. But to learn this present-moment awareness takes time. Thus we see a paradoxical dimension of Zhuangzi's thought. The achievement of the momentary awareness that enables the undoing of narrative temporality (and thus the realization of no-self) depends on cultivation, which can only be understood through narrative temporality. Whereas for the Confucians, narrative temporality is the framework for self-cultivation, for Zhuangzi, it is the framework for realization of no-self.

Receiving a Calling

What calls? As we have seen, for Zhuangzi, momentary temporality, contemplative practices, and attainment of the flow state, along with the absence of a structured narrative in the life journey, deconstruct the self. There is no stable temporal foundation on which it can be built. But without a self, what motivates our action? Since much of our motivation (e.g., our pursuit of fame, wealth, and status) arises out of our conception of "self," on what basis does a person act after the notion of the "self" is dissolved? What calls a person and how can they respond?

For Zhuangzi what guides people, rather than "self," is *nature,* the in-born spontaneous inclinations, tendencies, desires, preferences, and capacities (Zhuangzi uses the term *qi suo shou,* "what is received"). Zhuangzi believes different beings have different natures, and he often contrasts the natural tendencies of different beings. For example, "Creatures differ because they have different likes and dislikes. Therefore, the former sages never required the same ability from all creatures or made them all do the same thing" (W195). The unique nature of each being should be respected and allowed to manifest itself. Thus, when freed from the socially constructed "self," one's true nature is manifested in a way that is spontaneous (*ziran,* "so of itself"). Zhuangzi counsels, "Attentively guard your true nature" (M321), and says of the wise person, "If he believes that something may be harmful to his nature, declining, he will refuse to accept it" (M310).

Stepping back, we now see the different ways that Mengzi, Xunzi, and Zhuangzi view the relationship of self to nature. Whereas Mengzi's view is "self as realization of nature," and Xunzi's "self as reformation of nature," Zhuangzi's vision is of the "manifestation of nature through forgetting of the self."

For Zhuangzi, insofar as a "call" comes from something greater than ourselves, something that transcends us, it would be the natural Dao, the way of *Tian* (Nature writ large). But *Tian* also includes human beings. In Zhuangzi's view, when we realize that we are not separate from the Dao, it moves and guides us in an unobstructed way. Whereas Confucianism is effortful ("the burden is heavy and the road is long"), Zhuangzi's way is a form of yielding, of getting out of the way in order that Dao can move one. Human beings are a manifestation of nature, an expression of Dao living out our allotment of life in our own unique way.

A line in *Zhuangzi* reads, "Do not destroy the natural (*Tian*) with the human (*ren*)" (M159).[38] Nature provides the basic direction of our spontaneous predilections, and we stifle or act against them at great risk. For Zhuangzi, as opposed to the Confucians, we should not consciously strive to realize an ideal; we should yield to our nature. It is not a type of "self-mastery." In fact, there is no self-conscious control involved. For example, a millipede cannot even explain how he coordinates his numerous feet. He replies, "Now, I just move by my natural inner workings but don't know why it is so" (M159).

---

38. I translate *Tian* as "natural" here instead of "heavenly," which is Mair's choice. My argument for doing so can be found in Berkson, "Conceptions of Self/No-Self."

One of Zhuangzi's metaphors for calling is sound, as in music rather than words, which is illustrated in the "Pipes of *Tian* (Nature/Heaven)." Zi Qi, who is described as having "lost himself," describes the pipes this way: "The myriad sounds produced by the blowing of the wind are different, yet all it does is elicit the natural propensities of the hollows themselves" (12).[39] In this metaphor, each pipe is unique; because of the material it is made of, its size, and the way it is shaped, it will sound unlike any other pipe. Each pipe sounds only like itself (*qi ziji*). But it will only sound like itself when the "great breath" that blows through all pipes can blow through it without obstruction. It is the obstructions (e.g., the self, the striving mind) that cause some pipes to squeak or play flat in a way that spoils the sound for everyone (this can refer especially to the people who "blow their own horn [pipe]").[40] Despite the different sounds we make, the same breath blows through us all (we are all manifestations of nature). It is this very realization that allows the obstructions that block up the pipe to be removed. The pipe, then, makes its own unique sound, a sound that is not in unison with (which would be conformity), but is in harmony with, the other pipes. The natural Dao is the great harmonizer. For Zhuangzi, as opposed to the Confucians, harmony cannot be achieved by effort. It is only realized when nature, the ultimate harmonizer, does its work. When all things can simply express themselves without obstruction, they are "harmonized within the framework of nature (*he zhi yi tian*)" (23).

There is a seeming paradox here. It is only when experiencing the essential unity of things (the same breath blows through us all), by seeing through the boundaries (most importantly between "self" and "other"), that unique natures can emerge. Zhuangzi's writing features the play of unity and multiplicity, the emphasis on selflessness alongside the prominence of idiosyncratic personalities and the panoply of diverse individual natures. When we are no longer separated from the Dao, when artificial boundaries (the only kind there are) dissolve, then we experience the "oneness" of all things. This is *not* the kind of "oneness" that involves absorption

39. Watson's translation is, "Blowing on the ten thousand things in a different way, so that each can be itself" (32).

40. This metaphor is further developed in other stories within the *Zhuangzi*, with many examples of the natural expression of the Dao being blocked up by occlusions. "In all things, the Way does not want to be obstructed, for if there is obstruction, there is choking, if the choking does not cease, there is disorder; and disorder harms the life of all creatures" (W138). Elsewhere we see warnings to those who obstruct their natures: "He who is heedless of his nature . . . will find his nature choked with reeds and rushes" (260).

in undifferentiated unity, for it is at this point that the greatest connection to all other beings is felt and we experience our own uniqueness. Nor is it a union with some transcendent "other." Rather, it is a recognition that there are no boundaries between ourselves and the Dao. In other words, when I am without self, the barrier that my mind falsely constructs between "me" and the Dao disappears and I can experience myself as nature in a particular, unique instantiation.

Modern Challenges and Opportunities

The Confucian and Daoist traditions are characterized by worldviews and values that are often in tension with those of the twenty-first century, particularly in America. How can a person live out a Confucian or a Zhuangzian Daoist life today?[41]

The Confucian Revival in China

Confucianism is a resurgent tradition in the People's Republic of China. While Confucianism has played a continuously vital role throughout the modern period in South Korea, Japan, and Singapore (as a scholarly enterprise, a powerful cultural influence, and a worldview promoted by the state), it was vilified and suppressed during the first three decades of Communist rule in its birthplace of mainland China. It was considered a backward relic of a feudal age, and there were a number of anti-Confucius movements. However, there has been a Confucian revival in mainland China beginning in the early 1980s, which is still growing today. Confucianism has increasingly appealed to both intellectuals and the government, though for different reasons. Some intellectuals have used Confucian thought to critique

---

41. In regard to sectarian Daoism, there has been a Daoist revival in recent years in China, and sometimes the Chinese government finances the building or repair of Daoist temples in order to attract pilgrim and tourist dollars. There are a number of popular forms of Daoism in China and Taiwan today. Some center on priests who conduct rituals involving various deities. People hire Daoist priests for a variety of different rituals, from community agricultural festivals to funerals. The Daoist priesthood is often hereditary, with sons learning from their fathers and participating in rituals. There are also celibate Daoist monks and nuns who engage in contemplative practices and seek spiritual cultivation. See Isabelle Robinet, *Taoism: Growth of a Religion* (Stanford: Stanford University Press, 1997).

the government, and many have articulated a form of Confucianism that is compatible with democracy and human rights. The Chinese government, on the other hand, often employs Confucian ideas to emphasize loyalty to the state and social harmony, and to counter the influence of Western individualism. The government has created "Confucius Institutes" located in campuses around the world.[42] Courses on Confucianism are becoming popular on university campuses in China, and millions of students are being taught the Confucian classics in primary and secondary schools around China.[43]

One of the signs of Confucianism's popularity in China is the remarkable success of Professor Yu Dan's book, *Confucius from the Heart,* which has sold over ten million copies. Yu Dan's goal is to help people deal with the challenges of modern life through Confucianism. She writes about Confucian teachings as compatible with modernity and relevant to everyday life. "What we can learn from Confucius today is not . . . the Confucianism of the scholars, full of deep argumentation and fettered by textual research. What we can take away from the *Analects* of Confucius are the simple truths that every person knows in his or her heart, though they may not let them out through their mouths."[44] It is increasingly common in China for people to see themselves as living in accordance with—perhaps being called by— the Confucian Way. This does not mean that if we asked someone who lived in mainland China, or anywhere in East Asia, "What is your religion?" they would respond, "I am a Confucian." The approach to religious affiliation and identity is quite different in East Asia than it is in the US.

The Question of Religious Affiliation

Most Americans who describe themselves as "religious" identify with a single tradition. This is not the case in East Asia, where many people are connected to multiple religious traditions. For centuries in China, many people have had ties simultaneously to the Confucian, Daoist, and Bud-

---

42. There are currently around 350 campuses worldwide. The Chinese government says that these are for the purpose of educating people about Chinese culture and civilization. Some academics have raised concerns about Chinese government influence over these centers, and argue that the institutes are really ways to project Chinese "soft power" around the globe.

43. See Daniel Bell's *China's New Confucianism: Politics and Everyday Life in a Changing Society* (Princeton: Princeton University Press, 2010).

44. Yu Dan, *Confucius from the Heart: Ancient Wisdom for Today's World,* trans. Esther Tyldesley (New York: Macmillan, 2009), 5-6.

dhist traditions, as well as "folk religion." A popular saying that captures the nature of Japanese religion is "Born Shinto, Marry Christian, Die Buddhist." This approach to religious affiliation is labeled "contextualism," because one engages in the rituals and practices of a particular tradition based on the situation one is in.[45] Therefore, since most Chinese and Japanese people do not associate exclusively with one tradition, it can be difficult to find a representative "Confucian."

A study conducted in South Korea determined the degree to which Confucianism continues to guide the behavior and worldview of Koreans. The author Koh Byong-ik notes, "It is generally believed that at present Korea is the most Confucian country in all of East Asia."[46] However, less than 2 percent of Koreans described themselves as Confucians. The researchers found that this result did *not* indicate the lack of Confucian influence in Korea. The lack of self-identification is because Confucianism is not a tradition emphasizing "membership" in a Confucian institution.

However, the study found that while only a very small percentage of Koreans identify as "Confucian," the vast majority have values and worldviews deeply shaped by Confucianism. So the many Christians in Korea, for instance, are really "Confucian Christians." Furthermore, Koh observes, "A substantial majority of the supposedly nonreligious population is . . . actually Confucian; they observe the basic Confucian rituals, such as ancestral services and burial rites, and subscribe to Confucian values."[47]

While there are a growing number of schools that have adopted a Confucian curriculum in East Asia, Confucianism is largely learned in the home. Tu Weiming states, "Many people are not aware that they are Confucian, but they . . . live by some of the basic Confucian ideas, and they transmit some of these values to their children. . . . It's in the cultural DNA."[48]

---

45. One of the reasons that multiple religious identity is so common in East Asia is that people are affiliated with traditions more because of *practice* than because of *belief.* Affiliation through belief is more central to Christianity and Islam (asserting one's religious identity through reciting creeds and statements of faith is far more common in these traditions than in Asian traditions). Because the central belief claims of these traditions are often mutually exclusive (e.g., Christians assert the divinity of Jesus, Muslims deny it), it is almost impossible to imagine a "Christian Muslim." On the other hand, if affiliation is mostly about practice and participation in ritual, then there is no problem with going to a Buddhist temple one day and a Daoist temple or Shinto shrine the next.

46. Koh Byong-ik, "Confucianism in Contemporary Korea," in *Confucian Traditions in East Asian Modernity,* ed. Tu Weiming (Cambridge, MA: Harvard University Press, 1996), 191.

47. Koh, "Confucianism in Contemporary Korea," 192.

48. Bill Moyers and Tu Weiming, *World of Ideas:* "Interview with Tu Weiming" (Public

Another problem with finding people who regard themselves as "Confucian" has to do with the actual term "Confucian." In the Chinese language, those who transmit, teach, and write about this tradition, and those who have been ritual specialists, are called *Rujia,* which means the "School of the Learned, or Erudite." If the term "Confucian" is meant in this honorific way, then self-identification becomes a problem. As Tu Weiming says, "Sometimes, it's even wrong to say, 'I am a Confucian,' in the sense that I am a cultivated person or I am a scholar. Some other people may recognize you as such, but you don't make that kind of claim."[49]

The Confucian tradition is strongly associated with East Asia and with East Asians who live elsewhere. It is not as geographically widespread or ethnically diverse as Islam and Christianity, and it does not feature missionaries who seek to convert people of all nations and cultures. This raises the question of Confucianism's "portability." For instance, can a Confucian life be lived in America today? The features of American culture that would suggest barriers to the spread of Confucianism include individualism, the valorization of newness and innovation, feminism, egalitarianism, materialism, and the focus on profit and wealth characteristic of free-market capitalism. Given Confucianism's relational conception of the self, hierarchical social vision, emphasis on tradition and the past, suspicion of the profit motive, and history of patriarchy, it seems that there would be substantial obstacles to the flourishing of Confucianism in the US. I will conclude this chapter by highlighting the insights and perspectives from both traditions that I believe are valuable for us to consider, and by looking at examples of people who, I believe, are living Confucian and Zhuangzian Daoist lives today, including in America.

The Relevance of Confucian and Daoist Thought for Today

The Confucians pride themselves on being eminently practical people.[50] Zhuangzi, too, is primarily concerned not with metaphysical abstractions but with guidance for how to live. In the spirit of these great Chinese think-

---

Affairs Television, 1990), 3. The transcript of the interview can be found at http://www-tc
.pbs.org/moyers/journal/archives/docs/ming_woi.pdf.

49. Moyers and Tu, *World of Ideas,* 3.

50. This practical emphasis can be seen in the titles of two of the greatest neo-Confucian texts of the later imperial period, Zhu Xi's *Reflections on Things at Hand* and Wang Yangming's *Instructions for Practical Living.*

ers, I invite the reader to reflect on how these philosophical perspectives are relevant to us today. In what ways can they provide illumination and guidance on the significant choices we make in the areas of work, family, education, and even leisure? How can ancient Confucian and Daoist thought help us find our calling and live better lives in the twenty-first century?

Confucian Insights

Confucian thought teaches that, whatever our profession, the ultimate calling for each of us is to become a benevolent human being who expresses our full humanity in our relationships with others. From a Confucian perspective, our main task is cultivating ourselves, which means developing our heart and mind, body and character through ritual, education, the arts, literature, and physical practices. So we should not simply equate "calling" with "job" or "profession," but rather with the lifelong task of becoming a cultivated human being in relation to others.

The Confucians remind us to step back and think of our life in terms of a narrative of development with stages. We must seek out activities that are appropriate to the various stages of our life and prepare for future stages so that we can plan the trajectory of our education, career, family life, and retirement.

Education—particularly what we would call a "liberal arts education"—is fundamental to the Confucian worldview, and careers in the field of education are especially valued by Confucians. A commonly heard argument today is that education should focus primarily on preparation for a job, and that the worth of an education is equated with the earning power it provides. The Confucians remind us of the importance of an education for the sake of becoming a more informed, thoughtful, ethical human being and citizen.[51] Confucians believe that we must use our gifts in the service of others, which is why they emphasize civic engagement and public service.

In contrast to the widespread contemporary obsession with innova-

---

51. A strong argument can be made that a liberal arts education is vitally important for citizens in a democracy. Thomas Jefferson frequently wrote about the need for an educated citizenry in a healthy democracy. For example, he argued, "If a nation expects to be ignorant and free in a state of civilization, it expects what never was and never will be." Thomas Jefferson, "Letter to Charles Yancey," in *The Works of Thomas Jefferson*, vol. 11, ed. Paul Leicester (New York: G. P. Putnam's Sons, 1904-1905), 497.

tion, newness, and speed, Confucians remind us to maintain an engagement with and deep appreciation of ritual and tradition. Rituals have the power to slow us down and connect us with human beings (living and dead) who matter, and with the past, nature, and ourselves. Confucians also believe that we can enjoy the material benefits that come with a job (as long as they are obtained ethically), but they caution us against making the maximization of profit and wealth an overriding priority.

When it comes to finding the right kind of work for ourselves (or making any significant decision), Confucian thinkers highlight the importance of both inward reflection and seeking the guidance of others. Mengzi advises us to make time for quiet self-reflection and introspection in the midst of our busy lives. He tells us to examine our heart-mind regularly to see where it's guiding us; the call comes, at least in part, from within.[52] At the same time, as Xunzi argues, we must also look outward and ask those who know us best for advice. Often, others see things in us that we ourselves do not. We are all skilled at self-deception, and we must determine when we are hearing our "true self" speaking and when it's ego or greed motivating us.

Confucian Exemplars

To illustrate a Confucian life, I will profile someone who exemplifies the tradition and whom I have quoted a number of times in this chapter—Professor Tu Weiming, Professor of Confucian Studies at Harvard University and Director of the Institute for Advanced Humanistic Studies at Beijing University.

In many ways, he is an ideal living representative of the Confucian tradition. He was born in China, the birthplace of Confucianism, and raised in China and Taiwan, cultures that have a strong Confucian dimension. He is a scholar of Confucian classics, having begun his formal study of them at age fifteen (the same age that Confucius's autobiographical narrative begins in the *Analects,* when Confucius said, "I set my mind on learning"). Tu studied with eminent Chinese Confucian thinkers, and received a PhD

---

52. One such introspective practice is recommended in *Analects* 1.4: "Every day I examine myself on three counts: in my dealings with others, have I in any way failed to be dutiful? In my interaction with friends and associates, have I in any way failed to be trustworthy? Finally, have I in any way failed to put into practice what I teach?"

from Harvard, studying with leading American scholars in a number of fields.

In the Confucian spirit of public service, Tu has worked with the government of Singapore to develop the "Confucian ethics" school curriculum, and serves as a member of the UN's "Group of Eminent Persons" to facilitate "Dialogue among Civilizations." Prof. Tu says that his own work aims at "the development of Confucian philosophy as a living tradition rather than just as a historical phenomenon."[53] In addition, and of great importance in the Confucian tradition, he is father to two sons and two daughters.

Tu draws on the many resources of the Confucian tradition, joined by liberal democratic ideas, modern science, and feminism, to engage with the challenges of our time, including environmental problems, gender and economic inequality, and selfish individualism. He says, "There is virtually no limit, theoretically, to the Confucian tradition's ability to accommodate some brilliant feminist ideas, because Confucianism is not gender specific in terms of achievement."[54] Tu's project—his calling—is to bring the Confucian voice beyond China, beyond East Asia, and into the conversation of the world's cultures and religions. He says that Confucianism "cannot afford to be Sinic, it cannot even afford to be East Asian, it has to be global."[55]

Tu describes Confucianism as a form of "spiritual humanism," a "way of learning to be human." He states, "I try to envision the Confucian project as a faith in the improvability and perfectibility of the human condition through self-effort, but not effort by isolated individuals alone, but by the community as a whole."[56]

Tu Weiming exemplifies Confucianism not only because of his erudition and scholarly contributions, but also because he is representative of the vast majority of Confucian scholars throughout history—a male of East Asian ancestry. This is changing because Confucian patriarchy, and hierarchical thinking in general, is being challenged. Women are increasingly adding their voices to the interpretation of Confucian classics and working to rid Confucianism of patriarchical elements. One such scholar is Li Hsiang Lisa Rosenlee, author of "A Feminist's Appropriation of Con-

---

53. Anja Steinbauer and Tu Weiming, "Interview with Tu Weiming," *Philosophy Now* 23 (Spring 1999), accessed July 10, 2015, https://philosophynow.org/issues/23/Interview_with_Tu_Weiming.

54. Steinbauer and Tu, "Interview."

55. Steinbauer and Tu, "Interview."

56. Moyers and Tu, *World of Ideas,* 3-4.

fucianism."[57] Rosenlee writes, "The goal of making Confucian feminism, of course, is more than simply keeping Confucianism alive in the contemporary world. It is an affirmation of the dynamic nature of Confucianism, so that one can be a Confucian and a feminist without apology."[58]

While Confucianism is a tradition that highly values scholars and learning, one does not have to be a scholar to be a Confucian. One example is South Korean Ryu Chan U, the founder and former chairman of Poongsan Corporation, a major manufacturer of copper products, including ammunition for Korea's army. Ryu, who died in 1999, was called the "godfather of Korea's defense industry" and was awarded the "Order of Civil Merit" from the Korean government for his contributions to the defense industry.[59]

In a twice-yearly ritual, Ryu wore the robes and hat of a sixteenth-century scholar-official and paid his respects by making offerings and prostrating himself at an altar at his family's ancestral shrine to demonstrate his loyalty to his ancestors, the family business, and the state. These three things are connected, because an important ancestor of Chairman Ryu was the Defense Minister of Korea four centuries ago, and Ryu himself was a defense contractor. By founding a family business dedicated to the defense of his nation, Ryu ensured that family, work, and state are all served. In accordance with Confucianism's family emphasis, Ryu's son, Ryu Jin-Roy, took over the company's leadership. In a sign of Confucianism's evolution, Ryu's daughter, Mi Ahn, has served as president of one of the company's subsidiaries.

Ryu Chan U's leadership approach was both hierarchical and family-oriented in style. Each morning, his subordinates on his management team formed a line to bow before Ryu. Ryu said that he wanted his employees to "think of the company as a family," and that he tried to "create a family atmosphere."[60] Each year, he organized a trip for some of his managers to

57. Li Hsiang Lisa Rosenlee, "A Feminist's Appropriation of Confucianism," in *Confucianism in Context: Classic Philosophy and Contemporary Issues, East Asia and Beyond*, ed. Wonsuk Chang (Albany: State University of New York Press, 2011), 175-90.

58. Li Hsiang Lisa Rosenlee, *Confucianism and Women: A Philosophical Interpretation* (Albany: State University of New York Press, 2006), 159.

59. Choi Bo-shil, "Poongsan Corp. Chair Ryu Chan-U Passes Away," *The Chosunilbo*, Chosun Media, 11/24/99, accessed July 10, 2015, http://english.chosun.com/site/data/html_dir/1999/11/24/1999112461243.html.

60. Ryu was featured in the PBS documentary "Big Business and the Ghost of Confucius," part of the 1992 *Pacific Century* series written by Alex and Frank Gibney and produced by the Pacific Basin Institute and KCTS-TV.

travel to a Confucian Academy in his ancestral village where they received lectures on Confucian values and participated in team-building exercises.

Throughout most of its 2,500-year history, those who described themselves as Confucian have been people of East Asian ancestry. In the twentieth century, Confucianism became a significant intellectual tradition in the US. Today people who are not East Asian have been profoundly influenced by Confucianism, and some refer to themselves as "Confucian" or as having multiple religious identities such as "Confucian Christian." Robert Cummings Neville, a philosopher, theologian, and Confucian Christian, has written about what Confucianism and American culture can contribute to each other in the book *Boston Confucianism*. The term "Boston Confucianism" refers both to the community of Confucians in the Boston area, many of whom are non-East Asian, and also to the larger concept of American expressions of Confucianism. Neville aims to show that "Confucianism is not limited to East Asian ethnic application and can in fact be transported to a larger non-East Asian environment."[61]

Neville analyzes both the ways that Confucianism can contribute important perspectives and practices to American culture, and the way that Confucianism can be transformed by its encounter with American values. For example, American Confucianism would have to account for the multicultural, diverse character of the US, quite different from the far more homogenous populations of countries like Japan and South Korea. Neville writes that American Confucians "need to invent rituals for everyday life and government that foster inclusive cultural diversity, for without that, the respect required for humaneness cannot be expressed or exercised."[62] Another example is the way that the hierarchical Confucian ethos will be transformed by the more egalitarian ideals of America. He states, "The Confucian task in an egalitarian society is to develop social habits that recognize and reinforce equality while also addressing the unique persons playing egalitarian roles."[63]

The examples of Confucian Christians (and other multi-faith identities, like "Buddhist Jew" and "Zen Christian") illustrate the ways that notions of religious affiliation are changing in America today, in part due to the increasing familiarity of American Christians and Jews with Asian

---

61. Robert Cummings Neville, *Boston Confucianism: Portable Tradition in a Late-Modern World* (Albany: State University of New York Press, 2000), 1.

62. Neville, *Boston Confucianism*, 16.

63. Neville, *Boston Confucianism*, 16.

religions.[64] Multiple religious identity, which has been common in East Asia for many centuries, is becoming increasingly appealing to Americans. Neville writes that Confucian success in the West "will make multiple religious identity a forced option for Confucians."[65]

Zhuangzian Insights

Can Zhuangzi's idiosyncratic and often radical vision offer us any useful guidance? I believe that his subversive and sometimes outright bizarre vision provides important insights that can possibly transform our lives for the better. Zhuangzi teaches us to not hold tightly to the narratives, expectations, and norms given to us by society. We can use them skillfully, but we should not get trapped by them. Zhuangzi encourages us to accept the circuitous and unpredictable routes, as even seemingly "wrong turns" can be illuminating.[66]

Zhuangzi reminds us to be aware of how truly free we are. We should leave room in our lives for spontaneity, and remain open to possibility and change. Transformation is always possible, and is in fact always occurring.

Zhuangzi would advise each of us to allow our nature to manifest itself. We should think of the main movement of our life not as striving but as yielding. We should not try to shape, judge, stifle, deny, or reform our nature; we should simply let it guide us. We go against our natural predilections and tendencies at great risk to ourselves. Our approach should be to appreciate the unique natures of all beings without judgment or imposing ourselves.

When it comes to the realm of job seeking, Zhuangzi's radical thought can provide important guidance. He would tell us to seek out activities

---

64. The number of Americans who do not identify with any single religious tradition has increased dramatically in recent decades; in the most recent Pew religious landscape survey, 23 percent of Americans were "unaffiliated." See Pew Research Center, "America's Changing Religious Landscape," accessed July 10, 2015, http://www.pewforum.org/2015/05/12/americas-changing-religious-landscape/.

65. Neville, *Boston Confucianism*, 22.

66. Every year, Hamline University's religion department, which requires all of its students to take a course that focuses on vocational reflection, features a panel of people of very different ages (from their twenties to their sixties) talking about their work and the path they took to arrive in their profession. One theme that is common to virtually all panelists who have found a meaningful job and pursued a path they'd describe as a calling is that they took a very circuitous route to their destination. Many said, "I never would have guessed that I would end up doing this for a living when I was in college."

that maximize opportunities for flow (i.e., those in which you feel joyfully challenged, where the hours fly by). Each of us should have at least one art, craft, or sport in our life in which we are deeply engaged and through which we can attain the state of *wu wei,* effortless action. If we do not have a job that provides good conditions for attaining *wu wei,* we should develop practices (e.g., forms of meditation) that help us attain it. If we can't change our circumstances, Zhuangzi tells us, we can always change the way we experience them.

Zhuangzi also cautions us to not be seduced by jobs that will wear us down. Like Zhuangzi, we should be prepared to turn down or walk away from work that is harmful to our body, mind, or spirit. Zhuangzi criticizes the person who "is after the sham illusion of fame and reputation and doesn't know that the Perfect Man looks on these as so many handcuffs and fetters" (W68). Zhuangzi's advice is very useful for a cultural and historical moment in which anxiety plagues a large percentage of the population. He tells us not to worry or strive, but rather to nurture life and live out our full allotment of years with as much equanimity and contentment (and humor) as we can.

How is it possible for us to integrate the Zhuangzian perspective into our lives? My own overarching narrative is largely Confucian, as my family and job make it impossible for me to consider abandoning my "roles" and just go "wandering." However, Zhuangzi shows us how we can incorporate "free and easy wandering" into our lives of responsibilities. We need to preserve time for Zhuangzian moments of spontaneity and also to infuse all of our activities with a Zhuangzian perspective. Unlike other Daoists who believed that freedom could only be achieved by leaving society behind and finding refuge in the forest or some agrarian utopia, Zhuangzi demonstrates a kind of freedom that can be experienced anywhere. It is not based on external circumstances, but instead on a transformation of the mind. Many of Zhuangzi's sages live in the "world of humans," and they navigate it with playfulness, equanimity, and humor, without attachment, and with the skill of Cook Ding wielding his knife. This way, they can live out their years with ease. Wandering need not mean leaving things behind. It can be a way to walk more lightly, freely, and joyfully in the places we already live.

Zhuangzian Exemplars

Zhuangzi's influence can be felt in Daoist and Buddhist religious texts and poetry, and there are many people who acknowledge his influence. But are there people who are living a Zhuangzian life in contemporary America? What would that look like? I focus on one of the most Zhuangzian people I have encountered (through his books and in person), the poet Gary Snyder.

Snyder's worldview and practice have been shaped in significant ways by Chinese and Japanese forms of Chan/Zen Buddhism[67] (along with other influences, including Native American spiritual traditions). Chan Buddhism, which arose in China around the seventh century CE, was constituted as much by Zhuangzian language and ideas as it was by Indian Buddhism.

For me, Snyder's life and work often evoke the spirit of Zhuangzi. He is a masterful user of language, writing poetry that is thought-provoking, sometimes humorous, and informed by a deep commitment to the appreciation and care of nature. Like Zhuangzi, he aims to subvert many of our current norms and ideologies while moving his reader toward a greater appreciation of the natural world (and the entire cosmos, for that matter) and the human being's part in it.

Snyder's many jobs give a sense of his colorful life as well as the Zhuangzian themes of nature, "wandering," contemplation, craftsmanship, and skillful language. Snyder's jobs have included seaman (which exposed him to a wide range of cultures), timber scaler (at an Indian reservation in Oregon), fire lookout in the North Cascades, carpenter, trail builder in Yosemite, and, of course, poet. He spent time in Japan, where he became a Zen Buddhist, learning the practice of meditation that would remain a central part of his spiritual path ever since.

Snyder lives in the Sierra foothills in California in a place he named Kitkitdizze (the name Wintu Indians have for the aromatic evergreen shrubs known as bear clover that grow in the area). I had the opportunity to meet him and spend time in the remarkable community that lives in the foothills around him.[68] He designed and built his home himself. Despite being a man of letters who has spent his time in the academic world, he is completely at home outdoors. He said, "Nature is not a place to visit, it is home."[69] He exudes a rugged, capable demeanor. His calloused hands

---

67. The same character is pronounced "Chan" in Chinese and "Zen" in Japanese.

68. This was made possible by Mark Gonnerman, who has worked closely with and written extensively about Gary Snyder. See *A Sense of the Whole: Reading Gary Snyder's Mountains and Rivers Without End* (Berkeley, CA: Counterpoint, 2015).

69. Iain Sinclair, "The Man in the Clearing," *London Review of Books* 34, no. 10 (May 24, 2012): 35.

testify to his love of craftsmanship and manual labor. Iain Sinclair writes, "In Kitkitdizze, there are tools everywhere, racks and stacks of them, useful objects respected like artworks."[70] Snyder is equally at home chopping wood or writing poems, sitting in meditation or addressing an academic conference. He refers to his "permeable, porous life." He cares deeply about ecology and preserving wilderness, refuses to demonize those on the other side of the issues he fights for, and displays good humor and a trickster's spirit. Snyder writes, "Practically speaking, a life that is vowed to simplicity, appropriate boldness, good humor, gratitude, unstinting work and play, and lots of walking, brings us close to the actually existing world and its wholeness."[71] The freedom, humor, poetic voice, love of nature, and respect for craft are all shared with Zhuangzi.[72]

Snyder has long been a reader of Zhuangzi and draws on him explicitly at times.[73] Author J. J. Clarke writes that Snyder "allied himself with Zhuangzi and other Chinese thinkers in order to confront Western aggressiveness and destructive attitudes towards nature."[74]

Snyder's poems often combine a strong sense of place and rich description of the natural world, with humorous—sometimes subversive or satirical—critiques of contemporary society. These themes appear in poems like "Smokey the Bear Sutra" and "For All," which contains the lines,

> I pledge allegiance to the soil
> of Turtle Island,[75]
> and to the beings who thereon dwell

---

70. Sinclair, "The Man in the Clearing," 36.

71. Trevor Carolan, "The Wild Mind of Gary Snyder," in *Shambhala Sun*, May 1, 1996, 26.

72. Jack Kerouac modeled the character Japhy Ryder in *Dharma Bums* after Snyder. Kerouac's description of Ryder in the book is, to my mind, what a portrayal of a contemporary American Zhuangzi would look like: "He was wiry, suntanned, vigorous, open, all howdies and glad talk and even yelling hello to bums on the street and when asked a question answered right off the bat from the top or bottom of his mind I don't know which and always in a sprightly sparkling way." Jack Kerouac, *The Dharma Bums* (New York: Penguin, 1976), 10.

73. For instance, in one book, Snyder brings in Zhuangzi's story of Cook Ding as an example of how to "bridge the spiritual and the practical," showing "an image of how totally accomplished one might become if one gave one's whole life up to a work." Gary Snyder, *The Practice of the Wild* (New York: North Point, 1990), 147.

74. J. J. Clarke, *The Tao of the West: Western Transformations of Taoist Thought* (New York: Routledge, 2000), 82.

75. Turtle Island is the name some Native American tribes give to North America.

one ecosystem
in diversity
under the sun
With joyful interpenetration for all.[76]

Like Zhuangzi, Snyder's work is filled with animals, memorable characters, and an embrace of diversity, nonconformity, tolerance, and freedom. Snyder envisions a "true community of all beings . . . affirming the widest possible spectrum of non-harmful individual behavior—defending the right of individuals to smoke hemp, eat peyote, be polygamous, polyandrous, or homosexual."[77]

If one were to ask Gary Snyder, an appreciator of Zhuangzi, who *he* sees as living a Zhuangzian life, he might suggest fellow poet and walker of the wilderness, Nanao Sakaki (1923-2008). Snyder, who describes Sakaki as a "uniquely free and bold-spirited wanderer," writes, "His spirit, craft, knowledge of history, make him . . . an exemplar of a lineage that goes back to the liveliest of Daoists, Zhuangzi. His poems were not written by hand or head, but with the feet. These poems have been sat into existence, walked into existence."[78]

Sakaki spent three years visiting forests throughout Japan, which inspired him to write poetry about his relationship with nature. Gary Snyder called him "the unofficial examiner of the mountains and rivers of all Japan."[79] Sakaki later explored the mountains and deserts of the American West. He formed a countercultural community in Japan known as "The Tribe," which aimed to live free from the materialism that was increasingly overtaking his country. Gary Snyder was also a member. When a Buddhist priest once proudly proclaimed his lineage, Sakaki replied, "I need no lineage. I am a desert rat."[80]

Many of Sakaki's poems speak with a voice that echoes Zhuangzi's, and bring together an appreciation for nature, a sense of joy, and a space for quiet contemplation. One such poem gives us the following advice:

76. Gary Snyder, "For All," in *The Gary Snyder Reader* (Washington, DC: Counterpoint, 1999).

77. Gary Snyder, "Buddhism and the Possibility of a Planetary Culture," in *The Engaged Buddhism Reader,* ed. Arnold Kotler (Berkeley, CA: Parallax Press, 1996), 125.

78. Nanao Sakaki, *Break the Mirror* (Berkeley, CA: Blackberry Books, 1996), xi. I rendered the Chinese words into Pinyin.

79. Sakaki, *Break the Mirror,* x.

80. Sakaki, *Break the Mirror,* x.

If you have time to chatter
Read books
If you have time to read
Walk into mountain, desert and ocean
If you have time to walk
sing songs and dance
If you have time to dance
Sit quietly, you Happy Lucky Idiot[81]

Given the importance of humor and subversive social criticism in Zhuangzi, we would expect Zhuangzians in the world of comedy. A self-described Daoist, comedian Mark Saltveit often talks about Zhuangzi's influence on him. He says, "There is an attitude underlying comedy that shares a lot with (Zhuangzi's) thought: mischievous, suspicious of authority and pomposity, fond of humble citizens and workers, very aware of the limits of knowledge and problems of communication, self-challenging, and drawn to non-logical truth, the kinds of thought not taught in school. Daoism also celebrates a manner of action perfect for comedy: spontaneous, intuitive, humble, perfected through repetition and awareness. Every person and thing has its own intrinsic nature; not a fixed thing, but a process that develops and unfolds in concert with all the other unfolding natures. Not coincidentally, Daoism (and its descendant, Zen) are the only philosophies or religions that are frequently humorous." Here is one sample joke from Saltveit: "I've actually become a Daoist missionary. Which means I stay home and mind my own goddamned business."[82]

Concluding Comparative Reflections

As we reflect on the lessons that we can learn from the Confucians and Zhuangzi, we can see profound truths in both traditions, and also deep tensions between them. In his poem "Ash Wednesday," T. S. Eliot writes, "Teach us to care and not to care."[83] This is another way to approach the divide between the Confucians and Zhuangzi. The Confucians teach us

---

81. Sakaki, *Break the Mirror*, 3.

82. Warp, Weft, and Way: A Group Blog of Chinese and Comparative Philosophy, "Comedians as Daoist Missionaries," accessed July 10, 2015, https://warpweftandway.wordpress.com/2011/06/21/comedians-as-daoist-missionaries/.

83. T. S. Eliot, *Collected Poems: 1909-1962* (Orlando, FL: Harcourt, Brace, 1991), 83.

to care, to take things seriously. Zhuangzi teaches us not to care, to take things lightly. Eliot's words convey the importance of incorporating both perspectives into our lives.

The value of doing this is that each perspective will be tempered and balanced by the other. If we maintain a rigidly Confucian perspective, we can find ourselves imprisoned by social norms, expectations, and traditions. We can feel burdened by the weight of obligations and duties upon us. Zhuangzi allows us to see through these constructions and, when need be, free ourselves from them, if not by rejecting them outright, then at least by holding them more lightly or ironically, gently mocking them or playfully subverting them.

However, if we seek only Zhuangzian spontaneity and absorption in the moment, then we lose the goods that a narrative vision makes available to us. Narrative is what produces "the life" of each one of us and is thus necessary in creating and living out "a good life." Only through narrative can a self be cultivated, for our identity is shaped by our history and traditions. Furthermore, Confucians fully capture the importance of what we owe to our loved ones, living and dead, and to our communities. We must honor the commitments that arise from these deeply important relationships.

There is great value in struggling with both the Confucians and Zhuangzi. Each points us to important dimensions of existence and expresses powerful truths. Periodically, it is important to step back and see the course of our development over time. At the same time, we realize ourselves to the fullest when we are so absorbed in an activity that self and time disappear. We must both create ourselves over the course of our lives and forget ourselves in the greatest moments of our lives. And if we do the former well, we make the latter more likely. Living well, then, requires that we live the continuous paradox of cultivating the self and forgetting the self.

We must learn to see our lives from both of these radically different perspectives, as neither can be reduced to the other. Our lives are enriched when we embrace paradox and pluralism. We live best when we hold Confucian and Daoist perspectives in creative tension, a form of dual consciousness or binocularity that recognizes the wisdom in physicist Niels Bohr's statement, "The opposite of a fact is a falsehood, but the opposite of one profound truth may well be another profound truth."[84]

---

84. Quoted in William Thompson, *Self and Society: Studies in the Evolution of Culture* (Charlottesville, VA: Imprint Academic, 2004), 77.

Resources

The Works of the Classical Chinese Thinkers

Confucius. *Analects: With Selections from Traditional Commentaries.* Translated by Edward Slingerland. Indianapolis: Hackett, 2003.

Ivanhoe, Philip J., and Bryan Van Norden, eds. *Readings in Classical Chinese Philosophy.* Indianapolis: Hackett, 2005.

Mengzi. *Mengzi: With Selections from Traditional Commentaries.* Translated by Bryan Van Norden. Indianapolis: Hackett, 2008.

Xunzi. *Xunzi: The Complete Text.* Translated by Eric L. Hutton. Princeton: Princeton University Press, 2014.

Zhuangzi. *Wandering on the Way: Early Taoist Tales and Parables of Chuang Tzu.* Translated by Victor Mair. New York: Bantam, 1994.

Studies of Confucianism and Daoism

Crane, Sam. *Life, Liberty and the Pursuit of Dao: Ancient Chinese Thought in Modern American Life.* Malden, MA: Wiley Blackwell, 2013.

Ivanhoe, Philip J. *Confucian Reflections: Ancient Wisdom for Modern Times.* New York: Routledge, 2013.

Kohn, Livia. *Introducing Daoism.* New York: Routledge, 2009.

Slingerland, Edward. *Trying Not to Try: Ancient China, Modern Science, and the Power of Spontaneity.* New York: Broadway Books, 2015.

Van Norden, Bryan. *Introduction to Classical Chinese Philosophy.* Indianapolis: Hackett, 2011.

8

Vocation without the Supernatural

Calling in Secular Traditions

EDWARD LANGERAK

What is secularism? Deriving from the Latin word *saecularis*, meaning "of an age," the word "secular" meant to Christian medieval minds the realm of the worldly, which is temporal as opposed to the eternal matters that chiefly concerned the religious institutions. Religious people, of course, lived in the world, so there was no inherent conflict between the secular and the religious, though believers were warned to be *in* the world without being *of* the world, and to keep their priorities in proper order. The Protestant Reformation's insistence that religious calling did not restrict itself to the church, that it applied just as importantly to secular occupations, underscores the fact that until fairly recently there were no secular traditions separate from religious concerns. This is not to deny that throughout world history there were important philosophers and other intellectuals who were atheists or agnostics who had little regard for theological matters. But, at least in the West, they were not the founders of institutions or of traditions with distinct creeds and practices.[1]

Today secularism is often defined as the political view that insists on the separation of church and state or, more ambitiously, on the separation of religion and public life.[2] Under this definition, secularism remains controversial and continues to be debated in many countries, including the United States where separation of church and state has long seemed to

---

1. Eastern outlooks such as Confucianism, Daoism, and Buddhism complicate any effort to distinguish religious traditions from atheistic or agnostic ones.

2. Bhargava calls this "political secularism." See Rajeev Bhargava, ed., *Secularism and Its Critics* (Oxford: Oxford University Press, 1998), 494.

most citizens as American as apple pie.[3] However, without entering into this debate, it is clear that defining secularism as separation of church and state implies that many theists and other religious believers are secularists, since many religious believers and institutions insist that the health of both religion and state requires separation. In this chapter, in order to address distinctly secular traditions, I will focus on what has come to be called "secular humanism."

Secular Humanism

Humanism cannot be seen as a tradition distinct from religious and theological commitments, since religious humanism has been a strong current in Western thought since at least the Renaissance. Indeed, in the United States, the first *Humanist Manifesto,* drafted by John Dewey and others in 1933, was signed by as many ministers as philosophers (though they tended to be liberal Unitarian Universalist ministers) and treats religion very positively. The preface says: "Religions have always been means for realizing the highest values of life," while the manifesto alternates between referring to "religious humanism" and "humanism."[4] The much longer second manifesto, drafted largely by Paul Kurtz in 1973, tones down a bit this high opinion of religion: "In the best sense, religion may inspire dedication to the highest ethical ideals." However, this embrace of religion at its best was one factor that led many religious believers to assert that secular humanism was a religion and that teaching some of its scientific tenets in the public schools—such as the theory of evolution—was a violation of the separation of church and state. Hence in 1980 many secular humanists, including Paul Kurtz, founded the Council for Secular Humanism and issued *A Secular Humanist Declaration,* which denounced the rise of dogmatic religious opposition to secular humanism, though the authors ecumenically noted that "[m]any religious believers will no doubt share with us a belief in many secular humanist and democratic values, and we welcome their joining with us in the defense of these ideals."[5]

---

3. At least as a slogan, but the details of what is meant by "separation" is an ongoing debate. All sessions of Congress open with prayer, and "In God we trust" has been added to all US currency. The political climate makes it unlikely that divorce or separation is imminent.

4. All three humanist manifestos (1933, 1973, and 2003) can be found at the American Humanist Association website, accessed March 2, 2015, http://americanhumanist.org.

5. The Council was originally called "The Council for Democratic and Secular Human-

Some secular humanists emphasize *secular,* because they "maintain that there is so much in religion deserving of criticism that the good name of humanism should not be tainted by connection with it."[6] Others emphasize *humanist* because they worry about the largely negative perception of the "new atheists'" assault on religion,[7] which does not provide a substitute for the positive functions of religion. They think that appreciating the latter is an important part of understanding the challenges *for* secularism: "Secularism needs to become secular *humanism.*"[8] Of course, as secular humanists they deny the existence of supernatural or transcendent beings, being empiricist in epistemology and naturalist in ontology. However, they can be open-minded enough to think that science might conceivably discover something analogous to what those who say they are spiritual but not religious call "transcendence," even though secularists think such a discovery is unlikely and, in any case, it would not provide evidence for supernatural or transcendent beings such as those whom the religious identify as God or angels.[9] Thus they live in what Weber and others call a disenchanted world.[10] The question is whether they can be enchanted with the world in

ism" but was shortened after the fall of the Soviet Union and the consequent reduction in associating secular humanism with communism. See Council for Secular Humanism, accessed March 2, 2015, https://www.secularhumanism.org. The Council updated the Declaration with the *Humanist Manifesto 2000,* drafted by Paul Kurtz, who also published a book-length explanation of it, *Humanist Manifesto 2000: A Call for a New Planetary Humanism* (Amherst, NY: Prometheus Books, 2000), where he notes that "*A Secular Humanist Declaration* was issued in 1980 because humanism, especially *Humanist Manifesto II,* had come under heavy attack, particularly from fundamentalist religious and right-wing political forces in the United States. Many of these critics maintained that secular humanism was a *religion*" (10).

6. Fred Edwards, "What Is Humanism?" accessed March 2, 2015, http://american humanist.org/humanism. See also Tom Flynn, "Secular Humanism Defined," accessed March 2, 2015, https://secularhumanism.org/index.php/13.

7. For two examples, see Christopher Hitchens, *God Is Not Great: How Religion Poisons Everything* (New York: Twelve, Hachette Book Group, 2007), and Richard Dawkins, *The God Delusion* (New York: Houghton Mifflin, 2006).

8. Philip Kitcher, "Challenges for Secularism," in *The Joy of Secularism,* ed. George Levine (Princeton: Princeton University Press, 2011), 24. Emphasis in the text.

9. Kitcher, "Challenges for Secularism," 30; Kitcher, *Life After Faith; The Case for Secular Humanism* (New Haven: Yale University Press, 2014), 19–20, and 130.

10. If by living in a "disenchanted" world we mean only the loss of belief in magic, fairies, and demons, then monotheism, especially since the Reformation, was a major force in disenchantment. See Charles Taylor, *A Secular Age* (Cambridge, MA: Harvard University Press, 2007), 77. Secular humanists tend to be atheists; the disenchantment goes deep. See also Taylor's "Disenchantment—Reenchantment," in Levine, *Joy of Secularism,* 57–73.

other ways or at least have a functional substitute for it, thus avoiding or mitigating what Charles Taylor calls "the malaises of modernity."[11]

A widely discussed question is whether secular humanists can have a reasonable and well-grounded morality and be properly motivated to act on it. Does morality (or ethics) depend on religion (or theology)? One traditional view is the meta-ethical theory that ethics requires a theological foundation in order to avoid nihilism (no real values) or subjectivism (values are relative to each person). This requirement has been developed in at least two different ways, the first being what is called the "divine command theory of ethics." A venerable version of this theory is to claim that only God's will makes things right or wrong; it is sometimes stated as "X is good (or obligatory)" just means "God approves of (or demands) X." Divine command theorists admit that atheists and others can use moral ideas without realizing their foundation; people can use a building, for example, without giving a thought to its foundation. Only when they start questioning will they see the need for a foundation.

A philosophical problem with the divine command theory goes back to Plato's *Euthyphro*[12] dialogue. Plato believed that the question, "Does God approve of something because it is good or is it good because God approves of it?" is analogous to the question, "Does the gardener love a flower because it is beautiful or is it beautiful because the gardener loves it?" He thought that the answer was obvious: if the gardener's love is the foundation for beauty, if there is nothing in the flower that elicits the gardener's approval, then we end up with sheer arbitrariness. It would be as if God could choose murder to be good, thereby making it good. A religious problem with this version of the divine command theory is that when theists praise God as good, they seem to be saying something deeper than merely that God approves of himself. Although the debate continues, these difficulties are often cited by secular humanists (as well as many religious believers) as reasons to reject divine command as a moral foundation.

The second way that many thinkers assert a theological foundation for ethics is by claiming that the best—perhaps only—grounding for human dignity and universal human rights is that God creates all persons in God's image or that God loves all persons. When a United Nations committee

11. Taylor, *A Secular Age,* chapter 8. Some secular humanists insist that any substitute avoid the notion of enchantment; see Bruce Robbins, "Enchantment? No Thank You," in Levine, *Joy of Secularism,* 74–94.

12. In many translations and editions; see, for example, Plato's *Euthyphro,* accessed May 1, 2015, http://www.indiana.edu/~p374/Euthyphro.pdf.

was debating the Universal Declaration of Human Rights during the late 1940s, the committee chair, Eleanor Roosevelt, growing tired of listening to philosophers and theologians argue, insisted that they come up with a consensus on a coherent list of human rights, and then agree to disagree about their foundation. The document is thus called "A Universal Declaration of Human Rights" rather than a "Declaration of Universal Human Rights." (Interestingly, there were abstentions but no vetoes during the final vote.) The question is whether commitment to human dignity and rights can have a secular justification.

Entirely apart from the view that theology is needed for the *foundation* of ethics is the view of many believers that sacred scriptures reveal at least some of the *content* of ethics. Most of them agree that through reason and natural law humans can know some and maybe even most of morality, but claim that revelations provide distinctive features and emphases for moral and spiritual life. However, secular humanists believe they can provide an alternative well-rounded content for their ethic by appealing to, say, the commitments that are necessary for living together and flourishing as a group.[13]

Other religious believers think that we can know about morality quite independently of our religious beliefs, so they deny that ethics is epistemologically dependent on theology. Rather, they see the distinctively religious feature as one of motivation. We may have the proper convictions about what is morally appropriate or required, but will we be motivated to commit ourselves to do it? The oldest form of the claim that morality is motivationally dependent on religious commitment is the appeal to rewards and punishments, the "fire and brimstone" preaching by some Christians that "put the fear of the Lord" into people. "Fear" here is understood as being scared of God, which does not necessarily involve respect or love. This "reward or punishment" appeal, of course, is to self-interest—save your eternal skin—and is rejected by other believers who point to a different sort of motivation, such as a sense of calling nurtured by covenantal gratitude for creation and redemption. Indeed, as we will notice later in a

13. See, for example, Sisela Bok's *Common Values* (Columbia: University of Missouri Press, 1995). The literature on secular theories of ethics is vast. See the anthology *Is Goodness without God Good Enough?* ed. Robert Garcia and Nathan King (Lanham, MD: Rowman & Littlefield, 2009). I am convinced by books like Erik Wielenberg's *Value and Virtue in a Godless Universe* (Cambridge: Cambridge University Press, 2005) and Kitcher's *Life after Faith* that secular humanists can be appropriately committed to a well-reasoned ethic. The issue I will consider is whether such commitment can be associated with a sense of calling.

discussion of Wendell Berry's appeal to "gift," gratitude is commonly cited by contemporary Christians as the source of the calling that elicits moral motivation. Can secular humanism claim a similar sense of calling?

The question of moral motivation can be understood as the question, "Why should I be moral?" Notice that even someone who thinks there are good answers to the question "Why should *we* be moral?" (such as Bok's claim that commitment to some minimal values is necessary for societies to exist, and certainly to flourish) might still wonder why I (or any rational individual) should not cheat when I can get away with it. A good answer appeals to the folk wisdom that you cannot fool all of the people all of the time, so the best way to *assure* others that you are trustworthy is to actually *be* trustworthy. This folk wisdom, however, seems to base motivation on prudence rather than morality. Of course, if one gives a *moral* reason for being moral, it seems circular: "You ought to be moral because you morally ought to." One might note that such circularity is in good company. If one gives reasons in answer to the question "Why should I be rational?" one presumes commitment to rationality, and few regard this as a vicious rather than virtuous circle. Still, we can investigate whether at least some moral motivations flow from a sense of gratitude for gifts that enable one to live a meaningful and fulfilling life.

Secularism and Living a Meaningful Life

The challenge to a secular humanist's living a meaningful life has been dramatically stated by Bertrand Russell in his oft-cited essay, "A Free Man's Worship":

> That man is the product of causes which had no prevision of the end they were achieving; that his origin, his growth, his hopes and fears, his loves and his beliefs, are but the outcome of accidental collocations of atoms; that no fire, no heroism, no intensity of thought and feeling, can preserve an individual life beyond the grave; that all the labors of the ages, all the devotion, all the inspiration, all the noonday brightness of human genius, are destined to extinction in the vast death of the solar system, and that the whole temple of Man's achievement must inevitably be buried beneath the debris of a universe in ruins—all these things, if not quite beyond dispute, are yet so nearly certain, that no philosophy which rejects them can hope to stand. Only within the scaffolding of

these truths, only on the firm foundation of unyielding despair, can the soul's habitation henceforth be safely built.[14]

It seems the despair need not be unyielding, since Russell himself manages to develop a fairly optimistic outlook from this foundation, but one can see how others would decide the best thing for a person is too late—to not have been born.[15] Even Albert Camus's claim that, although life is absurd, suicide is ill-advised seems questionable when he offers a vision of Sisyphus futilely pushing his rock and asserts that we must imagine Sisyphus happy.[16] However, it does not take much imagination to see that Camus's image of repeatedly pushing a rock up a hill gives us a lopsided vision of the life available to a secularist, even assuming Russell's claims.

Camus thinks there is some sort of clash between our wild search for clarity and the relentless silence of the universe (since God does not exist), and that is what makes our life absurd like Sisyphus's. However, Thomas Nagel says that Camus mislocates the clash: it is not between us and the universe; rather, it is within ourselves. We are conflicted between our serious pursuit of goals and our ability to stand back and become spectators of our own lives and raise endless questions about those goals. But, says Nagel, that is no reason to pout; it is one of the most interesting things about us and calls for an ironic smile[17] or, more likely, a sense of humility.[18] Moreover Joel Feinberg[19] and Susan Wolf[20] convincingly argue that the goals secularists pursue can be much more important, engaging, and meaningful than those in the picture that Camus paints.

I believe we should grant that the goals available to a secularist can add up to living a meaningful life, certainly in the minimal sense that a

14. E. D. Klemke and Steven Cahn, eds., *The Meaning of Life,* 3rd ed. (Oxford: Oxford University Press, 2008), 56.

15. Nietzsche quoting Aristotle quoting Silenus's advice to King Midas, in Paolo Costa, "A Secular Wonder," in Levine, *Joy of Secularism,* 134. The next best thing, says Silenus, is to die soon.

16. "The Myth of Sisyphus," in Klemke and Cahn, *The Meaning of Life,* 81.

17. "The Absurd," in Klemke and Cahn, *The Meaning of Life,* 148–52.

18. Thomas Nagel, *The View from Nowhere* (Oxford: Oxford University Press, 1986), 222.

19. "Absurd Self-Fulfillment," in Klemke and Cahn, *The Meaning of Life,* 175: "Suppose, however, that the gods assign to Sisyphus an endless series of rather complex engineering problems and leave it up to him to solve them." And the solving is done in a social context with coworkers, friends, and family.

20. Susan Wolf, *Meaning in Life and Why It Matters* (Princeton: Princeton University Press, 2010).

person's life has a worthwhile purpose. It is true that a secularist cannot find purpose in service to God's kingdom. But as Kurt Baier points out, one need not be assigned a purpose by someone else; one can choose one's own purposes and goals.[21] Baier associates being given a purpose by God with being a robot manufactured in God's laboratory. However, theists think that a believer *accepts* God's call; it may be true that we were created to fit well into God's plans, and that therefore God issues an offer that is too good to refuse. But it is still a call or assignment that we are free to decline or accept. Even Rick Warren's best-seller, *The Purpose Driven Life: What on Earth Am I Here For?*, has a section on "Accepting Your Assignment."[22]

That theists must accept or reject God's call is an important point because sometimes theists claim that having secularists choose their own goals amounts to insisting that individual autonomy can usurp God's role and that the creature insists on being the creator. But for the theist to rebut Baier's claim that taking one's purpose from God amounts to denying human responsibility, the theist must agree that any call from God involves the decision whether to accept it. Even if the decision is seen as the result of saving grace rather than sheer gumption, one must affirm that it was grace from God that enabled the choice, and this affirmation must involve freedom if the theist is to avoid Baier's claim that receiving one's purpose from God turns theists into robots. So both the secularist and the theist affirm free decisions regarding goals. And if the values one uses to decide come from one's religious upbringing, one still needs to affirm these values for oneself. Of course, there is an advantage in responding to a call from someone else, someone who one thinks is especially wise and good. So even if we grant that secularists can choose to live a meaningful and purposeful life, we should ask whether there can be something analogous to a calling that *elicits* a sense of responsibility and direction.

Gift, Gratitude, Fulfillment, and Receiving One's Calling

Douglas Schuurman discusses various religious affections that nurture a sense of calling, such as the feelings of dependence, gratitude, obligation,

---

21. "The Meaning of Life," in Klemke and Cahn, *The Meaning of Life,* 101.

22. Rick Warren, *The Purpose Driven Life: What on Earth Am I Here For?* (Grand Rapids: Zondervan, 2002), 227–33.

and direction.[23] Secularists can and do certainly have a sense of dependence, not on God but on people and forces. Indeed, the forces, processes, and decisions that have resulted in their existence, from the big bang to the choices of billions of ancestors, can elicit the sort of awe, amazement, wonder, joy, and sense of the sublime that rivals that of theists. The latter have an awesome Deity, of course, but once you have an omniscient and omnipotent creator, the details of how God's providence produced you can be fairly unremarkable in comparison to the stupendous series of choices and random events that secularists think produced them and this amazing world.

Can this sense of dependence and awe elicit the sort of gratitude that associates with a sense of direction and obligation? Theists can and do emphasize gratitude as the source of covenantal responsibility, but what about others? It seems that others indeed can emphasize gratitude. Cicero, for example, says, "Gratitude is not only the greatest of virtues, but also the parent of all the others."[24] A theistic defense of such a sentiment can be found in Wendell Berry's essay "The Gift of Good Land."[25] Berry argues that the land, as well as everything we appreciate in our lives, should be experienced as a gift. More precisely, it is the *use* of the land and our other resources that is the gift; God owns the earth and all within it, and God gives us the usage. But this gift elicits the need to be worthy of it, which in turn elicits the sort of gratitude and humility that calls for neighborliness and good husbandry. I have often asked students whether they would rather *earn* something important (e.g., a college education, a career opportunity, or a house) or have it *given* to them. They almost invariably said they would prefer to earn it, especially if the gift was the usage and the usage came with sustainability strings attached. Preferring to *earn* something important is a thoroughly American attitude, of course; we like to see ourselves as individuals autonomously earning whatever we have or achieve.[26] But most of my students also admitted that much of what they

---

23. Douglas Schuurman, *Vocation: Discerning Our Callings in Life* (Grand Rapids: Eerdmans, 2004), 52–66. Schuurman is referring to James Gustafson's work on the affections.

24. In his *Oration for Plancio,* see Philosiblog, "Gratitude Is Not Only the Greatest of Virtues, but the Parent of All Others," accessed March 4, 2015, http://philosiblog.com/2013/01/11/gratitude-is-not-only-the-greatest-of-virtues-but-the-parent-of-all-others.

25. Wendell Berry, *The Gift of Good Land: Further Essays Cultural and Agricultural* (San Francisco: North Point, 1981), 267–81.

26. Today cultivating gratitude is something of a growth industry, with books such as Wendy Meg Siegel, *The Gratitude Habit: A 365 Day Journal and Workbook: A Tool for Cre-*

are, and *have,* and *achieve* is largely due to grace or luck combined with a lot of contributions from others. And they admitted that realizing this did elicit a sense of responsibility to use their gifts wisely, many of them translating that into covenantal responsibility to live lives of worth and service.

It is easier to see how this works when the gift comes from God than when it is blind chance. Can one thank one's lucky stars in such a way that it elicits a sense of calling, perhaps to stewardship? Ronald Aronson recounts what amounts to a secular "calling" story:

> Hiking through a nearby woods on a spring day recently, I followed the turning path and suddenly saw a tiny lake, then walked down a hill to its edge as birds chirped and darted about, stopping at a clearing to register the warmth of the sun against my face. Feelings welled up: physical pleasure, delight in the sounds and sights, gladness to be out here on this day. But something else as well, curious and less distinct, a vague feeling more like gratitude than anything else but not toward any being or person I could recognize.[27]

Aronson sees the problem with calling this feeling "gratitude," since we tend, especially in theistic traditions, to think that we are grateful *to* someone (he notes that he originally published this passage in an article titled "Thank Who Very Much?"). But he thinks that we can be grateful *for* something without being grateful *to* someone. Of course, there are plenty of someones to be grateful to. He says that at a thanksgiving dinner, we can be grateful "to our ancestors distant and recent and their struggles, whose labors have accumulated in the comforts we enjoy; and to countless other people, wherever they are, whose toil helped set the table at which we feast."[28] Mark Berkson's chapter in this volume, "The Cultivation, Calling, and Loss of the Self: Confucian and Daoist Perspectives on Vocation,"

---

ating Positive Feelings in Your Daily Life (CreateSpace Publishing, 2012). But my students' preference for *earning* something rather than being *given* it goes deep. In fact, many thinkers have claimed that there is no such thing as a free gift because gifts always elicit a burden of reciprocity and obligation. Some of the complexities involved in gift giving are explored in Gregory Walter, *Being Promised: Theology, Gift, and Practice* (Grand Rapids: Eerdmans, 2013), and in Douglas Schuurman, "Gratitude," in *Dictionary of Scripture and Ethics,* ed. Joel Green (Grand Rapids: Baker, 2011), 342–43.

27. Ronald Aronson, *Living without God: New Directions for Atheists, Agnostics, Secularists, and the Undecided* (Berkeley, CA: Counterpoint, 2008), 43.

28. Aronson, *Living without God,* 63.

explains that a feeling of indebtedness to ancestors, sages, and teachers yields for some a sense of calling from them, a calling that comes not from God or Heaven but from all who guide and support us and, ultimately, all other human beings: *We are all calling each other.* Thus atheists can feel a sense of calling from other people. However, apart from the fact that it is hard to see how we should feel called by villains and moral monsters who prey on others, to feel a sense of obligation as a call from all the rest of the people probably requires a more organic view of the unity of humanity (or at least of societies) than we find in more individualistic societies such as the only somewhat united US.

Aronson also insists on being grateful for the "natural forces that have made our own life, and this reunion possible."[29] He claims that "[a]llowing our relationships with nature to be mapped across time, from the big bang that created the sun, to the cosmic processes that created the earth, to the rains that created its oceans—yes, to the microbes in the water and in the soil, leading to the evolution of the other species of plants and animals—leads us to educate our sense of gratitude by becoming aware of our own sources."[30] So he endorses a response that elicits the determination

> to preserve the wilderness, and thus the possibility of such an experience for their children and grandchildren, and as their sense of time expands, even those living in the distant future. Other striking responses are a democratic sense—the belief that this heritage belongs to everyone and the desire to preserve this for everyone—and a feeling of this stewardship giving their life a meaning and purpose.[31]

Aronson's distinction between grateful *to* and grateful *for* enables him to agree with Robert Solomon that we need not personify the universe in order to feel grateful, a feeling that Solomon says is a philosophical emotion:

> So viewed, "opening one's heart to the universe" is not so much personifying the universe as reflecting on as well as feeling and expressing a cosmic gratitude, that is, expanding one's perspective, as the Stoics insisted, so that one comes to appreciate the beauty of the whole as well

29. Aronson, *Living without God*, 63.
30. Aronson, *Living without God*, 55–56.
31. Aronson, *Living without God*, 54.

as be absorbed in our own limited projects and passions. That is spirituality. It is, perhaps, the ultimate happiness, and it is an ideal expression of emotional integrity.[32]

It is not hard to see how this sense of gratitude can elicit a sense of responsibility to share and to be good stewards of what one has been the fortunate recipient. The calling would come not from God but from one's own conscience, one that says the more fortunate should help those less fortunate and that the only decent thing to do when one is gifted and lucky is to pay it forward. We will later consider some objections to this response, but first we should ask about practices that nurture it.

Practices and Communities

Not surprisingly, one practice that secularists nurture is experiencing the wonder and beauty of nature and of the entire universe, trying to keep in spatial and historical perspective the violence and suffering that it includes. Even the wildernesses that elicit feelings of the sublime are red in tooth and claw, to say nothing of containing deadly viruses. And when one thinks about the billions of ancestors (perhaps six billion in the last 12,000 years alone) that contributed to one's genetic endowment, appreciation must be tempered with the realization that many of them were marauders and rapists. The big picture has plenty of shadows, and one must work at stepping back to appreciate the overall context.

A related recommended practice is meditating on and reflecting on one's life and thought, sorting out what one is grateful for, and what one's responsibilities are. Of course, Buddhists and others also recommend the sort of meditation that empties the mind of such self-directed thoughts, and some secularists endorse this transcending of self and individual experience. For example, Sam Harris, often associated with the "new atheists," published *Waking Up: A Guide to Spirituality without Religion,* in which he discusses how to meditate, how to achieve mindfulness, and even the opportunities and dangers involved in psychedelic drugs.[33]

32. Robert Solomon, *True to Our Feelings: What Our Emotions Are Really Telling Us* (Oxford: Oxford University Press, 2007), 270.

33. Sam Harris, *Waking Up* (New York: Simon & Schuster, 2014). Harris discusses Breath Meditation on pp. 39–40 and psychedelics on pp. 186–200. His website provides a range of resources. See Sam Harris, accessed April 28, 2015, www.samharris.com.

Much more can be said about meditation, but of greater interest to me is the question whether secular humanists can have something like the group practices and sense of belonging to a community that are an important part of the way religion functions in the lives of believers. Though some atheists see little that is positive in religion, others admire its social function:

> Communities of believers connect their members, providing a sense of belonging and of being together with others, of sharing problems and of working cooperatively to find solutions. Religious involvement does not merely provide occasions for talk about important issues—although that itself is valuable—but also for joint action. . . . Engaging in common pursuit of a good endorsed by fellow strivers, and doing one's part in the shared effort, can be the source of deepest satisfaction.[34]

Communities of believers also care for their members through good times and bad, celebrating together, grieving together, and sharing each other's burdens in difficult times.

It is true that humanist organizations have developed materials that provide rituals for weddings and funerals and other notable occasions, but until fairly recently only the religious humanists, such as Unitarian Universalist congregations, nurtured the belongingness and mutuality and sharing that are the strengths of religious groups. Kitcher almost wistfully notes that

> [r]eligion does not have to be the main vehicle of community life. Thoroughly secular societies can contain structures enabling people to enter into sympathetic relations with one another, to achieve solidarity with their fellows, to exchange views about topics that concern them most, to work together to identify goals that matter to all members of the group and to pursue those ends through cooperative efforts.[35]

Can secularists develop the type of communities that Kitcher hopes could be alternatives to religious ones? There are the Ethical Culture groups with the motto "Deeds, Not Creeds" that meet on Sundays for a "platform lecture" and other activities, including youth education.[36] In the

34. Kitcher, *Life after Faith*, 119.
35. Kitcher, *Life after Faith*, 120.
36. See the American Ethical Union website, accessed June 8, 2015, http://aeu.org. This Union is in turn part of the International Humanist and Ethical Union, accessed June 8, 2015,

United States they are organized into the "American Ethical Union," which includes groups in twelve states, though they are mainly on the east coast (with eight of the twenty-two groups in the New York City area). Founded by Felix Adler in 1876, the Ethical Culture movement has not grown much over the decades, and seems not to attract the enthusiasm Kitcher notices in so many religious communities. So perhaps he can take heart in the recent rise of the Sunday Assembly movement. Calling itself "a global movement for wonder and good" and using the motto "Live Better, Help Often, and Wonder More," it has developed since 2013 from a single "godless congregation" in London to perhaps five hundred groups around the world.[37] Although the track record for secular communes is not nearly as good as for religious communes,[38] the Sunday Assembly movement is something new. It is not a commune, of course, but the Assembly seems to provide secularists with some of the social functions and benefits that religious congregations provide. Some liberal Christian churches emphasize that the religious life is a journey of *seeking* as much as *finding,* that unanswered questions have done a lot less harm than unquestioned answers, and that seekers journeying together can have the solidarity and the social benefits that traditional congregations provide.[39] Perhaps the Sunday Assembly

---

http://iheu.org/. Both groups affirm the 2002 "Amsterdam Declaration," accessed June 8, 2015, http://iheu.org/humanism/the-amsterdam-declaration/.

37. See its website, *Sunday Assembly,* accessed March 5, 2015, https://www.sunday assembly.com/. Of course, there are many civic organizations, clubs, and teams that anyone can join and thereby feel a sense of solidarity, at least regarding the specific goals of the group, but the Sunday Assembly movement seeks to nurture the mutuality and caring that is an intense feature of most religious communities. That secularists disagree about the need for Sunday Assembly meetings can be seen in the letters to the *New York Times* in response to a sympathetic account of visiting a Sunday Assembly meeting in 2015. See Molly Worthen, "Wanted: A Theology of Atheism," accessed June 3, 2015, http://www.nytimes.com/2015/05/31/opinion/sunday/molly-worthen-wanted-a-theology-of-atheism.html?_r=0.

38. Jonathan Haidt, in *The Righteous Mind: Why Good People Are Divided by Politics and Religion* (New York: Pantheon, 2012), has a chapter on "Religion Is a Team Sport," where he notes that religious communes have a 30 to 39 percent survival rate after twenty years while secular ones have 6 percent (most fail within eight years), 257. There seem to be no requirements or sacrifices for those attending Sunday Assemblies, which may be a problem given that for religious groups there seems to be a correlation between sacrificial demands and group success. However, Haidt notes that this correlation does not hold for secular groups; increase demands on secular groups, and their members simply do a cost-benefit analysis.

39. For example, the United Church of Christ's motto is: "God is still speaking; don't put a period where God has put a comma" at United Church of Christ, accessed April 28, 2015, http://www.ucc.org/god-is-still-speaking/.

movement can be seen as a secular version of a community of seekers. If so, it can be seen as an effort at retrieving elements from older religious traditions in order to reform secularism by emphasizing community.

Some Difficulties and Prospects

One problem is that some secularists do not think it is appropriate to thank impersonal forces: "[I]t seems evident to me that you can only thank a being whom it makes sense to ask something of. And it makes no sense to ask something of a non-personal being."[40] Feeling lucky might be appropriate, but not gratitude with whatever feelings of responsibility that may elicit. On the other hand, Ronnie de Sousa thinks that gratitude for sheer luck has a lot to be said for it, and it is more morally appropriate than gratitude to God for your life and gifts:

> For my part, having long passed the age at which most human beings who have ever lived are dead, I feel gratitude every day for being alive. But if I thought some God was to be thanked for that, as opposed to brute luck, I'd worry about the unfairness of it. Why should God privilege me, while condemning millions of innocent people to early and often horrible deaths?[41]

He objects to the irritating habit of theists who claim that God saved their lives during a catastrophe that killed many others; he says that the proper response would be embarrassment.

It is an empirical question whether people can and do feel gratitude for cosmic good luck, a gratitude that elicits an internal call to stewardship or sharing. The answer is that some do and some do not. A more normative

---

40. Ernst Tugendhat, "Thank the Impersonal?" First published in German in the *Neue Zürcher Zeitung,* December 9, 2006. It is noteworthy that gratitude is included in Sir David Ross's famous *prima facie* duties, but he rests it "on previous acts of other men, i.e. services done by them to me." *The Right and the Good* (Oxford: Oxford University Press, 1930), 21. Thus some secularists disagree with Aronson's use of the distinction between "grateful for" and "grateful to," probably thinking that "grateful for x" is simply shorthand for "grateful to y for the gift of x."

41. From a review of Solomon's *True to Our Feelings,* see Notre Dame Philosophical Reviews, accessed March 5, 2015, https://ndpr.nd.edu/news/23181-true-to-our-feelings -what-our-emotions-are-really-telling-us.

question is whether people *should* feel such a call. John Rawls thinks so. Referring to the "natural lottery," he claims that:

> The natural distribution is neither just nor unjust; nor is it unjust that men are born into society at some particular position. These are simply natural facts. What is just or unjust is the way that institutions deal with these facts. . . . In justice as fairness men agree to share one another's fate.[42]

Justice as fairness asks us to think behind "the veil of ignorance" where people choose the basic principles of justice while knowing all the relevant facts about the human condition but not knowing how fortunate or unfortunate they are in the natural lottery. In such a situation, we probably would agree to share each other's fates. But the question some of Rawls's critics raise is why we should feel obliged to think behind the veil of ignorance; we in fact often see what cards the natural lottery has dealt us, so why should we not bargain freely and fairly with others based on everyone's perceived strengths and weaknesses?[43]

Of course, quite apart from the veil of ignorance, decent people can be charitable toward those less fortunate, helping them not as a matter of justice but as a matter of humility and love. Erik Wielenberg argues that even in a godless universe "we can see that naturalistic humility, like Christian humility, leads to charity . . . naturalistic humility involves a recognition of the tremendous contribution of blind chance to the fates of human beings, and it is precisely such a recognition that should lead us to acknowledge an obligation to assist the less fortunate among us."[44] His use of "obligation" might suggest to some that he is making it a matter of justice, but a properly nuanced understanding of moral responsibilities allows for a call to obligation that goes beyond strict duties of justice.[45] Thus secularists can feel a calling to serve, whether as a matter of justice or of charity.

---

42. John Rawls, *A Theory of Justice* (Cambridge, MA: Harvard University Press, 1971), 102. Even a person's superior character, which enables him to work hard and succeed, is not entirely deserved, since it "depends in large part upon fortunate family and social circumstances for which he can claim no credit" (104). Thus we should see our gifts and good luck as social resources.

43. As libertarians argue; see Robert Nozick, *Anarchy, State, and Utopia* (New York: Basic Books, 1974).

44. Wielenberg, *Value and Virtue in a Godless Universe*, 115–16.

45. See Gregory Mellema, *Beyond the Call of Duty* (Albany: State University of New York Press, 1991).

We certainly have not settled the question whether secular humanists can argue that either gratitude for or humility at one's good fortune *should* yield a sense of calling to service and stewardship. However, we have seen why many secular humanists think that they have such a call, a call not from God but from one's own conscience. It can elicit what David Brooks calls the "summoned life,"[46] and that leads to another problem.

The details of what one's calling entails is a major issue for religious as well as secular traditions. It is clear that a vague sense of calling must be specified by reference to one's talents as well as to the opportunities and needs one sees around one.[47] David Brooks makes this point when he distinguishes the "Well-Planned Life" from the "Summoned Life." For the former, "life comes to appear as a well-designed project, carefully conceived in the beginning, reviewed and adjusted along the way and brought toward a well-rounded fruition." For the latter, "Life isn't a project to be completed; it is an unknowable landscape to be explored."

> The person leading the Well-Planned Life emphasizes individual agency, and asks, "What should I do?" The person leading the Summoned Life emphasizes the context, and asks, "What are my circumstances asking me to do?" The person leading the Summoned Life starts with a very concrete situation: I'm living in a specific year in a specific place facing specific problems and needs. At this moment in my life, I am confronted with specific job opportunities and specific options. The important questions are: What are these circumstances summoning me to do? What is needed in this place? What is the most useful social role before me? These are questions answered primarily by sensitive observation and situational awareness, not calculation and long-range planning.[48]

Brooks offers wise advice. Our calling involves not just free choice, but choice influenced by how circumstances summon us to respond appropriately. But what if one is oversummoned? The reality is that human needs, to say nothing of wider animal and ecological needs, are a bottomless pit, and

---

46. David Brooks, "The Summoned Self," accessed March 6, 2015, http://www.nytimes.com/2010/08/03/opinion/03brooks.html.

47. See Schuurman, *Vocation*, 140–50, his chapter in this volume, and Lee Hardy, *The Fabric of This World: Inquires into Calling, Career Choice, and the Design of Human Work* (Grand Rapids: Eerdmans, 1990), 80–106.

48. Brooks, "The Summoned Self."

there is no way a realistic person can expect that all or even most desperate needs will be met. As Kitcher puts it,

> Many, perhaps most, human lives do not go well. Among the contemporary global population, millions, if not billions, struggle to gather the necessities that enable them, and their children, to continue from day to day. For many more, secularist praise of autonomous choice of "one's own good" could only be heard as a tasteless joke.[49]

Kitcher is fair in noting that "[l]iteralist religions often do better than secular institutions in responding to the conditions dooming many people to lives marked by insecurity and confined to narrow horizons" but claims that their efforts are compromised by believing that present failures will be redeemed in the hereafter.[50]

The secularist worry is that religious belief in an afterlife can function as an opiate, not just to the oppressed, but also to those helping them, since when efforts at salvage faint or fail, salvation compensates. However, it is possible that belief in a compensating afterlife enables believers to work hard to salvage needy lives because they can avoid paralyzing despair in knowing that, in spite of their best efforts, they cannot make much of a dent in meeting the overwhelming needs. It is less like opium and more like backup medicine. A similar point is made by David Swenson, who was influenced by the Danish philosopher Søren Kierkegaard: "The hope of eternal bliss is not . . . a refuge from life; it is a challenge to live yet more deeply and intensely."[51] In particular, it enables a person "to wean [oneself] from the paralyzing effort of trying to shoulder the vaguely looming burden of tomorrow, or of all the tomorrows, in place of a concentration of effort and attention upon the definitely restricted burden of today."[52]

In other words, one can focus on a reasonably restricted summons to the needs of others, a focus that also allows for pursuing one's own projects and enjoying some leisure time, without thinking that such pursuits and enjoyments automatically violate one's call to a life of worth and service.

49. Kitcher, *Life after Faith*, 116.
50. Kitcher, *Life after Faith*, 118.
51. David Swenson, "The Transforming Power of Otherworldliness," in *The Meaning of Life*, 2nd ed., ed. E. D. Klemke (Oxford: Oxford University Press, 2000), 33.
52. Swenson, "Transforming Power," 37. Obviously Swenson is not addressing the plausibility of a Kierkegaardian leap of faith into this religious commitment; he is addressing only the this-worldly advantage of otherworldliness.

Obviously there are dangers here, and the human tendency toward self-serving restrictions on one's summons must be recognized as well as the urge of some to become an exhausted servant (or a mere means) for the needs of others. But at least the believer has an outlook that allows for living a balanced life. Can secularists decide among the almost infinite summons they might feel called to meet and still have time and resources for their own projects and fulfillment, knowing that the misery of those dying in destitution is all that there is for them?

Peter Singer provides a well-known argument that we ought to prevent something bad, such as severe poverty, whenever we can do so without sacrificing something of comparable significance.[53] Even if one has doubts about the details of this argument, it takes little imagination to see that most of us could do a lot more than we do to help those whose needs we in some way feel called or summoned to meet. How can secularists enjoy their comfortable lives, including the fine things in life that provide meaning and fulfillment, while knowing that they could do a lot more to help others in desperate need? As Jean Kazez says, "No matter how much of our lives we've devoted to fulfilling the demands of morality, there are going to be more demands"[54] and it seems we regularly override those demands in order to pursue our own projects, interests, and pleasures. She

53. Peter Singer, *Practical Ethics* (Cambridge: Cambridge University Press, 1979), 169–70. Singer originally made this argument in "Famine, Affluence, and Morality," *Philosophy and Public Affairs* 1, no. 3 (1972): 229–43. Singer admits that this obligation may be so severe that the only way to maximize the general good would be to publicly preach a less severe one, such as the obligation to tithe. But that would not change the stricter obligation that a conscientious person should feel (*Practical Ethics,* 181). Peter Unger in *Living High and Letting Die: Our Illusion of Innocence* (Oxford: Oxford University Press, 1996) defends Singer's basic outlook with what he calls a "Liberation" ethic. Singer believes that his conclusion applies more widely than only to his admittedly rigorous utilitarian ethic of maximizing the general good (a maximization ethic might imply, for example, that you are *permitted* to take a nap only when any other course of action would reduce the general good, that is, only when you are *obliged* to). He says it applies to anyone who accepts his premise that one ought to prevent a serious harm whenever one can do so without sacrificing something of comparable significance. One can deny this premise by asserting that one is responsible only for harms that one causes and not for (most) harms that one could prevent, but probably few people can conscientiously accept such a minimalist sense of responsibility. Zell Kravinsky is one who followed the relentless logic of Singer's premise, giving away almost everything, including body organs; see Ian Parker, "The Gift," *The New Yorker,* August 2, 2004, 59.

54. Jean Kazez, *The Weight of Things: Philosophy and the Good Life* (Oxford: Blackwell, 2007), 125.

thinks that most of the great moral philosophers "give morality a kind of ultimate value that would make it hard to ever say there was a good reason to desist from doing more" but that they allow normal life to influence their more modest expectations: "The contours of a normal life are pre-set; they include community, family, friends, an occupation, private interests, and pastimes."[55] Thus we simply allow other values and commitments to override moral ones:

> If the capacity for morality is more important to use than any other capacity, it doesn't follow that morality takes precedence in every situation. If I have done what's immediately required, and I've taken on responsibilities, and fulfilled whatever requirements they create, and I've devoted time to what's better, I am not contemptible if I also sometimes sink into my own life, disproportionately caring about whatever happens to be vital to me and mine. I can write poetry, play the piano, take my children to the movies, invest in a non-optimal career, without feeling like an abject sinner.[56]

Of course, not being contemptible or not feeling like an abject sinner is a rather low bar, one not conducive to sleeping well at night merely because one managed to get over it. However, I think she could combine this melancholy realism about the human condition with the claim that one can be a decent human being without being a saint or a moral hero. What she is discussing is value pluralism, the view that the sources of our reasonable loyalties are diverse and sometimes incompatible and incommensurable. Our loyalties and commitments include, of course, moral obligations that in turn include preventing harms by helping others and not just avoiding causing harms. But they also include pursuing valuable goals and personal projects that rub against moral devotion.[57]

The upshot is that everyone will encounter or hear about desperate needs that they decide they cannot or will not meet. Even though they at some level feel summoned to try to meet these needs, they will not, either because it is impossible or because of the other values in their

---

55. Kazez, *Weight of Things*, 124.

56. Kazez, *Weight of Things*, 127.

57. I discuss moral pluralism (our moral commitments sometimes conflict) and, more generally, value pluralism (sometimes nonmoral values override moral ones) and how to cope with them in *Civil Disagreement: Personal Integrity in a Pluralistic Society* (Washington, DC: Georgetown University Press, 2014), 38–62.

lives. Although secularists cannot have the hope that unfortunate people might in some way find fulfillment in an afterlife, they can be decent about providing a reasonable amount of help while gratefully pursuing and experiencing those worthwhile things that can make their lives meaningful and fulfilling. Those who are morally sensitive have to recognize the difficult, uncertain, and uncomfortable tradeoffs they make. Perhaps they can rarely feel completely good about themselves, but they can wonder about people who always do, given the sober realities of the human condition.

Conclusion

Secularism, at least in the West, does not have the long traditions with communities, institutions, creeds, and practices that most religious traditions have. Indeed, only in the past century or two could individual thinkers profess atheism without likely arousing significant hostility. And, as we saw, even the early associations that could be called humanist embraced liberal religious commitments. Only with the establishment of distinctly secular humanist organizations do we find a debate between those who would like to drop any religious overtones and those who would like to emulate some of the vitality of religious organizations, especially the sense of community and sharing. Secular humanists can commit themselves to a reasonable moral code quite independently of religious commitments, and can live a life of purpose and meaning. However, there is the important question whether secular humanists can feel something like the sense of calling that is such an important guiding and motivating feature of religious traditions, one that is often grounded not in fear of punishment or hope of reward but in gratitude for gifts given by God. Confucians and others feel themselves grateful for and called by ancestors, teachers, and all who have contributed to their well-being, and feel they should pay it forward by helping others. An intramural debate within secular humanism is whether one can and should feel gratitude toward the impersonal forces that have endowed one with life and opportunities, a gratitude that elicits a sense of stewardship and service. Practices and experiences that enhance a sense of gratitude and calling include appreciating the wonders of nature, meditating, and developing solidarity with others who share one's desire to live a journey of seeking, questioning, appreciating, and serving.

Resources

Aronson, Ronald. *Living without God: New Directions for Atheists, Agnostics, Secularists, and the Undecided.* Berkeley, CA: Counterpoint, 2008.

American Humanist Association, accessed March 4, 2015, http://american humanist.org.

Council for Secular Humanism, accessed March 4, 2015, https://www.secular humanism.org.

Kazez, Jean. *The Weight of Things: Philosophy and the Good Life.* Oxford: Blackwell, 2007.

Kitcher, Philip. *Life after Faith: The Case for Secular Humanism.* New Haven: Yale University Press, 2014.

Klemke, E. D., and Steven Cahn, eds. *The Meaning of Life.* 3rd edition. Oxford: Oxford University Press, 2008.

Levine, George, ed. *The Joy of Secularism.* Princeton: Princeton University Press, 2011.

Wielenberg, Erik. *Value and Virtue in a Godless Universe.* Cambridge: Cambridge University Press, 2005.

Wolf, Susan. *Meaning in Life and Why It Matters.* Princeton: Princeton University Press, 2010.

Further Selected Resources on Vocation

The resources listed below were originally produced under the auspices of The Collegeville Institute. The Institute, located at Saint John's University and Abbey in Collegeville, Minnesota, promotes scholarship, leadership, creativity, and community among people of faith. The Institute hosts a series of interdisciplinary, ecumenical, collaborative seminars that gathers researchers and practitioners to explore important issues facing today's Christian communities. Seminar members have explored Christian vocation in relationship to the lifespan, the professions, and other religious traditions. For more information, see http://collegevilleinstitute.org/the-seminars/.

Books

Cahalan, Kathleen A., and Laura Kelly Fanucci. *Living Your Discipleship: Seven Ways to Express Your Deepest Calling.* New London, CT: Twenty-Third Publications, 2015.

Neafsey, John. *Act Justly, Love Tenderly: Lifelong Lessons on Vocation.* Maryknoll, NY: Orbis, 2016.

Online Resources

Called to Life (http://called-to-life.com) and Called to Work (http://called-to-work.com), each a six-week small group program.

Lives Explored (http://lives-explored.com), video narratives on vocation.

Index

Abbasids, 91n9, 95

Abraham: calling of, 1, 15, 38, 57, 57n13, 60n19, 71; in Islam, 84, 85; and the sacrifice of Isaac, 15

Abu Bakr, 89–90; as the first *khalifa*, 91, 95n14

Acts, book of: calling of the first deacons in, 57n13; God's callings in relation to pivotal decisions in, 62, 62n21

Adams, Robert M., 55n8

Adler, Felix, 215

Africa, Islam in, 96, 97, 102

agape, 80; feminist view of, 80

ahkam al-jihad (Arabic: judgments pertaining to armed struggle), 105

al-Ghazali, 82–83, 91–94, 95, 96, 103; calling of, 92–94, 102; death of, 92; as one of the "men of religion," 91; and prayer, 102

'Ali b. 'Abi Talib, 95n14

al-islam (Arabic: the submission), 82

al-lah (Arabic: the god), 84–85

al-lat (Arabic: the goddess), 85; sphere of (*al-manat* [fertility]), 85

al-Mahdi, Muhammad, 95n14

al-manat (Arabic: fertility), 85

al-Qaida, 105

al-Shabab, 105

al-Tabari (Abu Ja'far Muhammad), 83, 85, 86

Ambedkar, B. R., 113n15; contention that caste and untouchability were fundamental to the Hindu tradition, 113; conversion of to Buddhism, 113

American Ethical Union, 214n36, 215

American Humanist Association, 203n4

Amos, calling of, 61n19

"Amsterdam Declaration" (2002), 215n36

Anabaptists, 56–57

Analects (Confucius), 186

anātman (Sanskrit: no-self), 139, 144

Andrew, calling of, 57n13

Antony, St., 31

Apostolicam Actuositatem (The Decree on the Apostolate of the Laity), 36

Arab tribal religion, 84–85; and *al-lah* (the god), 84–85; and *al-lat* (the goddess), 85; as polytheistic, 88

Aristotle, 208, 208n15

Armitage, David H., 42

Aronson, Ronald, 211, 212, 216n40

artha (Sanskrit: wealth), 124, 126

"Ash Wednesday" (Eliot), 199

Asia, Buddhism in, 150–51, 152

Athanasius, St., 31

atmān (Sanskrit: self), 107–8, 179n13